Not Your Mother's Mammy

Not Your Mother's Mammy

The Black Domestic Worker in Transatlantic Women's Media

TRACEY L. WALTERS

Rutgers University Press
New Brunswick, Camden, and Newark, New Jersey, and London

Library of Congress Cataloging-in-Publication Data

Names: Walters, Tracey Lorraine, author.
Title: Not your mother's mammy : the black domestic worker
in transatlantic women's media / Tracey L. Walters.
Description: New Brunswick, New Jersey : Rutgers University Press,
[2021] | Includes bibliographical references and index.
Identifiers: LCCN 2020029109 | ISBN 9781978808577 (paperback) |
ISBN 9781978808584 (hardcover) | ISBN 9781978808591 (epub) |
ISBN 9781978808607 (mobi) | ISBN 9781978808614 (pdf)
Subjects: LCSH: Women household employees, Black, in art. | Women household employees, Black, in literature. | African American women household employees in art. | African American women household employees in literature. | Arts, Black. | English literature—Black authors—History and criticism. | American literature—African American authors—History and criticism.
Classification: LCC NX652.A37 W35 2021 | DDC 704.9/496404608996073—dc23
LC record available at https://lccn.loc.gov/2020029109

A British Cataloging-in-Publication record for this book
is available from the British Library.

♾ The paper used in this publication meets the requirements of the American National Standard for Information Sciences—Permanence of Paper for Printed Library Materials, ANSI Z39.48-1992.

www.rutgersuniversitypress.org

Manufactured in the United States of America

This book is dedicated to my mother, Morne Elaine Edwards

Contents

Illustrations

Not Your Mother's Mammy

Introduction

> When I started my musical career I was a maid, I used to clean houses. My parents—my mother was a proud janitor, my step-father who raised me like his very own worked at the post office, and my father was a trash man. They all wore uniforms. And that's why I stand here today in my black and white and I wear my uniform to honor them.
>
> —Janelle Monáe

The domestic worker is one of the most exploited and victimized laborers in the global workforce. According to the International Labour Organization (ILO), there are more than one hundred million domestic workers worldwide. Many participate in an invisible multimillion-dollar shadow economy that devalues their skills and denies their rights as workers. As such, domestic workers are prone to enslavement, workplace violence, substandard wages, and racial discrimination. The dire nature of the employment conditions of domestic workers has been reported by activists who advocate for the establishment and enforcement of the labor rights of domestic workers and scholars who document the histories and examine the lives of these vulnerable laborers, many of whom are immigrants. While the work of organizations such as Domestic Workers United (DWU) and scholarship from academics like Pierrette Hondagneu-Sotelo, Judith Rollins, Dionne Brand, Tamara Mose Brown, Jacklyn Cock, Premilla Nadasen, and Danielle T. Phillips-Cunningham is essential for understanding the challenges confronting maids, nannies, and adult care workers, it is equally as important to recognize that members of the artistic community have in their own way also participated in the global and public discourse on domestic workers. Unlike texts by activists and scholars, which appeal to a specialized group of individuals (mostly scholars and those in grassroots organizations working on behalf of domestics), the literary and visual artists bring the experiences of domestic workers to a broader public audience. Since domestic work continues to be one of the leading forms of employment for immigrant women and men, especially those of African descent who are employed as domestics in their home countries and in the global marketplace, it is unsurprising that domestic workers feature so prominently in black visual and literary artwork chronicling the lives of poor and working-class women.

In recognition of the intersectional oppression that denies black women opportunities to control their own narratives, this multidisciplinary study examines how black artists—mostly women of the diaspora and many of them former domestics—reconstruct the black female subjectivities of domestics in black media. In doing so, they undermine and defamiliarize the reductive, one-dimensional images of black domestics as perpetual victims lacking voice and agency. Critical analysis of selected media by Alice Childress, Lynn Nottage, Kara Walker, Nandi Keyi, Mary Sibande, Renee Cox, Mickalene Thomas, and others provide examples of generations of domestics who challenge and co-opt their performative roles of subservience by engaging in subversive actions, thereby contradicting the image of the deferential black maid. In this study, multiple terms will be used to describe black women's labor in the domestic sphere. Occasionally, these terms are adopted according to the language used by a particular artist or the nomenclature of a particular period or culture. The book is centered around three core themes: representation, resistance, and performance. As such, the chapters feature visual and literary works featuring black female domestics engaged in performative acts of resistance that enable them to establish their identities as multidimensional individuals with a deep understanding of the world beyond the kitchen. *Not Your Mother's Mammy: The Domestic Worker in Transatlantic Media* brings visibility to stories of domestics often neglected in academic studies, such as the complexity of interracial homoerotic relationships between workers and employers or the mental health challenges of domestics that lead to depression and suicide.

Not Your Mother's Mammy builds on existing scholarship about the domestic worker in black media, in particular Trudier Harris's *From Mammies to Militants: Domestics in Black American Literature* (1982), Kimberly Wallace-Sanders's *Mammy: A Century of Race, Gender, and Southern Memory* (2011), and Ena Jansen's *Like Family: Domestic Workers in South African History and Literature* (2019). These groundbreaking interrogations of the representation of the domestic in media laid the foundation for my study. My intervention in this discourse on the marginalization and misrepresentation of black working-class women in media is reflected in the book's comparative, interdisciplinary, and geographic approach to the domestic worker. *Not Your Mother's Mammy* focuses on the global black female domestic worker as she is featured by artists *across* the African diaspora. Critical analysis of fiction, drama, film, and visual art also distinguishes this text from others.

A number of critical theories are essential for this interdisciplinary study. I apply these theories to the different works in question through the lens of cultural analysis, feminism, postcolonialism, cultural studies, and psychoanalytic theory, which provides the framework for an analysis of the intersectional oppression of black women who engage in various modes of resistance against their exploitation and oppression. Black feminist theory, specifically Melissa Harris-Perry's work on the politics of "misrecognition," Patricia Hill Collins's concept of the "controlling images of black womanhood" in media and society, and bell hooks's discussion of the "oppositional gaze," have been particularly useful in my analysis of how black women have been misrepresented in media, which promotes one-dimensional narratives about the black female experience.

Since slavery, black women have been subject to misrecognition. Harris-Perry contends that the misrecognition of black women has been consequential to black women's positionality in the public sphere as citizens. She argues that without recognition, or the ability to be seen accurately, black women are denied access to "social, political and economic" resources (42). Collins's seminal work, *Black Feminist Thought: Knowledge, Consciousness, and the Politics of Empowerment* (1990), suggests that black women's misrecognition is the result of what she defines as socially constructed myths attached to "controlling images" of black womanhood defined as the mammy, the jezebel, the matriarch, the angry black woman, and the welfare queen (69). These myths affect black women's lives politically, socially, and personally. Two of the earliest myths, the jezebel and the mammy, are most relevant to the critical analysis of the texts examined in *Not Your Mother's Mammy.*

During slavery, the failure to recognize black women as human justified the commodification of their bodies as breeding machines used to develop the wealth of Western nations and satisfy the sexual appetite of their slaveholders. Black women's inability to adhere to moral codes of the day, which dictated that women adhere to Victorian standards of womanhood—piety, chastity, and virtuousness—marked them as Other and earned them the label of jezebel. The black woman's body as a sexual object accounts for the falsification of her personhood as a sexual deviant, a stigma many women tried to repudiate. In the late nineteenth century, for example, black women made valiant efforts to prove their asexuality. They also established a respectability politics aligned with white society, which policed black women's bodies and denied them free expression of their sexuality.[1] The misrecognition of black women as Other also led to the consistent violation of black women's bodies. In the nineteenth century, scientists like J. Marion Sims, for example, used the bodies of enslaved black women as specimens to study their sexual organs and develop surgical procedures (without anesthesia). The French surgeon Georges Cuvier had his own fascination with the black woman's body and famously carried out his experimentations on the circus performer Sandra Baartman (also known as the Venus Hottentot). Baartman was a South African woman who was exhibited at fairs in London and Paris because of her supposedly abnormally sized posterior and extended vaginal lips. Naked from the waist up, Baartman wore a scant piece of material that barely covered her groin. Once her contract as a circus performer expired, Baartman allegedly became a prostitute. After her death, Baartman became a victim of scientific racism when Cuvier dissected her sexual organs in the name of science. When Cuvier's experimentation with Baartman's body was complete, she was displayed once again for public consumption in a jar at the Musée de L'Homme.

The entertainment value of the black woman's body—and more specifically, the jezebel—has continued through the centuries. Since the advent of film, in visual media the jezebel has been repackaged as the prostitute. From the blaxploitation era to contemporary music videos, the hoochie mama is pervasive in mainstream media. Feminist scholar bell hooks has been extremely vocal about the media's sexual objectification of black women's bodies. She has castigated musical icons from Josephine Baker and Aretha Franklin to Diana Ross and Beyoncé for their complicity in the exploitation of the black body. In 2016, her labeling of Beyoncé as a sexual terrorist led to prolonged public debate about redefining feminism in the twenty-first century.[2] Some would argue hooks's polemic denies these women sexual agency, but hooks contends that the sexual objectification of women is a dangerous prevailing image constructed and consumed by a white supremacist patriarchal society that seeks to oppress the black woman.

Antithetical to the image of the wanton jezebel is the mammy, another false myth linked to slavery. The mammy, a large, dark-brown African American woman, was conceived at the end of the nineteenth century, when supporters of the Confederacy sought to create a new narrative about the antebellum South and its defeat in the Civil War. Kimberly Wallace-Sanders observes as part of this flawed rewriting of Southern history that the mammy was created to represent mutual respect and loyalty between blacks and whites. Unlike the jezebel, the mammy's large body made her nonthreatening and sexually undesirable. Moreover, her supposed loyalty to the family she worked for helped create the idea of the domestic being like a family member and, subsequently in the eyes of the black community, a race traitor. The mammy image was perpetuated in a plethora of films. In fact, in 1940, the first Academy Award received by a black woman was given to Hattie McDaniel for her portrayal of Mammy in *Gone with the Wind*. Coincidentally, seventy-two years later, Octavia Spencer won the exact same award for her portrayal of a domestic in *The Help* (2012). Spencer's win was paradoxically praiseworthy and deeply troubling. The reality that black women were still playing the maid raised questions about the typecasting of black women in Hollywood. But the black community has also been complicit in their appropriation of the mammy image. In the cult classic *School Daze* (1988), Spike Lee used Hattie McDaniel's image as a mammy on placards in a dance number about beauty politics and colorism to signify less desirable traits of black womanhood. *Not Your Mother's Mammy* counters these negative images of the mammy with numerous examples of domestic workers in media who contradict and subvert the stereotypical mammy roles played by McDaniel and Spencer.

Unfortunately, the controlling images of black womanhood are global. In South Africa, attributes of the mammy and the jezebel are also represented in media. The comic strip *Madam & Eve*, created by American expatriate Stephen Francis and Rico Schacherl helped push the mammy stereotype in their comic strip, book, and television show. *Madam & Eve* is a satirical take on the dynamics of race and class in South Africa. Eve is portrayed as a cunning, sharp-tongued South African maid who is constantly outwitting her sometimes aloof but shrewd madam. Francis might aim to liberate Eve from her subservient position as the maid, but, as scholar Gail Smith argues, Eve embodies all the stereotypes about the maid and black women in general: she is sassy, hostile, and hypersexual. Smith decries the missed opportunity to use the comic strip to bring awareness to the real struggles of domestic workers: "Madam and Eve relies on black stereotypes that do not challenge white supremacy. It legitimizes white stereotypification of black experience. Eve is presented as a 'sassy black woman' when the reality of being black and woman means that 'sass' comes at a price, and for domestic workers that price could very well be your job" (34). According to Smith, *Madam & Eve* is so successful that, next to former first lady Winnie Mandela, Eve is one of the most popular women in South Africa. *Madam & Eve* is yet another example of why studies that showcase alternative representations of the maid are so important.

Finally, the advertising industry's appropriation of the mammy figure has profited from what bell hooks calls the commodification of the black woman's body. The mammy has been used to sell a variety of goods from pancakes to Pine-Sol.[3] K. Sue Jewell's study on cultural images and social policy says that dominant society looks to mainstream media and accepts its cultural images of black women (73). The inability to see black women for their true authentic selves leaves them subject to ridicule and invisibility. Burdened by controlling stereotypes of the mammy, jezebel, and matriarch, black women have been engaged in a perpetual fight for recognition. Harris-Perry argues that when black women are misrecognized, it impacts their lives personally and politically. As discussed in chapter 1, presumptions about the cleanliness and sexual immorality of black women, for example, led to governmental policies that policed black women's bodies. In addition, the pathologizing of single black mothers accounted for misdirected blame for the social inequality that plagues black communities. In 1965, for example, the Moynihan Report, a government study about urban blight and the breakdown of the African American family, deduced that the matriarch, a stereotype of an overbearing, controlling woman who infantilizes her black mate, and the welfare queen, who has multiple children out of wedlock, were the root causes for the dysfunction of the black community. The findings of Senator Daniel Patrick Moynihan (D-NY), which were supposed to convince the government to reinvest in the black community, backfired. Politicians who regarded the matriarch and welfare queen as culpable for the dysfunction of their community advocated against funding to improve the lives of destitute African Americans who were actually victims of failed government social programs.[4] Fortunately, black women have been able to, as Audre Lorde says, "transform silence into action" (40). In the nineteenth century, women's rights activist Sojourner Truth infamously reminded a room full of white women to recognize black women as victims of patriarchy and allies in the struggle for liberation. Along with Truth, writers like Anna Julia Cooper, Pauline Hopkins, and others demanded to be heard. Since then, as the works in this book illustrate, there has been no shortage of voices rallying the call to acknowledge and respect black women.

This discourse on the misrepresentation of black women provides the framework for a discussion of how black domestic workers in media are either silenced in novels such as *The Nanny Diaries*, mischaracterized in films such as *The Help*, or lack the complexity given to white domestics in television shows such as *Downton Abbey*, where maids are given storylines independent from their lives in the domestic sphere. The artists and writers in *Not Your Mother's Mammy* insist on portrayals of domestics that are often defamiliarized and antithetical to representations from the early twentieth century to the present in mainstream art, literature, and film. Capturing the authentic voice of these women is the essential motivation for this text, and as such, in the vein of black feminist tradition that connects the personal to the political, this study intentionally includes the works and voices of many creative writers and visual artists who were either domestic workers or the children of domestics. Novelists Alice Childress, Sindiwe Magona, Nandi Keyi, and Victoria Brown, for example, worked as domestics and draw from their experiences—as well as the experiences of the women whose stories they heard on the bus going to and from work—to bring to life fictional narratives about black women caring for children and cooking and cleaning in white homes. Their stories reveal much about the complicated relationships between white female employers and black employees working within the intimate confines of a matriarchal domestic sphere. The children of domestics have also responded to the topic of domestic work. Visual artists Mary Sibande and Zanele Muholi were the first generation of women in their families who did not work in service. Their art pays homage to the extended generations of women in their families who worked as domestics under South African apartheid. Through multimedia visual performances, they use their own bodies to give voice to their mother's stories.

This book is divided into three sections to denote groupings of works that share commonality around content, comparative readings, or stylistic conventions. The overarching themes of resistance, performance, and representation are presented throughout each section as a unifying thread connecting each of the works in the study. Chapter 1 is a historical overview of the global domestic worker. The chapter discusses the social and economic conditions driving black women to domestic labor and the systemic racist practices of mainstream society, which endeavored to deny Black women workers' rights, fair wages, and human dignity. The chapter demonstrates how working-class women fought back against white supremacy by establishing domestic workers' unions and pressuring governments to pass laws to protect the rights of domestic workers.

Part 1. Quiet Subversion: The Radical Acts of Working-Class Women in the Domestic Sphere

The first section is devoted to semi-autobiographical works by former domestics and children of domestic workers. Chapters 2 and 3 focus on the political and social activism in the work of women who were once domestics but later became writers who use their work as a didactic tool to enlighten readers about the exploitation of domestic workers who have limited protection under labor laws. The works lobby for legislation to protect domestic workers' rights and negotiate for fair wages. In chapter 2, for example, the character Mildred in Alice Childress's *Like One of the Family* urges domestics to advocate for themselves by joining unions and striking against abusive employers. In chapter 3, on the other hand, Nandi Keyi conflates workers' rights with immigration reform and provides insight into the lives of Caribbean women working as nannies in New York City. Keyi's *The True Nanny Diaries* (2009) and Victoria Brown's *Minding Ben* (2011) challenge the film industry's romanticized representation of the nanny experience in classics like Walt Disney's *Mary Poppins* (1964) or Emma McLaughlin and Nicola Kraus's *The Nanny Diaries* (2007). Keyi and Brown chronicle the harsh reality of immigrant domestics who face homelessness, deportation, and unemployment. In chapter 4, South African artist Zanele Muholi uses visual activism to tackle the invisibility of black South African women, especially domestic workers and those who are lesbian and transgender. Her artwork defamiliarizes the maid. Muholi's provocative photographic series entitled *"Massa" and Mina(h)* (2008) alters typical stories about white male sexual violence against black female employees with a story addressing the intimacy, sexual tension, and lesbian desire between maids and their employers. Muholi, a daughter of a domestic, uses art to give voice to her mother's stories and the multiple generations of South African women who never had an opportunity to share what it was like to live and work as domestics during the apartheid regime.

Part 2. We Wear the Mask: Servitude, an Art of Performance and Deception

The second section demonstrates how the artists in *Not Your Mother's Mammy* take care to create images of domestic workers who refuse to be defined by their status in society. The films, visual art, and plays in this section reflect upon the performative nature of servitude. This section interrogates the racial hierarchy and patriarchal power that contributes to the intersectional oppression of black women. Chapters 5 through 7 are intertextual readings of Genet's *The Maids* (1947). The domestics in these chapters acquire agency through their direct refusal to accept their assumed role as subservient. Chapter 5 explores how Ousmane Sembène's film *Black Girl* (1966) inverts the roles of maid and madam and defamiliarizes the symbolic representation of the power dynamic between employer and employee. The protagonist of Sembène's film insists on wearing her madam's cast-offs instead of a maid's uniform and refuses to perform her household duties. In turn, the madam is forced to take over the chores, thus leaving her questioning her role and position within the household. Chapter 6 turns to Hollywood to discuss black women's struggles to live beyond the role of the maid, Both on and off-screen. Lynn Nottage's *By the Way, Meet Vera Stark* (2011) uses extracts from the biographies of actresses of the 1930s and 1940s to reveal the precarious position of black actresses who either passed as white to secure nonstereotypical black roles or satirized the plantation stereotypes they were forced to play. In chapter 7, Mary Sibande's series of fiberglass mannequins and photographs contradict the notion that black South African women can only be maids. Her characters resist the mundane rituals of their domestic duties by playing dress-up in their madam's clothes and transporting themselves into worlds where they can enter white male professions and take on positions of power.

Part 3. Representing for Laure: African American / Caribbean Women's Reimaginings of Édouard Manet's *Olympia*

The last section confronts the absence of complex and accurate depictions of the black woman in Western art. The domestics represented by the artists in this section are seen beyond and beneath their aprons: they are mothers, housewives, and lovers. Several of the artists rework the art of old masters, such as Édouard Manet's *Olympia*, to give the unnamed maid (Laure) in Manet's portrait her own identity. In chapter 8, Mickalene Thomas and Renee Cox defamiliarize Manet's classical painting by transferring the role between the maid and her madam, so the maid moves from a marginal figure to a primary character in the foreground. Thomas and Cox force audiences to confront visually arresting, highly sexualized portrayals of the maid, who replaced the naked madam, with Laure, a glamorous woman who exudes strength and beauty. Cox's portrait series *The Discreet Charm of the Bougies* (2008) joins Genet's ruminations on domesticity, class, and performance with Manet's *Olympia* to challenge conventional images of black and white women in the domestic sphere. Cox's powerful image of a white maid serving her black madam disrupts standard images of black women as subservient to white women. Finally, chapter 9 discusses Kara Walker's sugar sculpture, *A Subtlety, or the Marvelous Sugar Baby* (2015), a thirty-five-foot-tall mammy constructed from sugar. Walker's large-scale piece underscores the efforts of all the artists in this book who fight to ensure that black women are seen in new and provocative ways that demand recognition.

1

Overview

The History of Black Women's Domestic Labor from the Twentieth Century to the Present

While domestic work is certainly not unique to black women, the texts in this book illustrate how the legacies of slavery and colonialism created a history of racial and gender oppression that kept black women in positions of servitude long after their white counterparts moved into other occupations. A brief historical overview of how colonialism, slavery, apartheid, and migration led to the predominance of black women in servitude across the globe provides important historical context for the following chapters. The nations discussed in this overview are reflective of the primary locations inhabited by the domestic workers in the study.

United States

While the end of slavery released black women from bondage, it did not free them from the backbreaking labor on the plantation. After slavery the distinction between the slave worker and the domestic laborer was purely economic. For the first time, slave mistresses had to negotiate wages with women who were now independent contractors. Initially, this shift in title meant little to plantation mistresses, who flaunted their authority and dictated the workers' wages, duties, and hours. Over time, those who could hired out their services for specific tasks, such as cooks, laundresses, or cleaners. Those who opted out of household work labored as sharecroppers alongside their husbands. Many women worked as domestics their entire lives, serving as surrogate mothers to multiple generations of the same family. The long-standing relationship between the domestic and her employers often established the false idea that the domestic worker was part of the family. The underpaid and overworked exploited black women, on the other hand, did not experience this familial connection.

At the turn of the twentieth century, life became more difficult for African Americans in the South. Domestic terrorism by white supremacists (lynchings, brutal beatings, and other fear tactics meant to keep blacks afraid to assert themselves politically and socially) and the lack of social mobility drove African Americans to the North and the Midwest. The promise of jobs in manufacturing plants and assimilation into deeply rooted black communities instigated the Great Migration, when African Americans moved in large numbers to Chicago, Pittsburgh, Detroit, Boston, and New York. Historians estimate that from 1910 to 1940, approximately 1.5 million domestic workers moved out of the South. While African American men integrated into northern cities as factory workers, bellhops, and train porters, most black women found themselves once again working as domestics. At the turn of the century, 89.3 percent of African American workers in the state of New York were domestics.[1] In contrast to the South, where African Americans were the predominant group working as domestics, in the North they had fierce competition with white immigrants, who were more desirable. Native-born white women, who were fewer in number and took domestic work as temporary employment until marriage, were the most preferred, followed by Irish, Finnish, and German women.[2] Black women who could not find work as domestics took related jobs in the service industry.

The Great Depression made it even harder for black women to end their predominance in the occupation. During this time, much like every other American, blacks faced mass unemployment. It was particularly hard on African Americans, as they were the first to be terminated from their jobs. Some domestics held onto their jobs, but even employers who could still hire household labor barely paid a living wage—in some cases wages were reduced to as little as ten to fifteen cents per day. In desperation, domestics resorted to hiring themselves out as day laborers on street corners known as "slave markets." In New York City, there were more than two hundred sites where women, primarily of African descent, gathered in the morning awaiting the inspection of white housewives to select them for a day's labor. These markets were spread across the boroughs, but the Bronx was the largest and the most well known. Women's groups, black and white, appealed to the government to intervene and disband the markets and provide economic relief for these women.

In 1935, Ella Baker and Marvel Cooke, African American journalists and advocates, wrote an exposé about the markets for *Crises Magazine*. They reported the desperation and immense poverty of these women. Their article underscored the double jeopardy for black women, whose race and gender ghettoized them as second-class citizens.[3] Aid finally came to the women when the slave markets began raising concerns for employers, who could not distinguish between the day laborers and the prostitutes who also occupied the street corners. Employers were fearful of employing the "wrong kind of woman." Finally, in 1939, Mayor Fiorello LaGuardia, who had long regarded the markets as a blight on the city's reputation, especially after local and national media began covering stories about the market, formed a committee to investigate them. Eventually, the committee resolved to open employment centers to get women off the streets, but this did not do enough to mitigate the economic realities for black women, who had the highest rates of unemployment. Over time, some women had no choice but to prostitute themselves to feed their families.

In the 1920s and 1930s, white women who joined groups such as the Young Women's Christian Association (YWCA) presented themselves as allies to black women, but their actions spoke otherwise. They created humiliating public health ordinances to regulate and stigmatize black women who were deemed sexually immoral.

Slavery accounted for the mislabeling of black women as lascivious. As enslaved women forced to have sex with male slaves and their slave owners, black women found it hard to adhere to Victorian ideals of womanhood (pious, chaste, moral). Over time, sexual myths about black women's sexual deviancy promulgated in the white community. During the 1930s, when the country contended with the outbreak of syphilis, poor and lower-class Americans, many of whom happened to be black, were suspected of being carriers of the disease. When white women raised the alarm about the potentiality of being unable to distinguish between a sex worker and a domestic worker, they were contributing to the public discourse on the sexually deviant black body.

Fear of domestic workers contaminating their homes led to government intervention. Politicians instituted public health policies in New York and New Jersey as safeguards to keep white homes sanitary, and the black women who worked in those homes were forced to prove themselves worthy of entry. In New Jersey, Thomas V. Crasner created an ordinance requiring Newark's domestics be tested for syphilis, while in New York, Charles Breitbart proposed a statewide bill requiring domestics to have blood work done prior to being hired. These public health schemes were as much about protecting the white family from contamination as they were about regulating black women's bodies. White women in the YWCA and the League of Women Voters backed these initiatives. Many of these white women, who regarded themselves as feminists devoted to the liberation of women, did very little to support black household workers. Angela Davis suggests these women had a crisis of consciousness: "The convenient omission of household workers' problems from the programs of 'middle-class' feminists past and present has often turned out to be a veiled justification—at least on the part of affluent women—of their own exploitative treatment of their maids" (Davis 96). To take Davis's point, when it came to black women, many white women operated in their own self-interests. They did not align themselves with black women's struggles because they wanted to maintain their access to cheap labor and they did not want regulations that might increase pay rates or give the workers more rights. This was evident in 1935, when President Franklin Delano Roosevelt implemented the New Deal.

The New Deal created initiatives to reinvigorate the economy so businesses could hire Americans citizens who could reenter the workforce and return to buying goods and services. White women, notably Roosevelt's wife, Eleanor, played a significant role in lobbying for legislation that would give women social and economic advancements. Once again, black women were slighted. When Eleanor hosted a "White House Conference on the Emergency Needs of Women," the particularity of black women's needs was ignored. Moreover, when Roosevelt signed the Fair Labor Standard Act (FLSA; 1938), which allowed for collective bargaining and a minimum wage, domestic workers (along with agricultural workers) were the only groups excluded from this law. The omission of these two groups, who happened to be predominantly workers of African American descent, suggested that refusing to cover them under the law was racially motivated. It took until 1974 for domestics to be included, by amendment, in the FLSA, which also includes overtime pay and other worker protections.

Black women were not defeated by the FLSA or any other legislation that did not represent their needs or the needs of the community in general. They were staunch believers in unionization and labor rights and for years took their position on the front lines, participating in the sharecropper's strikes and Tobacco workers' strikes. In the 1930s, African American domestic workers began mobilizing on their own behalf. One of the most effective unions was the Domestic Workers Union (DWU), founded in Harlem in 1934 and headed by Dora Lee Jones, one of the organization's most fearless organizers. Initially the group was integrated and represented African American and Finnish domestics. Under Jones's leadership, the DWU joined the American Federation of Labor. Jones was a strong voice for domestics who fought an uphill battle against white employers who did not want government oversight of domestic labor. Jones met with Mayor LaGuardia to discuss the struggles for domestics to earn a living wage and pushed for improved working conditions. The union also helped its members find jobs. According to Vanessa May, it is estimated that under Jones's leadership, 350 to 1,000 workers enrolled in the DWU (157).

The 1940s and 1950s produced a new crop of black feminist radicals who devoted their lives to advocating for black women. Communist activists such as Claudia Jones, for example, wrote extensively about domestic workers, their lack of union protection, and the need for access to Social Security law (116). Dorothy Bolden, a civil rights leader and founding member of the National Domestic Workers Union of America (NDWUA), tirelessly fought for a standard rate of pay for domestics. Bolden was instrumental in the bus boycotts, which instigated the civil rights movement. Tired of being disrespected by bus drivers, she opted to boycott the transit system. Women such as Bolden and hundreds of domestic workers courageously helped bring visibility to the oppression of black citizens by the white supremacists of the South. These women proved their economic power and political value to the movement. Essentially, their actions gave them a sense of pride, which marked a turning point for African American domestic workers. In the 1960s and 1970s, greater access to advanced education, increasing opportunities in the private sector, and a rejection of forms of employment akin to plantation labor led many African American women to disassociate from domestic work. By the 1980s, immigrants from the Caribbean, Latin America, and Asia became the more predominant domestic worker. These migrant domestics and labor advocates continued the legacies of Jones and Bolden; established the National Domestic Workers Union by 2002 under the leadership of Ai-Jen Poo; and in 2007 established the National Domestic Workers Alliance (NDWA), one of the most powerful advocacy organizations across the nation.

South Africa

The experiences of domestic workers from South Africa and North America are more similar than any other group. Historically, both groups lived and worked in societies governed by racial segregation and white supremacy, which made their jobs as domestics exceedingly more challenging. The native population in South Africa did not begin working as paid laborers until the Dutch settlers abolished slavery in 1834. Beyond farming, domestic work was one of the few options for African women. Native women entered domestic services in part because of a directive from the colonial government that determined the female population—black and colored (biracial) women—was well suited for domestic service, both on farms and in private residences. Similar to African American women, native South African women were competing with English migrant women for work. Fortunately for white women, because of a desire for social mobility that was often acquired through marriage, English domestics did not last too long in service. Next to white women, native men were even more sought after because of their strength and because they posed no threat to the madam's husband (van Onselen 29). Thus, initially, there were more native African men working as domestics than there were women, but when the mining economy began to boom, native African men were required to work in the mines. Domestics were sourced from hiring agencies, such as the South African Employment Bureau. Although the demand for domestic workers was unwavering, as even poor whites hired domestics, the government instituted a number of policies that made it difficult for domestics to find placements.

By the 1930s, native Africans were moving from rural areas to be closer to employment opportunities in urban environments. The government moved to curtail this mass urbanization with laws, such as the 1936 Land Act, which restricted the mobility of blacks, preventing them from entering neighborhoods designated as white areas.[4] In 1948, when the government instituted apartheid (Jim Crow–like government-sanctioned racial segregation), the lives of domestics became even more difficult. In 1950, the Group Areas Act, for example, restricted cohabitation of other races in private or public spaces. In addition, pass laws determined that natives, coloreds, and Indians needed legal documentation to prove eligibility to enter white areas. Another law, the 1952 Abolition of

Passes and Coordination of Documents Act required all South Africans over age sixteen to carry a passbook. Finally, domestics were required by the state to be registered by their employers. The employer and employee were both responsible for this registration, and those who stood in defiance of the law were fined.

Women reacted strongly to these laws. As early as 1913 they fought against pass laws in the Orange Free State (Boer state) because they knew the impact the law would have on their community. These laws put black women in a precarious situation. In order to seek work, one needed to enter white areas to find employers who would hire them. Women from both rural and urban areas protested these laws. With support from political organizations such as the African National Congress's Women's League, they staged stay-at-homes, strikes, and boycotts.

By the 1950s there were more than one hundred thousand domestics in South Africa. In-depth studies by scholars Jacklyn Cock and Shireen Ally illustrate that employment came with no clear guidelines. The state made rules only in the interest of racial segregation and disenfranchisement. They did nothing to protect the domestics who were treated more like servants than workers. Domestics worked for as little as seventeen cents and worked extended hours. In some cases, they were only given one day off, if at all, and some had no heat or were barely given enough food. Most importantly, they were denied the right to see their family or friends, who were restricted from entering white areas without registration papers. Living-in also meant employers tried to manipulate domestic workers into giving up personal time to perform tasks for the family: child minding or beginning the workday earlier or ending it later. Living on the premises also helped spur the idea in the minds of the employer that the employee was like family. Measures against urbanization meant some domestics had to travel long distances to work, so many chose to live in shed-like quarters in their employer's backyard, with a barely large enough space for their belongings and a bed. Not only were these spaces small; they were stiflingly hot in the summer and frigid in the winter. In the 1970s, when live-out work became more prevalent, domestics took the option, for it gave them autonomy and the opportunity to be with their children. Sociologist Judith Rollins points out that one of the few benefits of stringent apartheid laws were the miscegenation laws (Immorality Act of 1927, 1950), which made it illegal for blacks and whites to engage in sexual relationships; but in reality, black women were routinely abused by male employers.

The 1950s was a politically active time for South African women. Like their American counterparts, they were engaged in boycotts, and they defied segregation laws and pass laws. In the 1980s, more women joined labor unions such as the South African Domestic Workers Union (SADWU), which played a key role in the advocation of domestic worker's rights. In 1994, when apartheid ended, native South Africans no longer lived under the weight of racial oppression. Under Nelson Mandela, the nation's first black president, many native black Africans who had lived their entire lives in poverty and in fear of state violence, and were stripped of their land and reduced to menial labor, could now live with dignity. Opportunities for social mobility in the postapartheid state showed gains not only for the black race but also for women. One such advancement for women came in the form of labor laws. Under Mandela, new laws protected domestic workers. In 1995, two major pieces of legislation were put in place To protect workers' rights. The first was the Labour Relations Act (LRA), which granted the right to unionization and collective bargaining, and the Basic Conditions of Employment Act (BCEA), which regulated wages, hours, maternity leave, and sick leave.

One of the most important regulations under the BCEA was the introduction of labor inspectors to check the homes of employers (with consent). Shortly after the LRA and BCEA, the 2002 Sectoral Determination Seven law implemented contracts and determined a minimum hourly wage for the domestic worker sector, thus "solidify[ing] the post-apartheid state's efforts to transform 'servants' into workers and to establish one of the world's most comprehensive regulatory frameworks for paid domestic work" (Ally 68). At the time, South Africa's stance on domestic workers was far more progressive than were those of the United States and other Western nations. The new laws for domestics were effective, but some found employers resistant to the changes. Fortunately, unions were there to hear grievances and act on behalf of domestic workers. In 2000, SADWU was revamped and became the South African Domestic Service and Allied Workers Union (SADSAWU). This group helped institute employment insurance and grant assistance to women.

The end of apartheid held the promise of greater possibilities for black women in South Africa, but it did not change life for the majority of South Africa's black women, who were still the poorest and the least educated. Women had free rein to move into a plethora of occupations in the public and private sector, but according to Ally, fifteen years after apartheid there were almost one million women working as domestics. Moreover, in the twenty-first century, many of these native-born women have been joined by migrant workers from Zimbabwe and other nations. These migrant women are now facing the same kinds of discriminatory practices and exploitation native black women faced, this time from white and *black* employers.

Migrant Domestic Workers

Over the past sixty years, the United States, Canada, and continental Europe have served as primary sites of migration for black female domestic workers. Since the 1980s, global migration from developing countries has been on the rise due to global recession. According to studies by the ILO, by the 1990s the numbers of migrants living and working in foreign countries rose to more than one hundred million. Many of these migrants—skilled and unskilled, documented and undocumented—were forced to take jobs in the service sector. Those without documentation were highly vulnerable, depending on where they resided. Since the beginning of the twentieth century, Caribbean women migrants from English-speaking countries have been migrating in mass numbers. From the turn of the century to the 1960s, many went to England, especially after World War II, but during the 1960s, with immigration reform in the British Isles, the United States and Canada were viewed as better options. Immigration to the United States came in three waves: the first wave between 1900 and 1920, the second between the 1930s and 1960, and the third wave from the 1960s to the 2000s. According to historian Philip Kasinitz, while the first two cohorts were middle class, the last group was from various socioeconomic levels. In earlier years, in the 1920s and 1930s, educated Caribbean migrants entered professions as doctors and lawyers and purchased large amounts of real estate in heavily populated black neighborhoods. During the 1960s, their options decreased as overall immigration to the United States rose.

After World War II and through the 1970s, changing economic conditions in the United States and Canada attracted large numbers of black female laborers from the Caribbean. Their proximity to North America and recruitment from the Canadian government made migration a viable option. Since the second half of the twentieth century, Caribbean women have migrated to Canada to work as domestics. From the 1950s through the 1980s, many arrived through various employment schemes between the Canadian government and corresponding Caribbean countries.[5] Even after formal arrangements between nations ended, women continued migrating to Canada for domestic work. Unstable economies and limited chances for social mobility in the Caribbean factored into the domestic workers' departures from their countries of origin. Like many other migrant domestic workers, they faced hardship. They were often overworked, underpaid, and treated as dispensable by their employers.

Economic conditions in Caribbean countries also necessitated migration to the United States. In the case of Jamaica, for example, an economic downturn occurred during the 1970s and 1980s due to a decline in tourism, exports, and remittances. Fortunately, the migratory wave of Caribbean women came at a time when African American women in northern cities were moving into other occupations and making room for these new immigrants. By the 1980s, Caribbean women found high rates of employment in professions such as nursing and administrative employment, and the numbers of domestic workers declined[6] (Kasinitz 104). Undocumented Caribbean women saw domestic work as advantageous. Many could be paid under the table, and they were incentivized by the potential to gain naturalization through their employers. Many were eager to take this option to have the opportunity to become citizens and petition for their own families to gain resident status. Some women were also attracted to the live-in opportunities, which alleviated the stress of finding immediate housing.

While immigrants transitioning from one culture to another often encounter difficulties with alienation, cultural estrangement, and homesickness, many Caribbean women who move to large cities with dense black immigrant communities have been able to survive due to kinship communities of domestic workers. Sociologist Tamara Mose Brown's research illustrates that these women congregate in parks and playgrounds, where they share news from home, food, and culture. Domestics help situate new workers and through their "nanny network" help others find employment. Caribbean women have also been politically active in organizations such as DWU.

African and Caribbean Migration to Europe

In France, migrant domestic labor increased after World War II, when men from North Africa and sub-Saharan Africa were recruited to fulfill a continental labor shortage. Initially, most men traveled alone, but after a family reunification program allowed their wives to join them, the rates of African women increased. In the 1960s, during the period of African independence, greater numbers of women traveled to pursue their educations and secure employment. Unfortunately, African migrant domestic workers in Europe have faced difficulty securing employment. In comparison to Caribbean migrant domestic workers in the United States, who readily replaced African American domestics, African migrant domestics suffer high rates of unemployment due to overt racist discrimination. According to scholar Judy Scales-Trent, Spanish and Portuguese women are more desirable than African women, so African women have found that racial barriers limit their ability to secure employment. Some employers go to great lengths not to hire African women by asking for their last names or requesting a picture prior to the interview.[7]

Since the twenty-first century, African domestics have found greater success working for diplomats from Middle Eastern countries or their own relatives from their countries of origin. Unfortunately, many have suffered extreme abuse under these arrangements, especially since they are undocumented and have no legal right to French protection under the law. According to scholar Encarnación Gutiérrez Rodríguez, since 2006, domestic work has been "the largest employment sector for migrant women entering the EU. The majority of these workers are undocumented. They arrived as refugees, for family reunification, or with a tourist visa, thereby losing their legal status because of restrictive asylum and migration laws"[8] (65).

While France has a sizeable number of African domestic workers, the United Kingdom is also beginning to see a rise in the numbers. Despite its own role in colonialism and the postwar labor shortage, Britain did not experience an influx of black female domestics until the 2000s. Prior to the 1980s, most black women migrating from the Caribbean and Africa to the United Kingdom secured nursing positions or factory work or cleaned offices and hospitals. Moreover, black nannies and housekeepers were rarely employed in white households. Instead, they worked for African and Caribbean relatives or South Asian and Middle Eastern families. The vulnerability of these migrants has led to oppressive working conditions often extreme enough to be categorized as slavery. The U.K. Home Office determined that since the millennium, there has been a surge in reported cases of slavery. Reports indicate that in 2012, the U.K. Human Trafficking Centre received 2,255 reports of human trafficking, "an increase of 178 (9%)" from the previous year (www.bbc.com/news/uk-25048307).[9] These slaves, often women, men, and children from Eastern Europe, Africa, and Asia, are trafficked and held captive as sex-slave workers, hair braiders, and domestic workers.[10]

Advocates for enslaved workers maintain that British laws have not adequately protected immigrants entering the United Kingdom on work visas. In 2012, for example, the government implemented the "tied visa" law, mandating employees who arrived in the United Kingdom on a work visa sponsored by their employer to live and work with their sponsor for six months before resigning from their post or seeking new employment. An employee who was terminated or resigned from their job would have no legal right to work or remain in the United Kingdom. Supporters of the law maintained that the 2012 law was implemented to safeguard against employee abuse. The employer and employee have to sign a "declaration of the terms and conditions of their U.K. employment, theoretically preventing an abusive relationship being imported to the UK" ("Hidden Away"). Those against the law argued that the policy was detrimental to these workers because it emboldened employers to manipulate employees who were beholden to them for their future prospect of gaining residency in Britain.[11] The 2015 Modern Slavery Act (MSA), the first in Europe, sought to improve the previous law. In an effort to thwart the practice of enslaving workers for many years, employees on "tied visas" were only permitted to work in the United Kingdom for six months. The "new slavery" was serious enough to warrant a public service campaign, "Help Free the U.K. from Modern Slavery," which educated the British public about enslaved individuals living and working in neighborhoods across the nation. A website and hotline were established to both help identify common traits of enslaved persons and provide access and resources for those seeking to liberate themselves from their enslavement.

In sum, this transatlantic history of the domestic worker is retold in the literature, film, and visual art of the writers and artists discussed in *Not Your Mother's Mammy*. The following chapters illustrate how artists interweave history with autobiography and creative license to create and recreate the lives of women who have for so long been unrecognized and underappreciated.

PART 1

Quiet Subversion

The Radical Acts of Working-Class Women in the Domestic Sphere

2

Let's Hear It from the Maid

Alice Childress's Like One of the Family

"What does it feel like to raise a white child when your own child's at home being raised by somebody else?"
—Kathryn Stockett, *The Help*

The 2011 film adaptation of Kathryn Stockett's *The Help* (directed by Tate Taylor) was celebrated for its honest and poignant meditation on the relationship between white women and their black maids. While both the movie and novel were hugely successful and well received by many audiences, some were deeply offended by the story's stereotypical representation of black female domestic workers. The Association of Black Women Historians wrote a scathing open letter to the public condemning the film's historical inadequacies and glaring omissions. The statement on their website read, "Despite efforts to market the book and the film as a progressive story of triumph over racial injustice, *The Help* distorts, ignores, and trivializes the experience of black domestic workers" ("An Open Statement"). Others decried the submissive portrayal of black maids and the privileging of the white female perspective. This critique came in response to the movie's black maids playing a supportive role to a young, empathetic white protagonist who gathers and records interviews from the "help" to further her career as a budding journalist. The controversy surrounding *The Help* led to connections to other tales about domestic workers, such as Alice Childress's short stories, "Conversations from Life with Mildred."[1] Childress's stories were first published in *Freedom* newspaper, edited by famed actor, singer, and activist Paul Robeson. Eventually, they were put together in *Like One of the Family* (1956), a book-length collection of monologues set in New York during the mid-1950s, at the nadir of the civil rights movement.[2] The stories in *Like One of the Family* defamiliarize the plantation stereotypes in *The Help* and present the domestic worker as a strong, intelligent, and politically conscious woman.

The 1950s offered most black women few employment opportunities beyond domestic work. Twenty years prior to Childress's publication, Louise Thompson Patterson's 1936 essay, "Toward a Brighter Dawn," published in *Woman Today*, a Communist Party USA (CPUSA) journal, brought attention to the private sector's marginalization of black women. According to Patterson, in 1936, approximately "85 percent of all Negro women workers [were] domestics, [making up] two-thirds of the two million domestic workers in the United States." Patterson maintained that black women's oppression limited their social mobility. Since factory work and domestic work were the most prevalent jobs for black women, they were stymied by their inability to advance professionally or economically. Patterson urged black women to advocate for better wages and called for unionization to protect worker's rights. Several years later, Patterson's study was followed by the *Daily Compass*'s "I Was Part of the Bronx Slave Market" (1950), a five-part exposé on journalist Marvel Cooke's undercover social experiment as a domestic worker. Cooke detailed how black female domestics participated in what was akin to the slave auctions of the antebellum period. She described the "undignified" and "vicious" daily routine of black women who huddled together each morning, on sidewalks near department stores, waiting for white women to choose one among them to work for the day. Cooke discovered that many of the white women preyed on black women's desperation by undercutting adequate wages for their labor. She reports, "Twice I was hired by the hour at less than the wage asked by the women of the market. Both times I went home mad—mad for all the Negro women down through the ages who have been lashed by the stinging whip of economic oppression" (Cooke). Like Patterson, Cooke stressed the importance of securing worker's rights for domestics: "We must carry on the continuous and militant fight to bring domestic workers under the protection of the minimum wage and maximum hour laws, and under the workmen's compensation and social security acts." Social activists like Patterson and Cooke laid the foundation for successive generations of advocates to mobilize women to fight for labor rights. Some women did this through union activity, and others, like Childress, used their art to reach the masses.

Mildred: A Heroic Figure for Working-Class African American Women

I am not *just* like one of the family.

—Mildred, *Like One of the Family*

The title of *Like One of the Family* is an ironic refutation of the statement that domestics are treated by their employers "like one of the family." Mildred, the protagonist of the stories, emphasizes the disconnection between the sentiment and the reality, arguing that while white madams might claim their black maid is like family, their blatant disrespect and exploitation contradict this idea. Mildred coldly chides her employer for believing she is treated like family: "You think it's a compliment when you say, 'We don't think of her as a servant . . .' but after I've worked myself into a sweat cleaning the bathroom and the kitchen . . . making the beds . . . cooking the lunch . . . washing the dishes and ironing Carol's pinafores . . . I do not feel like no weekend guest. I feel like a servant" (Childress, *Like One* 3). Mildred underscores the essential factors that evidence her outsider position within her employer's household; she is a worker and is treated as such. The power dynamics established between the employer, who directs the various tasks that must be completed before day's end, and the worker, who feels overworked and underappreciated, will never convince the maid she is equal nor will she ever feel like family. Mildred's belief that she was more like a workhorse than a family member was a reality for many black women in the 1950s.

In an interview with historian Elizabeth Clark-Lewis, Nellie Willoughby, a maid who worked for a prominent political family in Washington, D.C., for twenty-five years, proved this when she shared her experience with these employers, who were convinced they treated her like a family member. Upon entering Willoughby's home, Clark-Lewis noticed family portraits of Willoughby's former employers displayed on the walls and when entering her bedroom saw in the wardrobe the uniform Willoughby was required to wear during her many years of service. Clark-Lewis was surprised to learn Willoughby showcased the pictures and saved the uniform not out of sentimentality but rather as a bitter reminder of her hatred for this family (187). Willoughby noted that while the family supposedly regarded her as one of their own, they went to great lengths to ensure she was aware of her "place" in the household. Thus when they moved from a house to a condominium, the husband "paid a contractor to have the plumbing rerouted so they could cut a back door in the hallway" to ensure she would not enter through their front door as an equal (Clark-Lewis 187). In the interest of keeping her job, Willoughby remained silent and never confronted her employers for treating her as inferior. The stifled voices of women like Willoughby are brought to life through the conversations of Mildred, a fictional, Northern, day laborer who *is* able to speak to both her employer and friends about the various offenses that occur while working as a domestic in New York City. Ultimately, Mildred is a heroic figure for black, working-class women who knew firsthand what she was facing.

The conflicts Mildred encounters with her employers are recollected through one-sided conversations with her friend Marge, both on the phone and in person and—most importantly, as scholar Sonja Lancaster notes—"outside of the white woman's kitchen" (122). Marge, an active listener, never contributes to the discussions, but she is essential for Mildred's storytelling because

Mildred needs a willing and empathetic audience to hear what she had endured during her day. Lancaster surmises, "Marge represents the original readers of these conversations, who read them as weekly newspaper columns in African-American newspapers. Marge supports Mildred by listening sympathetically to her stories and reacting to the indignities Mildred describes" (122).

The episodes in the collection feature Mildred chastising and shaming her white female employers for their offensive mistreatment. While Mildred's wit and assertiveness give the book a comical tone, it is important to recognize that at the heart of the stories is a serious effort to teach maids to assert themselves and reject their employer's humiliation and abuse. Furthermore, Mildred is a woman who defies the notion that a woman should be defined by her job. Her musings on various social and political issues of the day serve to educate Marge and readers about the civil rights movement, the nascent anti-apartheid movement, and ongoing efforts to recruit domestics to membership in established trade unions. In essence, Mildred becomes a subversive voice for black female domestics working during a period when the political consciousness of African Americans was being transformed by the civil rights movement and Marxist and other left-wing ideologies.

In fact, in 1956, when the stories were released as a book, black women were experiencing a pivotal moment in U.S. history. In 1956, the nation (and the world) witnessed the power of black women's political activism when they courageously challenged segregation laws with a statewide boycott of the Montgomery, Alabama, transit system. For one year (December 5, 1955, to December 20, 1956), domestics who participated in what is known as the Montgomery Bus Boycott demonstrated their economic power and their tenacity as they walked miles to work and carpooled to support the efforts of the boycott. Rosa Parks, who instigated the boycott by violating the law mandating that black bus riders sit at the back of the bus, is the name and face synonymous with the boycott. Even so, long before the boycott, many women had already engaged in their own quiet protests. According to historian Premilla Nadasen, one such woman was Georgia Gilmore, who decided to stop taking the bus after being humiliated by a bus driver (27).[3] Gilmore, an ardent supporter of the boycott, founded Club from Nowhere, an organization made up of domestics and service workers that sold meals to fund the boycott (Nadasen 29). Hundreds of women participated in what is considered by historians as one of the most successful mass boycotts of the twentieth century. Domestics who were involved in the boycott had a lot at stake. Not only did they risk being fired by unsympathetic employers who were against the boycott and the radicalization of their employees, but they were also risking their lives. White supremacists who were fearful of losing their power were apt to brutalize men and women who dared defy Jim Crow laws or express political views. Despite facing punitive consequences, maids boycotted for twelve months. Not only did the boycott lay the foundation for the civil rights movement, but it also emboldened black women domestics across the nation to wield their political power. Thus, during its time, *Like One of the Family* made an important creative contribution to black women's political activism. This political and intellectual advocacy was, as scholar E. S. McDuffie asserts, "a politics that centers working-class women by combining Communist party positions on race, gender, and class with black nationalism and black radical women's lived experiences, embedded in their writing and activism" (34).

Black Marxist feminists like Claudia Jones were instrumental in publishing essays underscoring the interconnectivity of race, class, and gender with scholarship and activism. Jones's influential essay "An End to the Neglect of the Problems of the Negro Woman" (1949), for example, was an important treatise on the oppression of black working-class women and the essentiality of labor legislation to protect domestics.

Childress was acquainted with social activists such as Jones and Cooke in Communist Party–related activities. She worked with them as part of a collective of black women on the left who paired their national struggle with a Pan-African fight for liberation.[4] Just as Patterson, Cooke, and Jones used their work to speak out against worker inequality and black women's oppression, with *Like One of the Family*, Childress engages in this discourse on the victimization and inequality facing working-class black women. Her short comedic pieces, which appeared routinely in local African American newspapers, reached a broad audience of readers who could readily identify with scenarios that closely matched situations they experienced or witnessed. The brevity and accessibility of her short stories enabled her to speak directly to working men and women who did not have the luxury of time (or disposable income) to purchase and read lengthy novels. Literary scholar Paul Lauter's analysis of working-class literature of the 1950s suggests that working-class artists and audiences had similar views about society and the function of artwork:

> They saw artistic production within the context of that shared experience, of the world here and now. Art was not a means of lifting people outside the world in which they lived, or a means of producing "catharsis" and thus achieving "stasis." . . . Rather, it was a means of making working people conscious of their world and actions within it, of extending their experiences of that world, indeed of enlarging the world they could experience. (65)

Lauter's observation neatly frames Childress's motivation for writing her stories. She wanted to depict the lives of domestics and give them a platform and, at the same time, inspire them to change their circumstances.

Mildred, the protagonist of *Like One of the Family*, was a strong, militant voice for domestic workers. Like many domestics who migrated from the South to the North, Mildred took full advantage of the freedom of speech afforded to northern African Americans who encountered racism but did not live under the tyranny of southern Jim Crow. As is evident in *The Help*, southern maids had to be more cautious about how they spoke to their madams. When the film characters Minnie and Aibileen confront and retaliate against their madams for their ruthless behavior, both are terminated for their subordination. (In the novel, however, readers must wait until the end to see Aibileen muster the courage to speak out.) Conversely, in the North, Mildred felt free to speak candidly.

Mildred's demeanor was not too different from Childress's own attitude toward her white female employers. According to literary critic Trudier Harris, prior to becoming a writer, Childress worked briefly as a domestic. Harris reports that Childress took no nonsense from her employers, and those who grieved her paid handsomely (introduction, xxii).[5]

Later, Childress used these experiences as the foundation for *Like One of the Family* (Harris, introduction, xxii). Confident her stories could embolden her readership, Childress "articulated the radical potential of this workforce, helping to foster in domestic workers a subjectivity of dignity and resistance" (Nadasen 17). Her radical stance concerning the labor rights of domestics and the working class in general was an extension of her leftist views, which were expressed not only in *Like One of the Family* but in her plays and novels too. Childress's ability to write in a variety of genres exposed her art to a diverse audience. While mainstream audiences attended her plays and read her novels, *Like One of the Family* was exclusively for a black readership. Childress was very intentional about where she published the Mildred stories, and she was clear about her intended reader and how they could be reached.

Like other black leftist artists of the day, Childress used her cultural production to challenge images of black womanhood. The vignettes, originally titled "Conversations from Life with Mildred," ran in *Freedom* newspaper. *Freedom* newspaper was the ideal space for black radicals such as Childress to advocate for racial, economic, and gender justice. "Conversations from Life with Mildred" was placed alongside stories about union strikes and national and international politics. Positioning Mildred's stories next to articles about labor negotiations and revolutionary activities in Africa reinforced the radical nature of Childress's series. Moreover, much of the political rhetoric of the news stories was echoed in Mildred's conversations, thus creating a dialogical function for the stories. Mildred's conversations with Marge lend themselves to a participatory relationship with readers who can readily identify with Mildred's workplace drama. Mildred also engages in social critiques on a variety of issues of the day that bring her readers into a political discourse independent from Mildred's experience. According to critic Mary Helen Washington, the stories in "Conversations" were "collaborative text[s] . . . effective because of their relationship to the other articles in *Freedom*, each article and column anticipating the next one, encouraging and supporting political risk and pursuing the paper's goal of developing a politically informed black community" (189). Obviously, readers of *Freedom* were politically conscious individuals, and as such, Mildred's militancy appealed to their sensibilities.

"Conversations from Life with Mildred" ran in *Freedom* from 1951 to 1955. In 1956, the anecdotes were published as a book with Independence Publishers. Later, Mildred appeared in the *Baltimore Afro-American* under the title "Here's Mildred" from 1956 to 1960. Initially, Childress ran the stories for free, which as Lauter explains, is typical of working-class literature that "is offered not for its exchange value . . . but for its use in the lives of the people of whom it is directed" (64). Later, she made an arrangement with the *Baltimore Afro-American* to run one story per week for twenty-five dollars each titled the "Childress Papers." Carl Murphy, president of the *Baltimore Afro-American*, congratulated Childress for writing stories that gave domestic workers a sense of dignity.

Feminist scholars such as Patricia Hill Collins also stressed the importance of Childress's stories for readers of the day, writing, "Mildred's identity as a Black working-class domestic and the form of publication of these fictionalized accounts illustrates an increasingly rare practice in Black intellectual production—a Black author writing to an African American, working-class audience, using a medium controlled by Black people" (109). Mildred's stories were very popular with working-class readers, and some actually wrote to Childress about the series. A reader of the *Baltimore Afro-American*, for example, suggested having a comment section in the paper for readers to reflect on their own personal experiences represented in Mildred's encounters. Ultimately, as Harris observes, Childress's readers lived vicariously through Mildred: "The many domestic workers who subscribed to that paper and who found themselves in situations equally or more restrictive than Mildred's could applaud her victories; the conversations thereby transcended their individuality and responded to a collective consciousness" (introduction, xxxvi). In essence, Mildred becomes like the blues singer who similarly used her music to express a black feminist poetic, creating a new vision of black womanhood that defied conventional ways of living and being in the world. Like these women, she was independent, she spoke out against injustice, and she inspired a generation of women who found themselves in the pages of her stories.

Mildred Finding Humor in Humiliation

The vignettes in *Like One of the Family* touch on a range of subjects, and Childress employs humor to soften the sting of humiliation felt by Mildred and her readers, a rhetorical device often used in black writing. As historian Lawrence Levine explains in *Black Culture and Black Consciousness*, in the black community humor has often been used as a way to mitigate the hardships of daily life (344).[6] Mildred's wittiness is reminiscent of the cartoon character Candy featured in Jackie Ormes's 1942 comic strip of the same name. Like Mildred, Candy, an African American domestic worker, always gets a laugh at the expense of her employer. Mildred often marvels at the audacity of employers whose privilege and false sense of superiority blind them to their callousness. While stories like "I Liked Working at That Place" give a favorable image of white employers, most others emphasize white women's efforts to demean their employees and establish a power dynamic within the household. Knowing that only her race and class place her above the black female, the white woman works hard to mirror the patriarchal racist attitudes of white men. To this end, domestics "saw themselves as a frenetic audience forced to attend the mistress's performance. The home was the wife's stage; it was the only setting in which she could feel legitimate. Domestics saw the white woman's domination of household workers as a transparent exercise of the only kind of power she had" (Clark-Lewis 109).

Mildred frequently witnessed white women's efforts to prove their superiority. In "Mrs. James," for example, her employer tries to legitimize her superiority by referring to herself in the third person. In another story, an employer questions the morality of black women. Childress understood that most white women were willfully ignorant of the commonality between themselves and the women who entered their homes for twenty to thirty hours a week. She knew that many white women regarded black women as dishonest, unclean, and unintelligent, and she undermined such attitudes, relentlessly upholding her crusade to inform white women that she did not regard herself as inferior. "The Pocket Book Game" is a clear example of how Mildred rebukes the women's superior attitudes and petty behavior. In this episode, each time Mildred reports for work to clean Ms. E's home, the woman clutches her pocketbook, fearful Mildred will steal its contents. Mildred very quickly acknowledges Ms. E's stereotyped perception of her as a thief. In retaliation, one afternoon when Ms. E asks Mildred to leave the apartment to convey a message to the building's superintendent, Mildred seizes the opportunity to address the unspoken allegation of her dishonesty. Mildred steps away from the apartment but re-enters hurriedly, loudly stating that she had to rush back to retrieve her pocketbook. The woman recognizes that Mildred is aping her own display of distrust and becomes defensive—"I hope you don't think I distrust you"—to which Mildred retorts, "That's all right Mrs. E . . . I understand. 'Cause if I paid anybody as little as you pay me, I'd hold on to my pocket book too!" (Childress 27). Mildred succeeds in both addressing the affront and, with her comment about Mrs. E paying low wages, exposes her for underpaying employees. As Harris observes, Mildred relishes the opportunity to play the trickster figure, outwitting the women and reversing their insults and racism. However, Mildred, as scholar Zita Dresner asserts, is no ordinary trickster.

In comparison to other trickster figures, "Mildred assumes no mask for herself. Rather, she continually repudiates the masks that whites attempt to impose on her and compels them to confront the incongruity between their preconceptions and the reality of who she is. In doing so, she turns the disparagement directed at her into laughter at the disparagers and acquires an aura of at least personal invulnerability" (Dresner 226).

In many cases, even when Mildred gets the upper hand, she still feels deeply offended by her employer's insults. "The Health Card," for example, reveals just how cutting employers could be to their maids. The story tells of an incident with an employer who asks Mildred to provide her medical card to verify her cleanliness. Mildred agrees to bring the card the next day, but not before informing the woman that her exposure to the family's soiled laundry and their beds makes her concerned for her own health. As such, she requires the woman, the woman's husband, and children to produce their own health cards so she can check their health status to determine if they are clean enough for her standards. While Mildred is vindicated, she still has the knowledge that her employer has questioned her hygiene. This health card incident would certainly have resonated with readers, many of whom had likely spent several years fighting against various health ordinances imposed on them by the state, as discussed in chapter 1.[7] Ultimately, "The Health Card" is not simply an entertaining story but also social commentary and historical documentation of the various social policies and practices occurring at the time.

Interestingly, *The Help* also references policies related to black women's health and sanitary standards. In the narrative, one of the white characters is convinced black people are inferior and carry diseases harmful to white families. To address this public health concern, she pressures local politicians to approve an ordinance mandating that all African American household employees use specially designed outside bathroom facilities. Most workers reluctantly adhere to the rule, but during a torrential rainfall, Minnie, a black maid, ignores the rule and uses the bathroom inside her employer's home. Unsurprisingly, her disobedience leads to her termination. Minnie's defiance bears similarity to Mildred's feistiness. Readers might also imagine Mildred ignoring the mandate and either using the indoor bathroom or refusing to work for the employer. Unfortunately, the two characters handle such situations in markedly different ways. In *The Help*, Stockett strips Minnie of her dignity and humanity. After losing her job, Minnie retaliates by serving her employer a generous slice of homemade pie, deceptively laden with feces. While Minnie's actions were intended to be humorous, Stockett endorsed the very stereotype that justified the ordinance: black people are unsanitary and inferior. Stockett obviously disregarded the implications of such behavior.[8] Childress, on the other hand, fully understands the politics of representation and avoids such mischaracterization. In *Like One of the Family*, at no point does Mildred engage in behavior that sacrifices her dignity or morality; as such, the employer is always portrayed as the one lacking integrity.

The Value of Black Women's Labor

While a number of readers may certainly have drawn inspiration from Mildred's recalcitrance, Childress endeavored to make Mildred more than a sassy black woman who could handle her employers. She broadened the character's perspective beyond individualized experience and engages in a serious interrogation of the domestic's place in society and the dangerous stereotypes attributed to black women household workers. In "Those Colored Movies," for example, Mildred tells Marge she is fed up with seeing the maid portrayed as an unintelligent, passive woman unconcerned with events in the world. Ultimately, she challenges the notion that working-class black women are disconnected from the politics of the day. Mildred's objection is shared by Jones, who expressed her frustration with the media's constant characterization of the black woman as a mammy rather than "her real role as breadwinner, mother, and protector of the family" (111–112). Jones argued that this perennial stereotypical image of black woman as "the Negro slave mother" was long past its expiration and "must be combated and rejected as a device of imperialism to perpetuate the white chauvinist ideology that Negro women are 'backward,' 'inferior,' and the 'natural slaves' of others" (112). Furthermore, "All about My Job" gives Mildred the occasion to prove why such antiquated portrayals of the maid compromise their dignity and diminish the value of their labor and their contribution to the workforce and community. At an event showcasing the black community's advancements in the workplace, Mildred is asked about her occupation. When she informs the inquirer that she is a housekeeper, the woman is dismissive. Mildred sternly educates the woman about the social and economic value of the black maid's labor. She informs the woman that domestic workers were instrumental in the establishment of the economic foundation of the black community. In effect, without the maid there would not be the black professional, tradesman, or artist. She insists black woman's labor allowed the black community to build schools and churches and feed the poor. With this diatribe, Mildred celebrates the working-class domestics' significant contributions to the workforce, thus giving readers a strong sense of pride in their accomplishments.

Two other pieces—"We Need a Union Too" and "On Leavin' Notes!"—also emphasize the value of domestic labor and production. Typically, working-class literature focuses on work—"especially work for wages, organizing with other women, and the fear of desertion and physical violence—[and] completes the picture of women's lives that most bourgeois forms only show in fragments" (Lauter 68). Along with encouraging unionization, Mildred taught readers about various ways to prevent employers from devaluing their labor. In "On Leavin' Notes!," Mildred recounts an incident when the mistress leaves a note asking her to take home three dresses to wash and iron (Childress, *Like One* 154–155). While Mildred is unconcerned with the request, she is annoyed by the woman not asking her in person. Moreover, the woman insults Mildred's intelligence by asking her to do the task for $1.00, when the Laundromat charges seventy-five cents per dress. The woman would thus save $1.25. But Mildred will not be manipulated. Addressing the woman in person, Mildred asserts she will not wash the dresses for less than seventy-five cents a dress. Realizing that she cannot deceive Mildred, the woman states, "Well it looks as if I can't use you" for such chores (Childress, *Like One* 155). Childress uses this example to remind domestic workers to be aware of efforts to devalue their labor. Mildred firmly believes cleaning and washing are acquired skills, and as Dresner says, "by treating her skills as a commodity with market value Mildred dictates that she should receive adequate financial compensation for her labor" (227). Furthermore, as Mildred insists in "We Need a Union Too," with union representation, employers would not be able to take advantage of domestics' labor.

Reading more like a speech than an essay, Mildred's "We Need a Union Too" is one of the most important pieces in the collection. Mildred does not recount a particular incident with an employer; instead, she moves from singular to plural as she meditates on the importance of domestic workers' rights and the unionization of domestic workers. As Washington and others have observed, Childress's essays were "virtual dramatization[s] of the issues in [Claudia] Jones's essays" (186). In 1956, black women had unions, but going back as far as 1935, they were denied protection under the Fair Labor Standards Act. While many women joined other organizations to advocate for their rights, they wanted their own representation so their specific needs could be addressed. Childress believed unionization was key for the empowerment of the black female workforce. By outlining the major problems with domestic work as an occupation and by defining its place in the American labor force, Childress proves the urgency of immediate action. She positions the argument from a feminist intersectional perspective, charging that domestic work was not only a gendered activity but also the burden of the poor (and specifically black women), who were forced to take on housework and childcare because white women and black men had employment options that allowed them to avoid this "loathsome" occupation. Fuming to Marge, Mildred laments, "We got a job that almost nobody wants" (Childress, *Like One* 140). While it is unstated in the book, the only women who would have willingly taken the job without resentment were the Caribbean women who were immigrating in waves, steadily moving into domestic work, and replacing some of the African American women who were fortunate to find other jobs (i.e., factory work).

The undesirability of domestic work was not simply because of exploitation, mistreatment, and/or low wages. Fundamentally, the job lacked credibility as a legitimate form of employment. Although there were numerous domestic science training programs sponsored by women's organizations and local governments, social attitudes rejected housework as work, a claim that in the 1960s and 1970s was rejected by Marxist feminists like Mariarosa Dalla Costa and Selma James, who recognized the reproductive value of domestic labor. These women joined women's rights activists such as Silvia Federici to advocate for wages for housework.[9]

Unlike other jobs, there were no opportunities for advancement and promotion. As such, women were routinely ignored in matters of labor legislation. Presenting her case to Marge, Mildred explains the benefits that come with unionization, such as "set hours and set pay just like bus drivers and other folks" (Childress, *Like One* 140). She also explains that union support is essential not only to negotiate for fair wages but also to protect domestic workers from harsh and dangerous working conditions—like waxing floors by hand, a job that is best handled by machine. In her view, employers should contact the union to hire men to take on strenuous work ill-suited for women. While Mildred proposes a number of important benefits to be derived from union membership, she acknowledges the shortcomings that come with organizing women to join unions or participate in union activity. First, domestic workers, especially live-out workers, had different work schedules, which made it challenging to settle on a meeting time that could accommodate their schedules. There was also the reality that some women were averse to joining unions. Cooke's study revealed that some women did not join unions because working on the books might potentially cut their welfare payments, leaving them without adequate income to cover expenses. Others had family obligations and their own households to clean. Mostly, women did not want to compromise their ability to be hired by employers who were against hiring union employees. Mildred urged these women to stop working for such employers. She insisted domestic workers must expose employers who reject union workers. In her opinion, domestics have the power to handicap the employer by simply refusing to show up for work and going on strike. Ultimately, she explains that a domestic workers' union might mobilize all the women who work in particular neighborhoods to unite in protest against women who refused to hire union workers. Moreover, she suggests they could make public the names of anti-union employers so that maids would know which employers to avoid. She explains to Marge, "Well then the union calls out all the folks who work in that buildin', and we'll march up and down in front of that apartment house carryin' signs which will read, 'Miss So-and-so of Apartment 5B is unfair to organized house workers!'" (Childress, *Like One* 141). Mildred insists such actions will be effective because other employers will be inconvenienced by the absence of their own maid, who is marching for the cause instead of being at work. This revolutionary rhetoric is emblematic of Childress's Marxist views about the lack of workers' protection for domestic workers. Ultimately, she endeavored to show these women that not only could they be strategic, but also with union representation and simple tactics they would have the leverage needed to negotiate the terms of their employment. In effect, "Childress was giving them a theory of labor rights, an authorization for dissent and a language to speak against injustice, constructing them and herself as bona fide figures of the left" (Washington 198). Although her readers may not have detected her didacticism, she was teaching domestics to take charge of their lives.

Mildred has several conversations with political overtones. Her political views on civil rights issues of the day bleed into the narrative to include her impressions on apartheid in South Africa and the Montgomery Bus Boycott. Mildred's reference to these historical moments serves as another example of Childress's conscious effort to use her narrative didactically. What is important to note here is her pan-African sensibility as she recognizes the shared plight of blacks suffering under white supremacist governments in Africa and in America. Mildred's voice is ironic and humorous, and important for its time, but what is most important is her voice for the community that relates to her experiences. She gave the domestic worker an authentic voice, dignity, and the tools to organize and fight for workers' rights. Sixty years after its initial printing, Childress's book, reprinted in 2017, continues to serve as a model for literature about black female agency and self-determination.

3
Dirty Work
The Representation of Undocumented Caribbean Domestic Laborers in Nandi Keyi's The True Nanny Diaries *and Victoria Brown's* Minding Ben

In 2019, when Alfonso Cuarón, the renowned Mexican film director, screenwriter, and producer, won an Academy Award for directing the film *Roma*, a moving portrayal of the life of a Mexican domestic laborer in Mexico City, he shared concerns about the marginalization of domestic workers in the national imaginary. During his acceptance speech, Cuarón applauded the Motion Picture Academy for recognizing a film that sheds light on the exploitation of an indigenous Latin American domestic worker, who is "one of the 70 million domestic workers in the world without work rights" and "a character that had historically been relegated in the background in cinema. As artists, our job is to look where others do not. This responsibility becomes much more important in times when we are being encouraged to look away" (Miranda).

Indeed, Hollywood has failed to bring stories like *Roma* to the fore. While there is a long history of domestic workers represented on-screen, these tales of domestic life have been glamorized in popular twentieth-century classics like *Mary Poppins* (1964), *The Sound of Music* (1965), and *Nanny McPhee* (2006). In *Mary Poppins* and *The Sound of Music*, the attractive, young white protagonists of these films are not labeled maids but governesses called upon to rescue parents with wayward children, which they do with good-natured fun and adventure. In addition to balancing the demands of their wards, they are also often swept away by an available bachelor, who puts the bow on the fairy-tale ending of these romanticized versions of domestic life. In 2007, the film adaptation of *The Nanny Diaries* attempted to modify the fantastical *Mary Poppins* narrative with a more authentic portrayal of domestic workers. While the film definitely succeeds in shedding light on the struggles faced by childcare workers, it continues to privilege the perspective of the white domestic while marginalizing the voices of the thousands of black and brown domestic laborers who actually make up the majority of the domestic labor force.[1] Thus *The Nanny Diaries* illustrates the need for increased visibility in media of black and brown working-class women whose stories of life in service lack representation.

While chapters 1 and 2 discussed the experiences of African American domestics prior to and during the civil rights movement who endured racism, the humiliation of Jim Crow laws, and exploitation of their labor, chapter 3 focuses on the Caribbean women domestics who replaced the African American women who left domestic work in the 1970s and 1980s for administrative positions and other types of employment. Caribbean novelists offer an insight into the lives of domestic workers, specifically migrant domestics, that is markedly different from stories like *The Nanny Diaries* or *Like One of the Family*. An examination of Nandi Keyi's *The True Nanny Diaries* and Victoria Brown's *Minding Ben* reflects the struggles of domestics, many of whom are undocumented workers employed off the books as part of the so-called shadow economy (work for wages that are not reported or taxed), which leaves them vulnerable and easily exploited. A comparative reading of *The Nanny Diaries* with *The True Nanny Diaries* and *Minding Ben* shows that the migrant domestic workers' race, class, and immigration status account for a very different story about life as a domestic. The authors present everyday struggles of women contending with harsher realities than those in *The Nanny Diaries* film, such as housing insecurity and deportation. Moreover, their stories emphasize the need for legislation for these workers who are without protection under labor laws and are therefore vulnerable laborers.

The novel *The Nanny Diaries* (2002) was a *New York Times* best seller by Emma McLaughlin and Nicola Kraus, two American-born white women who were nannies on New York's Upper East Side for more than seven years. The book is a social critique of nannying in New York City. In a *New York Times* interview, McLaughlin reports *The Nanny Diaries* was conceived after she and Kraus worked as nannies to help pay for college (Hayden-Guest). In 2007, the film adaptation introduced McLaughlin and Kraus's story to a wider audience. The film, described in the trailer as "a comedy about life at the top as seen from the bottom," features the stars Scarlett Johansson (Annie Braddock) and veteran Laura Linney (Mrs. X) and was billed as an updated version of *Mary Poppins* ("Trailer"). To stress this point, in an early scene in the movie, the protagonist replicates Mary Poppins sailing down from the sky holding her iconic umbrella. Earning $50 million worldwide, the film was a success for the distributors (Weinstein Company), who premiered it at the Venice Film Festival and lobbied for it to be a contender for awards like the Golden Globes (Mohr). The film's comedic tone and young white protagonist made this story about the harrowing experience of domestic workers palatable to audiences who might have been less comfortable finding amusement in a narrative about the power dynamics between a black or Latina domestic and her employers.

Although *The Nanny Diaries* was a contemporized rendering of Mary Poppins, it lacked some of the former's glamour. The fantastical happenings of Mary Poppins, who teaches the mischievous but lovable Banks children to find joy (and song) in the mundane, has little in common with this film's harsh social critique of how the elite abuse their class privilege and power. Within two years of the film's release, several novels about Caribbean immigrant domestic workers living and working in New York City were published; first, Nandi Keyi's *The True Nanny Diaries* (2009) followed by Victoria Brown's *Minding Ben* (2010). Keyi and Brown belong to a tradition of Caribbean authors who have written about challenges for Caribbean domestics in North America, such as Paule Marshall's *Brown Girl, Brownstones* (1959), Dionne Brand's *Sans Souci* (1989) and Jamaica Kincaid's *Lucy* (1990). Of these three, Kincaid's *Lucy*, which was serialized in the *New Yorker*, was one of the first novels to bring a story about the Caribbean migrant's experience as a domestic worker to a broad audience. Thematically, Lucy's tale about a young Antiguan girl who migrates to New York to work as an au pair overlaps with Keyi's and Brown's novels. The major difference between Kincaid's novella and Keyi's and Brown's novels is the visa status of her protagonist. Lucy is an au pair (an elevated title that sets her apart from the maid) and a documented worker. Her status changes the trajectory of her novel because she is not faced with the same challenges encountered by the undocumented migrant protagonists of *The True Nanny Diaries* and *Minding Ben*. Moreover, unlike them, the light of the American dream does not blind her.

Keeping It Real: The Real Nanny Diaries

Although Keyi's self-published novel did not receive the kind of media attention granted to *The Nanny Diaries*, through self-promotion her book found its own audience and was published in multiple languages. The title of Keyi's novel reads as a challenge to *The Nanny Diaries* and suggests that her text offers a more authentic rendition of life as a babysitter in New York City. Like the protagonist Valdi, Keyi (a native of Trinidad), who migrated to New York from Canada, turned to domestic work as a last resort. In an interview with scholar Brenda Greene, she explains, "It was something I didn't want to do. Being Afrocentric it bothered me, and I know it also bothered African American women." Black women's uneasiness with domestic work is, as Keyi's protagonist, Valdi, explains, sometimes perceived as an affront to the civil rights movement: "I didn't want ferrying this boy around them judgmental black Harlemites who would perceive my efforts at making a living as prancing on the graves of Martin and Malcolm: kicking Rosa off the bus; cancelling the Thirteenth, Fourteenth, and Fifteenth Amendments. . . . But again it was about a rock and a hard place. It was sink or swim" (Keyi 106). Like Valdi, Keyi sought domestic work because, like so many migrants, she found it was the quickest route to employment. She was surprised by how easy it was to find a family: "There's almost like a don't ask don't tell policy. Nobody even asked for ID. I found these women on *Craig's list* [*sic*]" (Greene).

The impetus for *The True Nanny Diaries* came from a university Professor who Keyi had confided in about her struggles on the job. Her professor advised, "Instead of complaining, write about it" (Greene). Keyi heeded the advice and set pen to paper. Although the work is semi-autobiographical, Keyi is clear it is fictional: "There's a lot of me in it [and] there are sketches of real people I met on the playground" (Greene). Keyi published *The True Nanny Diaries* to give voice to the authentic experiences of a diverse array of immigrant domestic workers of Caribbean descent, who by choice or necessity remain tied to domestic jobs for almost half their lives, often overworked and underpaid. Many of these women are constrained by motherhood, lack of education, or immigrant status and often go unrecognized as they blend into our streets and homes.

Minding Ben was published shortly after *The True Nanny Diaries* and also chronicles the plight of the undocumented migrant domestic. Unlike Keyi, Brown was fortunate to receive a book deal with Hyperion, a major publisher, and as a result, received endorsements for the book jacket and reviews by major news outlets, including the *New York Times*, *Kirkus Reviews*, and *Library Journal.* Her publishers also went as far as to market the book similarly to *The Nanny Diaries* and *Mary Poppins*—the book jacket features a nanny holding the infamous umbrella. As a memoir combined with the stories of other domestics, *Minding Ben* is a cautionary tale about the American dream and the insecurity of undocumented domestic workers whose status makes them vulnerable and exploited. The idea for the book came while Brown was working on her thesis at the University of Warwick in England. As she began laying the foundation for her novel, *The Nanny Diaries* was released and temporarily dampened her enthusiasm for her own project: "I remember reading the review and freaking out . . . I just kept yelling, 'They wrote my book!' It exploded and I thought the nanny story is done, no one is going to want to read this. And then a year went by and I realized that my story is my story" (Sidman).

Like all the writers included in this study, Brown's motivation for the book came from a desire to bring visibility to domestics. She recalls her own experience of being ignored and disregarded: "'I was one of those anonymous women pushing a child on the upper east side,' Ms. Brown recalled. 'I'd be in the building's lobby with the little boy and the neighbors would say hello to the little boy but not to me. There was a degree of invisibility. It might sound corny, but I wanted to give these women some inner life'" (Lee). In *Minding Ben*, Brown succeeds in making domestics more than interchangeable figures standing behind strollers.

The publication of *The Nanny Diaries*, *The True Nanny Diaries*, and *Minding Ben* indicated a pressing need to tell these stories and a receptive audience to buy them. Coincidentally, these novels appeared during a pivotal moment in the history of labor organizing for domestic workers. The work of labor activists and domestic workers was gaining traction in playgrounds, in Congress, and in academia. In fact, in 2007, the same year *The Nanny Diaries* was released, Ai Jen Poo founded the New York Domestic Workers Alliance (NYDWA), an organization advocating for domestic workers' rights. According to sociologist Tamara Mose Brown, of the 1,300 members, 300 were active at that time (133).[2] Poo, along with NYDWA founding member Allison Julien, from Barbados, took to the streets of New York City, marching for immigrants' rights, passing out flyers, and recruiting domestics to join their organization. Later, the grassroots efforts of Poo and Julien merged with academics and other activists advocating for labor rights.

On June 6, 2008, Barnard College held the first National Domestic Workers Alliance Conference, bringing together scholars, activists, and organizations committed to both empowering domestic workers and establishing the *Domestic Workers' Bill of Rights* that would protect domestic workers under New York state's labor laws.[3] This movement sought to extend similar protections to domestic workers in the state of New York. Concurrently with the efforts of activists and scholars, New York state representatives debated and crafted legislation for a *Domestic Workers' Bill of Rights*, which was eventually passed August 31, 2010, and signed into law by African American governor David Patterson (D). Under the new law, workers were granted the labor rights advocates had demanded: vacation days, sick days, overtime wages, and so on.[4] Each in their own way, *The Nanny Diaries*, *The True Nanny Diaries*, and *Minding Ben* contribute to the discourse on labor rights for domestic workers from the perspectives of those who do the work.

On the surface, the plotlines for *The Nanny Diaries*, *The True Nanny Diaries*, and *Minding Ben* are similar. All the works portray young, educated women living in New York City and working as nannies for elite families; all of the characters are subject to abuse at the hands of their employers, both men and women; and all cope with personal issues independent from their jobs. But there is a fundamental difference between the story told by McLaughlin and Kraus and the stories told by Keyi and Brown: the white American protagonist in *The Nanny Diaries* has race, class, and citizenship privileges that protect her from some of the experiences that make life much more difficult for migrant workers, especially those who are undocumented. In general, women who work as childminders join the occupation because of their love for children or because they have few other options. Some women go through agencies and others through local informal networks of nannies and parents. Although domestic work is often viewed as not professional or "real" work, most of the individuals who do this work take their jobs as seriously as laborers in any other occupation.

In its Hollywood fashion, *The Nanny Diaries* trivializes domestic work by making Annie's foray into childcare by happenstance a fun project. The protagonist is a young, recent New York University college graduate who has failed her first round of job interviews.

Although she holds a business degree, she is fearful about entering corporate America and undecided about her career aspirations. Conversely, Annie is eager to put to good use her college minor in anthropology, and after she inadvertently becomes a nanny, she engages in an unofficial anthropological study of the stereotypical Park Avenue neurotic, demanding, Upper East Side housewife and socialite. Annie's foray into domestic work commences after a character known only as Mrs. X witnesses Annie comfort her son Grayer, who had fallen in the park. Mrs. X assumes Annie is a nanny and, because she is desperate to replace her current child-minder, offers Annie a job. Annie half-heartedly tries explaining the misidentification, but jobless, she attends the follow-up appointment and finds herself drawn in by the opportunity to hide from her responsibilities and step into the lives of the city's elites. Very quickly she learns that she is not only unprepared for the challenges that come with minding children, but she is ill-equipped to interact with the parents as well.

Domestic work is one of the most racialized professions in the service industry. Globally, women of color make up the largest numbers of domestics. Scholar Shellee Colen notes that "domestic work is often assigned to racially or ethnically distinct groups who are accorded low status in an ideological context that turns difference from those in power into inferiority. Conversely, performing this disdain work reinforces low status" (180). The perceived low status of domestics determines the rate of pay for specific ethnic groups. Given that educated white women domestics are the minority in large cities like New York City, Boston, Los Angeles, and San Francisco, as the film suggests, they are the most desirable and can command wages higher than most women of color. Annie attests to this when she describes herself as equivalent to a designer bag—the "Chanel" bag of nannies. Annie's positionality within the domestic work industry mirrors inequity in the private sector between white women and women of color. Even when black and white women have the same qualifications, white women earn more and have more advantages. According to Raine Dozier, since the 1980s, the wage pay gap between white and black women has steadily increased, "becoming two and a half times larger by 2002" (18–34).

Annie not only earns more than the other women, but she has the luxury of taking the job by choice; it is something she can do while trying to figure out life, in contrast to the protagonists of *The True Nanny Diaries* and *Minding Ben*, both of whom are undocumented workers who have few alternatives beyond service work. Valdi and Grace migrate to America seeking the American dream. Neither sets out to work as a domestic, but after unexpected difficulties, it is the only option, and the job is relatively easy to find, requires few skills, and allows laborers to work off the books as part of what is known as the shadow economy. According to *New York Times* journalist Lauren Hilgers, "It is estimated that only about five percent of domestic workers in the United States are paid on the books." Some women see the job as temporary, a means to an end, but often they find themselves tied to the job for years. In *The True Nanny Diaries*, Valdi enters the United States legally. She arrives in New York a twenty-five-year-old graduate student from Trinidad on a student visa to attend Columbia University. After the organization that gave Valdi a scholarship abruptly terminates the program that brought her to America, she loses her ability to pay for school and thus her visa. Valdi chooses to remain in the country, but without papers, she must work off the books, and domestic work is one of the few jobs that comes easily. But what was supposed to be temporary turns into a more than ten-year career, a fact that makes her bitter:

> My America was peeping at other people's Kodak moments at play dates, in playrooms and parks, feeling like wet bread. My America was the grinding minutiae of dreams unfulfilled . . . I had gone from studying at a prestigious institution to baby-sitting and playing with little white children, by the steps of an old sundial, on the grounds of that very institution. (Keyi 52–53)

While Valdi is unable to transition from life as a domestic and has little to show for her time in the service sector, her associates believe in the American dream, a belief that charts a pathway to their success: Ava, for example, is able to earn her degree while working as a domestic and is offered a job as a school psychologist (the employers who paid for her education have other plans). Another character, Madame Lucien, is a shrewd businesswoman who spends her days caring for three children and her nights earning money on the side with a microbusiness baking bread. By the end of the novel, she has saved almost $9,000 to build a home back on her home island, St. Lucia.

In *Minding Ben*, Grace's arrival in the United States is also predicated on the American dream. She needs money to help her ailing father. Grace leaves Trinidad for America after she is invited to visit by her cousin, but the family member never arrives at the airport to meet her. Fortunately, Grace is taken in by Sylvia, a fellow island woman who takes pity on her but also exploits Grace's situation by coercing her into serving as her babysitter in exchange for lodging. When Grace's visa expires, she is compelled to remain in New York, wholeheartedly believing in the American dream.

Neither Valdi nor Grace considers returning home when their visas expire. Their decision to remain in the United States is driven by the reality of Trinidad's fragile economy and intergenerational poverty. Valdi's and Grace's stories of migrating to the United States from the Caribbean and falling into domestic work are typical narratives. Prior to the civil rights movement, domestic work was a field occupied primarily by African Americans until they left the profession for manufacturing jobs and administrative work. High rates of unemployment and politics drove waves of Caribbean women to the United States in large numbers in the 1960s and 1970s. Those who could went into nursing or social work. Others secured childcare work through employment agencies, such as the Frances Green Employment Agency (Nadasen 157). Later in the 1980s and 1990s, many worked through informal employment networks. Mose Brown notes that, according to the census figures, there has been a steady increase of women as childcare workers: "In 1980 such workers numbered 980, in 1990 they numbered 1,752, in 2000 they numbered 7,007, and in 2006/08 they numbered 9,232" (27).

Many women who came to the United States forty years ago believe the same thing as women who migrate today: domestic work is a pathway to citizenship. In fact, for some it was and continues to be an option. U.S. immigration law allows employers to sponsor workers for U.S. Permanent Resident status by filing paperwork indicating their intention to offer the foreign national permanent employment. When Grace is hired, for example, the Bruckners dupe her into believing they will complete this process to help her become a Permanent Resident Alien (green-card holder). For months the Bruckners deceive her and pretend they have submitted the required forms. At one point they even show her the completed paperwork. Although friends caution Grace to be wary of the Bruckners, to her detriment, Grace is naive. A year later she learns her employers never intended to sponsor her; they were using the promise of the green card as a manipulative tool to guarantee her labor.

Scholar Mary Romero explains how employers use promises and their resources as psychological control: "Employers' rewards and inducements bind the worker in an emotional and economic trap. Simply the promise or expectation that the employer might pay more, provide gifts, or help the employee get a green card obliges the worker beyond the boundaries of the contractual work arrangement" (151). Both Keyi and Brown illustrate that those who cannot secure residency legally find other methods, such as falsified documents or arranged marriages. At one point, Valdi considers marrying the uncle of one of her good friends, but she waits too long for him to ask her, and he instead marries her friend: "Uncle Ram said he would do anything to help someone get settled in America, especially a woman with children like Monica" (Keyi 23). In this instance, the arrangement works out, not simply as a business arrangement but as a real marriage. Even then, Monica complains that her husband uses the green-card marriage as a form of control: "Monica implored Ava to talk to uncle Ram about his controlling ways. Ava agreed, but told Monica not to expect a change. 'That's why he had no wife when you met him. I warned you to keep it strictly business. A green-card marriage is a green-card marriage Monica, there's no pleasure in that'" (Keyi 204). For Monica, this marriage allows her to sponsor her own children to move to America. Transnational mothers who migrate from their countries to earn money sometimes regret their decision to leave. An important scene in *The Nanny Diaries* offers this perspective: "I left my country because I thought I could give this boy and my mother a better life. I thought I would be here two to three years tops. While I've been raising these stranger's children my own child has grown up without a mother" (30:12–31:00)

Grace is skeptical about entering into a green-card marriage. The idea is presented to Grace both by her employer, who suggests she proposition the doorman, and by Bo, her housemate's brother. Bo knows Grace is in an awkward position and sees a green-card marriage as a capitalist opportunity. Although he tries to convince Grace to accept a $3,000 deal for the sham marriage, Grace declines.

Legislation Now!

Domestics who participate in the shadow economy, especially those who are undocumented, take incredible risks working without papers. A vengeful employer displeased with their productivity (or personality) can easily report a known undocumented worker to immigration services. Some employers, for ethical or tax purposes, opt not to hire off the books. Valdi and Grace are both rejected by employers who will not work with undocumented workers, but they gain employment with others who are the beneficiaries of their cheap labor. Sometimes being undocumented makes the worker an easy target for harassment. On several occasions, Grace is sexually harassed by Miriam's husband, Sol, who openly flirts and often roams the home partially clothed. Grace says nothing for fear of retaliation from his wife, Miriam, who is insecure and jealous of Grace. Grace also experiences microaggressions from Miriam and other relatives about her race and nationality, but she shrugs at their ignorance. Valdi, despite her predicament and because of her age, demands her employers' respect. Like Mildred in Childress's stories, she will not be mistreated. Unlike Grace or Annie, she is free from sexual misconduct but does find herself enduring verbal abuse from her employer's husband, who calls her a "nigger."

Annie endures her own share of abuse. In addition to being emotionally abusive, Mrs. X forces Annie to take on extra responsibilities, and she monopolizes her time by having her accompany the family to her weekend home, only to learn that she is expected to be the caretaker for other people's children. Annie is also sexually harassed by Mr. X, a philandering husband. The sexual harassment experienced by Grace and Annie and their silence in the wake of this harassment speaks to concerns of the #MeToo movement. Unfortunately, the headline news was mostly made by Hollywood starlets who were violated while domestics were often excluded from national news stories about women who endured sexual harassment in the workplace.

Fortunately, smaller news outlets like *Vice News* ran stories about the harassment of domestics and agricultural laborers.[5] Bernice Yeung's publication *In a Day's Work: The Fight to End Sexual Violence against America's Most Vulnerable Workers* (2018) is also a much-needed in-depth study of assault on farmworkers, janitors, and domestics. Brown, McLaughlin and Kraus, and Keyi only give a snapshot of the horrors experienced by domestics. Even still, some question if novels like these are more hyperbole than reality. A reviewer of Brown's novel wrote, "The Bruckners' casual cruelty beggars belief, but Grace's inability to fight back is even more implausible" ("Minding Ben"). Clearly, this person missed the larger point, which is that some domestics cannot defend themselves against such infractions, no matter how trivial or serious, because they are undocumented, fearful of retaliation, or have a strong attachment to their ward. Carol Pier and Orville Schell point out that "many workers choose to endure human rights violations temporarily rather than face deportation. Others endure the abuses because their cultural and social isolation—lack of knowledge of U.S. law, few local contacts and friends, and [in some cases] inability to communicate in English—make the steps required to flee their employers, find alternative housing, and seek legal redress prohibitively daunting."

As much as domestic workers might remain in toxic workplace environments, they are also wary of the temporality of their employment. Domestics exist in a profession predicated on the age of their charges. Once a child (or children) reaches a certain age, a nanny is expendable. There is a complicated dance between employer and employee, who are both aware of the tacit agreement that at some point (often before or after preschool) full-time care will no longer be needed. Childcare workers who have a good rapport with family might discuss transitioning to a new position so they are not terminated without warning, and likewise, employers might feel obliged to advise their employees to seek a new job due to changing needs of the family. Sometimes both parties prepare for this situation, consulting with friends, with other nannies, or on social media sites. Not all employers feel obliged to inform employees that they are terminating their services. Some are afraid to disclose their plans too soon, in case the nanny opts to leave immediately, jeopardizing childcare. Other employers simply regard domestics as dispensable.

The disposability of childcare workers is addressed by all three writers. *The True Nanny Diaries* opens with Valdi in a coffee shop looking for jobs on the bulletin board. A particular posting for a "Live-in Nanny Position" catches her eye: "Our babysitter needs a home. She crawls on the floor! She dances! She clowns! She wrestles! She makes faces! My girls really adore her but our needs have changed and we want to pass her on to a good family" (Keyi 2). Even before Valdi reaches the end of the advertisement, she realizes it is herself being described in it. She is outraged by her employers' characterization of her as infantile and equally offended by her obvious disposability and her employer's cowardice. As an undocumented worker, Valdi has no legal contract and cannot challenge her termination. The same kind of dismissal happens to Valdi's friend, who has worked with a family for many years. Once again, it is Valdi who spots the posting. Conversely, Grace plays a role in her own firing (during an emergency, she defied her employer's rule never to take their son to Brooklyn). Even though her actions warrant termination, later she learns the family was planning to leave without informing her of their departure. Finally, Annie is fired after the sexual harassment incident. Of these three women, the situation is most dire for Valdi and Grace, both live-in workers. Annie can return to her mother's home in New Jersey, but Valdi and Grace are at the mercy of others.

The issue of housing insecurity and domestic workers is one that does not usually surface in mainstream news stories about the challenges faced by domestics. Few take into account how many domestics take on this work precisely because it offers housing, which can in some ways mitigate other issues. Live-in nannies are often desired by parents with several children under school-age or parents who travel. Working as a live-in has its advantages and disadvantages. Housing is convenient for domestics who do not earn the income to cover rent, especially in major urban centers where rent is extremely high. The proximity to the family also means lack of privacy and the potential to be "on call" to parents after hours. After Valdi learns she is soon to be fired, she begs her employer to stay a little longer, so she can find alternative lodging. Grace, on the other hand, knows she can always return to Sylvia's, but even her arrangement is not ideal or guaranteed. For the undocumented worker, the lack of housing makes them extremely vulnerable. In many states, they are not entitled to any social services programs for the unemployed: healthcare, food stamps, and temporary housing. The unpredictability of housing and employment causes great stress for undocumented workers. Constant worries about their families back home can also add to their burden and lead to emotional turmoil, especially for those without a support network. Women who cannot confide in other domestics, their relatives, or even their employers can feel isolated. This is shown in *The True Nanny Diaries* when Valdi, after losing her job, goes into a depression. Fortunately, her friends help her find both a new job and an apartment. Some women are not as fortunate.

Dionne Brand's short story "No rinsed blue sky" provides an excellent example of the severity of the duress experienced by immigrant domestic workers. The unnamed protagonist of Brand's story struggles to cope with separation from her baby daughter and the knowledge that she cannot pay her mounting bills. Each day when she returns from work, she secludes herself in the apartment, growing paranoid by thoughts of the walls closing in and an incessantly ringing telephone. Over time, she becomes irrationally terrified, with a fear of immigration services arriving at her home to deport her to the Caribbean. The woman has a few friends, but she is too prideful to share her troubles. When the weight of her stress becomes too much to bear, she contemplates taking her life. Each day is a struggle, but she finds the courage to persevere. While this woman is able to make it through difficult moments, as we'll learn in chapter 5, some migrant domestics feel so worthless and undervalued that they eventually do make the decision to end their lives. Studies on mental health and immigration report that migration comes with the risk of "acculturation stresses" due to factors such as "family upheaval, social isolation, violence, addictions, language and cultural barriers, employment, certification processes, and lack of access to programs and services that many encounter . . . and gender is implicated in these migration processes" (MacDonnell et al.). The challenges for migrant workers are also linked to the larger issue of labor laws and the absence of adequate policies for these workers.

All three novels speak to a fundamental problem with reproductive labor: the lack of protection for workers and the relationship between labor rights and immigration. Each day, the nation benefits from the labor of millions of undocumented workers whose contributions to the economy enable our society to function. Sometimes the government overlooks these workers in the service industry, agriculture, and manufacturing, and other times they do not. In 2019, under President Trump's administration, for example, the government has been more vigilant in its efforts to arrest, detain, and deport undocumented workers. Advocates for domestic workers argue that denying work visas restricts domestics from alternative kinds of employment beyond domestic work or other low-paying jobs in the service industry. Some domestics suspect the government does little to provide working visas or green cards because, as mentioned previously, many private industries exploit cheap labor (Mose Brown 146). Ultimately, given that domestic work is one of few jobs available to immigrant women, they are forced to accept low wages ($7.25 federal minimum wage and $10.40 minimum state wage in New York) and less than ideal working conditions because it is what keeps them from deportation.[6]

Keyi directly addresses her readers about the urgency of fighting for their rights. Rather than integrate a call for the then-pending *Domestic Workers' Bill of Rights* into the plotline, Keyi used the novel's foreword to explain why the bill is important. The book's foreword, by Kevin Parker, a former New York state senator, outlines the importance of the legislation (Senate Bill S2311) of which he was a sponsor. He writes,

> Although the labor of approx. 1.5 million nannies, maids and housekeepers is still central to the ongoing prosperity of this nation, they remain among the most marginalized in the US. . . . If passed, it will amend New York State's labor law to give thousands of housekeepers, nannies and companions to the elderly, inter alia, one day off each calendar week, seven days of sick leave and five vacation days each year. It would include domestic workers and their employers in the New York State human rights law. (Parker qtd. in Keyi ii)

Finally, he acknowledges the link between the bill and the millions of undocumented workers who were without protection: "Senate Bill S2311 must serve as a challenge to engage comprehensive immigration reform and create a pathway to citizenship. It is imperative that we protect these workers who, though undocumented, give their all so that Americans can conduct their own important work outside of the home" (Parker qtd. in Keyi ii). Again, by using the senator's statement as the foreword, Keyi signals the seriousness of the bill, which is not to be taken as fiction but as a political tool on behalf of domestics. As previously noted, the bill was signed into law in August 2010.

It has been ten years since the *Domestic Workers' Bill of Rights* was enacted, and the fight for nationwide And global workers' rights for domestics continues. Hollywood has also been slow to change.[7] Unfortunately, they are still in the business of Disneyfying the nanny experience with heart-warming musicals like *Nanny Poppins Returns* (2019) instead of grittier stories about the everyday struggles of domestics reaching for the American dream. Fortunately, the publishing industry continues to recognize the importance of black women's perspectives in relationship to telling narratives about the domestic worker. Nicole Dennis-Benn's *Patsy* (2019) is another work about a Caribbean domestic in New York. Dennis-Benn's novel brings a fresh approach to the Caribbean domestic's story by exploring new themes about motherhood, gender, and sexuality. Several other new works about domestics in service show a widening of the pool to include the perspective of African domestics: Chimamanda Adichie Ngozi's *Americanah* (2014) and Imbolo Mbue's *Behold the Dreamers* (2017) serve as two good examples.

At its essence, the absence of immigrant domestic women's stories in the American national imaginary speaks to the privileging and reproduction of specific standpoints (here working-class white women). In her discussion of feminist analyses of labor studies, scholar Evelyn Nakano Glenn determines, "When they [academicians] portray reproductive labor only as gendered, they assume there is only one standpoint—that of white women. Hence the activities and experiences of middle-class white women become generic 'female' experiences and activities, and those of other groups become variant, deviant, or specialized" (145). The same argument can be applied beyond feminist circles to Hollywood producers who insist on reproducing the image of the working-class domestic as exclusively white. Fortunately, novels like *The True Nanny Diaries* and *Minding Ben* present everyday struggles of women contending with harsher realities than those in Hollywood blockbusters. Hopefully, one day novels like these will make their way to the big screen.

4
Forbidden Kinship
Homoerotic Desire between the Maid and Mistress in Zanele Muholi's "Massa" and Mina(h)

In 2010 South African photographer Zanele Muholi participated in Gabi Ngcobo's installation in *PASS-AGES: References & Footnotes* (2010), a series of works about South Africans living under the apartheid state (Bethlehem). Muholi's contribution, *Work as Usual*, was a series of photographs representing domestic workers, one of whom was her own mother, Bester Muholi. Bester is featured in a short newspaper article similarly entitled "Work as Usual for Bester," which spotlights her experience working for forty-two years as a domestic for two generations of the Harding family. The article portrayed Bester as grateful for the chance to have worked for the Hardings. Bester, who was at the time of the interview still employed by the Hardings, unsurprisingly only had good things to say about her employers but lamented that she was separated from her children. She recounted how Mr. Harding tried to console her by saying she was "one of the family" ("Work as Usual for Bester"). As noted in chapter 2, Alice Childress argues that even if the sentiment is genuine, as long as the relationship between maids and their employers is hierarchical, they can never be equals. Muholi had similar thoughts about her mother's relationship with the Hardings. Certainly, she did not doubt the kinship between her mother and Mrs. Harding, but she was aware of the limitations of the relationship, especially during apartheid, when whites deemed blacks inferior. Moreover, these women were supposedly great friends, and yet Mrs. Harding paid Bester meager wages that could barely support her family and overlooked the extended working hours that kept Bester apart from her children. But still, there was something to be said about their lifelong friendship, which prompted Muholi to look more deeply at the bond between domestics and their employers. This chapter discusses how throughout her career, Muholi has curated a collection of self-portraits in homage to her mother and the great sacrifices she and other maids made to provide for their families. In addition to exploring how Muholi's portraits enable her to preserve her mother's legacy, this chapter also considers how provocative artwork like *"Massa" and Mina(h)* (2008) invites audiences to think more broadly about relationships between women in the domestic sphere. Muholi envisions some maids and madams in platonic and homoerotic relationships that stand in defiance of racial and sexual norms. These radical images in *"Massa" and Mina(h)* are as much about maids and madams as they are about the queer encounters between women whose expression of same-sex desire is denied public recognition. In *"Massa" and Mina(h)*, as well as in *Somnyama Ngonyama, Hail the Dark Lioness* (2012–2017) and other pieces, the lives of both the black maid and the LGBTQI+ individual are documented and put on display so that they can be seen beyond the labels that define their personhood.

Muholi is a self-described lesbian and visual activist. She was educated at Ryerson University in Toronto, where she completed her MFA in documentary media (2009) and wrote her thesis on the postapartheid black lesbian experience. Muholi's documentaries and portraits are intended to document her own life and also, in her words, "make a visual statement" about the rampant homophobia leading to the victimization and marginalization of lesbians and gays because of their transgender identities or same-gender loving relationships. At the same time, archiving their experiences and allowing them to be seen as themselves, with their partners, without shame, subverts the subjugation that denies them public visibility. Along with highlighting the lives of members of the LGBTQI+ community, Muholi has been equally as passionate about spotlighting the stories of domestic workers, most notably her mother. Throughout her career, her portraits of maids have brought dignity to a generation of women who, like members of the LGBTQI+ community, lack representation and recognition. In almost every interview, Muholi references her muse, her mother Bester. In a 2018 interview she explains why it is important to give Bester a voice: "My mother never had an opportunity to own her own voice until she died" (*Artnet*). Muholi, who did not spend a great deal of time with her mother, attempts to reconstruct parts of her mother's life through the general history of black women in South Africa and through memory, not simply as memories existing solely in her own mind but in the collective memories of all those who knew her. In her self-portraits, Muholi becomes the physical manifestation of Bester, who is given voice and agency. Unfortunately, Bester died from cancer on September 27, 2009, and never had the opportunity to see any of her daughter's completed work.

Muholi knew the great burden carried by women like her mother and countless other victims of the apartheid state whose poverty, lack of access to education, and forfeiture of land rights forced them into a profession that exploited their labor for decades. Bester worked for almost her entire life under apartheid, a caste system of racial segregation mandated by the government (1948–1994). During apartheid, white settlers, although the minority, controlled the country's government, land, and the nation's lucrative resources, including gold and diamond mines. Black South Africans were denied the right to vote, move freely, or live with basic human dignity. Black women in particular bore the brunt of apartheid. In addition to their intersectional oppression, they suffered the burden of raising their children as single parents while their husbands worked for several months of the year as migrant laborers in gold and diamond mines, or they were, like Bester, domestics or agricultural laborers away from home, making the equivalent of less than $1 an hour. The apartheid regime was designed to regulate the bodies of black South Africans, and they achieved this aim through the restriction of their movement. In 1866, pass laws were instituted to ensure native South Africans settled in areas specified by the government. Those who were discovered outside the confines of their residential areas without a pass from their employer could be arrested. Pass laws created problems for those who worked in white-only spaces or wanted access to relatives living and working in white-only spaces. Duma Ndlovu and Mbongeni Ngema's play *Sheila's Day* (1998) dramatizes how desperate women compromised their dignity and defied the law in order to secure passbooks. The playwrights uncover the cruelty of white employers and government officials who used the pass laws as a manipulative tool to control women. If, for example, a woman was sent to jail for working without a pass, she might be forced to trade sexual favors in return for her freedom. For more than thirty years, Bester Muholi lived and worked according to these pass laws that limited access to her children, who could not freely visit her at work. Sociologist Shireen Ally observes that "when the state urban contractual apparatus made it illegal for any black person to be on a white premises without being a registered employee, employers were able to completely cut domestic workers off from their families" (47).

Over the years, South African women have not remained silent about the oppression of the indigenous community and the victimization of women in particular. They fought back against the pass laws, apartheid, and the sexual assault on black women. Women like Florence Matomela, an activist who spoke out against discriminatory laws, were bold revolutionaries who put their lives on the line for just causes. Others were, like Bester, quiet radicals using the meager profits of their labor to co-opt the system by transforming the lives of their daughters and sons through education or bolstering their children with enough love and self-esteem to live like Muholi and be their authentic selves without apology.

For Muholi, domestic workers are the unsung heroes of the nation whose stories deserve to be told. She was among the first generation of South African women who did not have to work as domestics. Using herself as the subject, she transforms into Bester and imagines life from her subjectivity: "By performing the same role as her mother, Muholi makes a chain of gestures including but not limited to that of paying tribute to her mother" (Ngcobo 5). In many ways her mother's story is connected to her own narrative about life as a South African woman whose alterity as a black person and gay person subjects her to the same racialized oppression as blacks living under apartheid. In Toni Morrison's *Beloved*, the protagonist Sethe's intimate connection with her daughter is reminiscent of how Muholi uses her own body to express the inextricable link between mother and daughter: "You are my sister / You are my daughter / You are my face" (255).

In two unnamed pieces unearthed by curator Ngcobo, who is an unofficial Muholi archivist, Muholi imagines Bester in a number of different scenarios. First, a sepia-toned image shows Muholi standing alone in a field dressed in her standard maid's uniform. The picture reminds us of the past, perhaps invoking the memory of a younger Bester. Behind her there is a pylon that obscures the faint image of a house in the background. A barbed-wire fence to the left connotes her status, the limitation of her mobility, or lack of access to the land stolen from her ancestors. In its simplicity, the picture begs for answers. Who is this woman, how is it that she came to be in this field? It is clear that she is a domestic worker. Her pristine and unrumpled uniform indicates that she is en route to work, and perhaps she has taken a long journey through the field to arrive at her destination. More importantly, someone stopped her to take her image; someone deemed her worthy of being captured in that moment.

In *Face a Face* (2017), a collaborative project with Laurence Prat (in collaboration with Gloria Pourpre), Muholi is depicted as a domestic radical, ready to advocate on behalf of the voiceless. Dressed in a light blue maid's uniform complete with white apron and cap, she stares steadily at the camera with one hand raised in the black power salute, the other hand on her midriff. Bright pink work gloves in a pocket contrast with the blue uniform. This image manages to more fully express the kind of defiance detected by the maid in Irma Stern's well-known portrait, *Maid in Uniform* (1955), which features a discontented South African maid seated at a kitchen table, her arms crossed, her eyes slanted, and her jaw taut. In this tribute to her mother, Muholi acknowledges women's fight for justice, for wages, and for humanity. On her blog, she thanks her friend Prat for having her in the *Warriors* series, again acknowledging that the piece is directly Related to her mother. She says the picture is a

> tribute to my late mother Bester Muholi who worked as a domestic worker for more than 42 years to raise 8 children on her own with a meager salary. Allow me, also to acknowledge all those women who are doing domestic work to fend for their children in South Africa and beyond, as we continue to celebrate National Women's month in SA. (Muholi, "Photo of the Day")

The political tones of this work are also seen in an untitled performance piece, where Muholi demands recognition for the overworked and underpaid domestics whose labor is taken for granted by the women who fail to acknowledge their existence in their homes.[1] According to Ngcobo, Muholi staged this public intervention at an Association for Women's Rights in Development (AWRID) conference that included many activists who had gathered to tackle the systemic oppression of women and yet could not see that their own privileged position made them complicit in the marginalization of other women. Ngcobo reports that Muholi entered the meeting disguised as a maid and spent her day attending sessions and taking pictures of the attendees. Despite the fact that she was dressed in a maid's uniform and had no documents permitting her access to the conference, no one questioned her attendance. Muholi's nonexistence in this space—her race and her uniform—emphasized her alterity and spoke to the heart of the issue: black women were synonymous with servitude and therefore undetected minorities in society. Finally, in a Sojourner Truth–like moment, Muholi addressed the delegates and reminded them that they were beholden to the women who cleaned their homes and relieved them of domestic duties so they could attend that very meeting about women's rights. Unfortunately, Muholi's radical performance was not captured on film, but hopefully it was etched into the memories of the participants of the conference. This performance piece, along with all her other pieces about domestics, calls attention to the ongoing plight of domestics in South Africa and globally.

Similarly to domestic workers in the United States, South African domestics fought for several decades for labor rights. For years women did not earn a living wage nor receive sick days or vacations. Moreover, as noted previously, pass laws created difficulties in seeking and gaining employment and kept them separated from their children and partners. With time, domestic workers mobilized and pushed for worker's rights even in the face of governmental regulations that tried to censor their labor activist efforts. According to Romero, under apartheid, "the government banned working class, predominantly black unions," but SADWU, however, was a group that "provided a space to organize workers, align women's interests and advocate for basic employment rights within the private household" (238). Domestic workers were on the frontlines making their voices heard by engaging in a number of strikes, such as the June 1, 1989, strike organized by SADWU. Here "domestic workers from all over South Africa called for laws to protest for domestics and farm workers. They presented petitions to the offices of the Commissioner of Manpower in every city in the country. They fought against child labor, for improved accommodation, negotiation of contracts, and increased wages" (Meer 62). Shortly after apartheid ended, in 1995, the Domestic Workers Act was passed and outlined conditions of employment for domestics, including pay rates, sick days, age requirements, and so on. Domestic workers earned R8,34 (approximately seventy cents an hour). While these laws were binding for domestics, they did not guarantee that workers' rights would not be violated or that workers would report workplace malfeasance. In 2013, the South African government ratified the ILO Domestic Workers Convention, including Sectoral Determination Seven, which for the domestic worker covered wages and hours, but domestics remain the lowest paid workers.

Some of Muholi's early works reflect a theme of justice for domestic workers that is continued in later collections, such as in her 2017 series *Somnyama Ngonyama*, which is clear in its objective to include domestics as part of a meditation on a host of social issues such as homophobia, racism, discrimination, the environment, and representation of the South African woman. This collection of self-portraits, some of which Muholi took daily for a year, present snapshots of the daily lives of black South African people. Muholi explains that *Somnyama Ngonyama* (Zulu for *Hail, the Dark Lioness*) is "a statement of self-preservation through portraiture. The entire series also relates to the concept of MaID (my identity) or, read differently, 'Maid' the quotidian and demeaning name given to all black women in South Africa" (Muholi, *Somnyama*). This identity (maid) imposed upon the bodies of working-class women is co-opted by Muholi who takes creative license to portray the body differently; she gets to name it, humanize it, and give it beauty and reverence.

The portraits in the series are all black and white and feature close-ups of Muholi, who uses lighting to make her skin appear darker. In the images with maids, she dons elaborate headwear and garments made from items that have a direct association with domesticity and the everyday labor of black women, who are in effect reduced to the utilitarian items with which they work. Scouring pads, strands of mop rope, latex gloves, clothing pegs, and what looks to be the rubber hoses used in washing machines or vacuum cleaners adorn her head or drape over her body. As per usual, several works honor Bester. *Bester I, Mayotte* (2015), for example, is an intense image of Muholi with a headful of pegs. Pegs are also placed on her ears and used to clip the fabric around her shoulders. Her eyelids, lash line, and lips are painted chalk white, which makes her appear regal or haunting. The shadows that make her skin appear darker mute her features and highlight the props, thus emphasizing the point: women's subjectivity and individuality is obscured by their occupation. (The piece bears remarkable similarity to Mary Sibande's *Long Live the Dead Queen* [2009] series that will be discussed in chapter 7, which also pays tribute to motherhood with self-portraits.) As with all her images, Muholi/Bester's stare is focused on the camera. Muholi's maids always look back and engage in what she calls the "returning gaze." She explains,

> Through the medium of the visual, and more specifically the photographic, I try to take seriously the question of the gaze; I attempt to develop what bell hooks calls the "critical gaze" by returning the colonizing gaze, and responding actively to the heteronormative and patriarchal constructions of black queer bodies, our genders and sexualities. (Muholi, "Ngibonile" 42)

In another work, *Bester V, Mayotte* (2015), the pegs are replaced with scouring pads designed to make an elegant headdress. Art historian Tamar Garb explains that "the materiality of steel wool, arranged on the head, is metaphorized to stand in for the stare, the hair, the toil, the trials that this mother and daughter have borne" (Garb 17). All of these women are outside of the confines of the domestic arena, independent from their employer and their uniform, and yet their tools still signify their designation in society. Other pieces titled *MaID* feature Muholi in a range of costumes independent from the markers of domesticity in the Bester portraits. In *MaID X Durban, South Africa* (2015), for example, an elaborate headdress and choker connote a celebration of Muholi's culture and heritage, an important part of her "ID." The versatility of these images make a strong statement about the diversity of South African women's experiences. The women tell a story about South Africa past and present. The props and costumes demand a close look and do not permit making assumptions about the women as merely black and servile. All the portraits described thus far evidence Muholi's life's work: archiving the maid's existence and giving them visibility. In *"Massa" and Mina(h)*, Muholi interweaves her passion for representing both the maid and the LGBTQI+ community in a series of prints presenting homoerotic scenarios.

"Massa" and Mina(h) is comprised of a newspaper clipping and three photographic images of a domestic worker—two pictures of a maid with her madam and a third picture of the maid with a dog. The series is meant to acknowledge "all domestic workers around the globe who continue to labor with dignity, while often facing physical, financial, and emotional abuse in their place of work. There continues to be little recognition or protection from the state for the hard labor these women perform to feed and clothe and house their families." Again, Muholi becomes both object and subject of her artwork. She explains, "I turn my own black body into a subject of art. I allow various photographers to capture my image as directed by me" (Muholi, "So They Have 'Eyes to See'").

The article "Work as Usual for Bester" exposes the tragedy of life for domestic workers who, due to systemic racism and sexism, are trapped in an occupation that strips them of voice, family, or an identity beyond domesticity. The title "Work as Usual for Bester" glibly reflects on the typicality of Bester's existence; her life is one defined by working, more specifically working as a maid for the Harding family. The spotlight is not an exposé on maids or intended to interrogate Bester; instead, it is meant to highlight the special devotion of this black woman to her white family. The first half of the article emphasizes Bester's long years of service. Bester recounts that while working for another family, she "dreamed of" working for the family. When the Hardings prepare to move to a new neighborhood, they invite Bester to go along, and she accepts the offer. Bester appreciated the Hardings because, in her words, they "took me in [their] heart[s]." The Hardings are portrayed as being equally as fond of Bester. The writer records, "according to Kathy Harding, her children adore Bester" ("Work as Usual for Bester"). After forty-two years in service, Bester continued traveling to different parts of town, working for various members of the Harding family. At the time of the article's publication, Bester was working for two of Mrs. Harding's children in different parts of town. While Kathy Harding retired, Bester, probably not much younger than she, continued working. The writer tells us that even though Bester collects her pension, she has no plans to retire because, as she says, "I like working" ("Work as Usual for Bester"). It is interesting to note her choice of words. She does not say she likes working for the family—she states she likes working, earning a wage. By all accounts, Bester experienced a good working relationship with the Hardings, so much so that she delays retiring so she can continue working for this family. While Bester's responses to the interview are probably genuine, it is also clear that this woman was still employed by the Hardings and was not in a position to expose conflicts she may have experienced while working for them.

As Ngcobo argues, perhaps what is most important is "not what is said, but what is not said" (Ngcobo). In her review of the exhibit, Ngcobo finds the newspaper article problematic. She says it is unclear if the piece is only spotlighting Bester or celebrating her achievements:

> If it is celebratory, it is not clear who is being celebrated[,] for Muholi's mother appears as a shadowy figure of her employers without whom she may not fully exist as a person, at least in their eyes. In a way, the article enshrined its hero to her "place"; a place where though "adored" by her master's children they had to at some point be taught to distinguish that Bester belongs to a different social class. (Ngcobo)

The second part of the essay includes biographical details that serve to humanize Bester and show her as more than the family's maid. The writer details where she was born, her marriage to her husband, a Malawian immigrant, and number of children (six surviving) and grandchildren (twenty) in the family. Bester is a daughter, wife, and mother. Of these three roles, the most important role is as mother, but for forty-two years, Bester was without her children. Each day, she took the long commute to work from her township. She was forced to take on work because, as she says, "In our time there were very few factories and the only option open to women was to clean houses" ("Work as Usual for Bester"). Like many women of that generation (1950s–1980s), she had to make hard sacrifices that affected her children's lives. Muholi recognized her mother's sacrifice and the opportunities it gave her family, noting, "She managed to support us with her meager salary and still pay for our Bantu education" (Muholi, "I Have Truly Lost" 23).

When we juxtapose the first half of the news clipping with the second half, it is clear that as much as Bester appreciated the Hardings and dedicated her life to the family, she also suffered. She shares this when she admits how much she worried about her children. A well-intentioned Mr. Harding would tell her not to worry because "you're one of the family" ("Work as Usual for Bester"), but his paternalism did not make up for the hours spent away from her family. Moreover, trading one family for another offers little consolation for Bester. As much as Mr. Harding meant well, his gesture does not ease the guilt of knowing that, for forty-two years, Bester cared for two generations of another family's children while her own were neglected. Even as a live-out, she would have to leave for work very early or return home late and barely see her children. Muholi shares that while she knows her mother sacrificed so much for her children, she was also resentful of her mother's absence.

Although Bester does not get to share the full story of her experience as a maid, semiautobiographical fictional narratives by South African writers such as Sindiwe Magona help fill in the gaps of Bester's life. In *To My Children's Children* (1990) and *Living, Loving and Lying Awake at Night* (1991), Magona recounts the everyday experiences of the black female labor force in South Africa, specifically the trials of domestic workers and their interactions with their madams and fellow workers during the apartheid era. The story "Atini" bears resemblance to Bester Muholi's story. Atini is a young mother who spends restless nights fretting about her starving children, fearful of another day with no food. Her husband's absence leaves her with the misfortune of bearing sole responsibility for their children. When Atini is unable to provide for them, she puts them in the care of their grandmother and journeys (without a pass) to the white areas to seek employment. Parting from her children is difficult, but it is her only option for improving their lives.

Magona's description of Atini's heart-wrenching decision to leave her children describes the pain Bester articulates when she shares how much she worries about being away from her children. The vignettes in *Living, Loving and Lying Awake at Night* also recount the routine humiliation faced by maids and the physical and psychological abuse they suffer at the hands of the white madams who attempt to establish their superiority and strip maids of their personhood. At the time the newspaper article was published, Bester was not at liberty to say if she endured offense while employed by the Hardings, but it is clear her experience with previous employers was less than optimal, since she was eager to leave and work for the Hardings. In her own words, she was "looking over the fence thinking, 'I like that missus there'" ("Work as Usual for Bester").

The anecdotes in Magona's stories provide a plethora of reasons why Bester might have been driven to work for the Hardings. Magona illustrates that maids are subject to all kinds of assault: from being stripped of their names and being called Sophie or Sheila because their employers found it easier to pronouncing than their given African names, to looking through the maid's belongings to ensure they had not stolen from the madam, to insisting maids use their hands to wash floors and toilets rather than allowing them to complete these jobs with brushes and mops. While maids often remained silent about the insults they faced, they found ways to resist such mistreatment. In "Surviving Life as a Woman: A Critical Ethnography of Violence in the Lives of Female Domestic Workers in Malawi," scholar Lucy Mkandawire-Valhmu et al. write,

> One way in which women attempted to maintain their self-worth was by actively resisting their employers' demands in a way that did not jeopardize their employment. Even though the women could not openly defy their employers, they found ways of covertly resisting their employers as a way of surviving without creating further difficulties for themselves. (796)

An example of this covert resistance is described by Magona in the story "Stella." Stella's madam leaves a note telling her to hand wash the dirty underwear left in the bath water. Stella does not confront the madam in person. Instead, she writes a note chastising the madam for her lack of decorum. She writes, "Please excuse me but I do not think anyone can ask another person to wash their panty. I was taught that a panty is a most intimate thing . . . my mother told me no one else should even see my panty. I really don't see how I can be asked to wash someone else's panty" (Magona, *Living, Loving and Lying* 17–18). Stella's refusal to wash the underwear is couched in a tone of moral conviction rather than insolence. This sly innocence is reminiscent of the trickster antics of the character Eve from the highly popular South African comic strip *Madam & Eve*, featuring Eve, an outspoken maid who often plays naive so she can outwit her madam.[2]

Other stories in *Living, Loving and Lying Awake at Night* tell of harsher abuses, such as the sexual victimization of domestics. "Virginia," for example, not only alleges that Mr. Reed, Atini's employer, sexually abuses the domestics, but she also reveals that she was coerced into trading sexual favors with a white inspector to secure her legal pass to work in the town. Virginia's honest revelation exposes the daily sexual exploitation and sacrifice endured by maids who did what was necessary to remain employed. The most tragic account of sexual abuse is relayed by a character who tells Atini about her madam's collusion with a gynecologist to deceive a former maid into having a hysterectomy. She explains that the maid assumed the doctor performed a much-desired abortion. Unfortunately, she learns that the doctor, with the consent of the madam, removed her uterus, leaving her barren. These examples of sexual abuse show the vulnerability of domestic workers who are not solely victimized by their madams but also by the white males.

While most of the stories report madams to be harsh and demeaning, even those who avoid mistreating their maids engage in maternalistic practices that infantilize and exploit the women. There are hints of this kind of maternalism in Bester's article and from Mrs. Harding herself, who appears in Muholi's auto-documentary *Difficult Love* (2010). Mrs. Harding recounts how she bought Bester a house and helped pay school fees and bought clothing for the Muholi children. When women like Mrs. Harding gave lavish gifts, they were not always purely acts of gratitude; rather, they often served to pacify the maid and seek her undying loyalty. Magona's stories also reflect on the maternalistic behavior of employers. In *Living, Loving and Lying*, one of the employers purchases a home for her domestic. From the domestic's perspective, the house is a conditional gift paid for with her labor and loyalty. Moreover, although she is a proud homeowner, her lengthy workday barely even leaves her time to enjoy the house.

Characters in Magona's stories warn against feeling beholden to women who infantilize their workers. Toward the end of the narrative, Magona, like Childress, uses her story to motivate domestics to recognize their position in society and to take action to improve their circumstances. Joyce is a young student who would have been similar in age to Muholi and detests working as a domestic, which to her stands in the way of her dream of medical school. Joyce is adamant that she will not be domestic forever. In a feminist manifesto of sorts, she chastises white women who claim to be feminists and yet demean the women whom they employ. She indicts these white women for their maternalism, a manipulative tool that allows them to justify their failure to properly pay their maids. She says, "Children grow up, but domestic workers remain children to their death. . . . Pay her and pay her justly. Then and only then does she become—even in the eyes of the medem [*sic*]—the adult she is" (Magona, *Living, Loving and Lying* 39). Magona's fictional work emphasizes the complicated relationships between domestics and their employers. In *Difficult Love*, Bester claims she had a good relationship with the Hardings, who supposedly treated her "like family," and yet she never earned enough to support her family, and the Hardings seemed oblivious to her struggles.

In the *Difficult Love* documentary, Muholi endeavors to show the closeness of the relationship between Bester and Mrs. Harding.

Mrs. Harding reflects back fondly on the wonderful relationship between the Muholi's and the Hardings, who "did everything together" and were in her eyes "like family." As Mrs. Harding recounts all of the wonderful things she did for Bester, including helping educate Muholi, she laments one thing: her inability to convince Bester to have her tubes tied so she would stop having so many babies. She makes the statement in jest, unaware of how appalling her words sound to the viewer. In this one statement, Mrs. Harding revealed everything about the true nature of that relationship. Bester was *kind of like family*. Similar to the madams portrayed in Magona's stories, Mrs. Harding is not only maternalistic, but she treated Bester as though she owned her body and her labor. Her comment about Bester's fertility, which yielded eight children, read as an inconvenience impacting Bester's ability to do her job.

Mrs. Harding's words echo much of what was discussed in Magona's stories, most frighteningly, coercing maids to have hysterectomies. While it might not have been Muholi's intention, the brief interview with the Hardings revealed harsh truths about the power relationship between maids and madams. Putting this into perspective, Muholi notes that while Mrs. Harding's generosity and true overtures of friendship were admirable, it does not change the fact that her mother was not treated as an equal: "It was always curious to me that two women could share parts of their personal lives and struggle despite the years of apartheid that kept one woman in the perpetual role of servant and the other in the life long role of Madam" (20). The article on Bester and Magona's collection of short stories provide insight into the relationship established between Bester and Mrs. Harding. Muholi's recognition of the intimacy of these two women underscores their commonality as women, wives, and mothers but also shows that race and class differences compromised the relationship. Given the mores of the day, Bester would never be publicly equal to Mrs. Harding, but privately, they may have had their own arrangement. In *"Massa" and Mina(h)*, Muholi suggests that the relationships between maids and mistresses are more nuanced than they appear.

"Massa" and Mina(h): Same-Sex Desire in the Domestic Sphere

Three portraits make up the *"Massa" and Mina(h)* series, which merges two of Muholi's passions: maids and the LGBTQI+ community. *"Massa" and Mina(h)* is about the potential for homoerotic relationships between black and white women in the privacy of the domestic sphere. Multiple images make up the series, detailing a maid's secret fantasies about her mistress. The public representation of same-sex desire in South African society is taboo, but it has not deterred Muholi from creating artwork that presents a provocative image of the domestic and her employer, and it definitely brings visibility to the LGBTQI+ community, which is ostracized by many in South African society. Before analyzing *"Massa" and Mina(h)*, it's imperative to provide insight about the vilification and silencing of LGBTQI+ individuals in South Africa.

Prior to 1996, same-sex partnerships in South Africa were unprotected under the law. The end of apartheid granted new rights for the LGBTQI+ community. Under the 1996 Constitution, for example, sexual orientation was included under the Equality Clause, making South Africa one of the first nations to protect gay rights under the Constitution, and it was among the first countries to pass a Civil Union Act (2006) and legalize gay marriage. Despite these laws, as in other parts of the world, homophobic attitudes largely fostered by religion and culture led to discrimination and victimization of the LGBTQI+ community. Today, those who are not closeted routinely face punitive actions for their homosexuality, which is viewed as "unAfrican." As authors Morgan and Wieringa put it,

> This homophobia is based on the perception that same-sex relations are alien to African culture and an import from the depraved West. This perception is based on current African leaders being ignorant of the fact that a range of same-sex practices in Africa have existed for a long time. (17)

In order to protect themselves from violence, many people live closeted and in silence. According to the *Guardian*, a 2008 report by

Triangle, a South African gay rights organization, showed a rising number of hate crimes against lesbians, who have been murdered, ostracized from communities, and victims of "corrective rape." One of the most famous cases of brutality—which drew national attention to the phenomenon of corrective rape—involved Eudy Simelane, a young lesbian woman who was training as a referee for the 2010 FIFA World Cup. In April 2008, she was gang-raped and stabbed to death in Johannesburg.

The assault and murder of Simelane, and the LGBTQI+ community in general, is personal to Muholi, who has lost friends to this kind of violence. As such, she uses her art as a radical act to disrupt the imposed code of silence that forces lesbians and members of the transgender community to live in a shroud of secrecy. She explains, "For me, photography is not a luxury, but visual activism. I produce photographs to advance my political agenda, which is to contest the invisibility of LGBTI communities in the mainstream media; to rewrite / revisualize / represent black queer bodies in an amicable way" (Muholi, "Ngibonile" 41). Muholi's first major collection, *Faces and Phases* (2010), serves as an example of how she fights against the invisibility of the LGBTQI+ community. The collection is a portrait series of lesbians and transgender individuals in South Africa who are brutally victimized or live under a code of silence that mutes their voices in the collective experience of living in South African society. Some have died from AIDS or were murdered. Most of the portraits in this collection were shot outdoors. Taking the portraits in public gave these individuals the freedom to openly express themselves and be seen in spaces which are generally hostile to their presence. Muholi's photographs are meant as a radical act to disrupt "the enforced privacy and secrecy of black queer life. One must note that hate crimes against LGBTI persons reported in South African and international newspapers typically include the discovery of the victim's body in a public space" (Efeoghene 187). Thus, by photographing the community, Muholi maintains an archival record of their being, which undermines the efforts of those who think killing members of this community totally erases their existence.

For her part, Muholi has been fortunate to be raised in a household with a mother who did not react negatively to her lesbian lifestyle. In a very personal essay written after her mother's death, Muholi revealed,

> My ex-lovers are still welcomed at home even though my mother is gone, because she [Bester] taught my family to accept and respect the intimacy and love between me and them. She accepted each one, not as a friend or as my sister, but as my lover. I never had to officially "come out" to Mama. . . . My sexuality has never been up for too much discussion among my relatives because my mother always responded positively and with respect on my behalf. (22)

While Muholi's lesbianism is accepted by her family, she has faced her share of prejudice from others in the community. A most telling example was in 2009, when Lulu Xingwana, minister of arts and culture, abruptly left the opening of *Innovative Women*, an art exhibition showcasing the lives of South African women. Newspapers reported that Xingwana left the event early because she was disturbed and offended by what was described as Muholi's "pornographic" artwork (Evans). In addition to facing these kinds of insults by government officials, in 2008, Muholi's computer hard drives, which contained master copies of her work from 2008 to 2012, were stolen out of her home. The thieves wanted to send a clear message that her work around issues involving the LGBTQI+ community was an affront to African values. The effort to censor Muholi's work and cast members of the LGBTQI+ community in the shadows is precisely what motivates her subversive actions. The *"Massa" and Mina(h)* series is an example of her effort to make visible and revisualize the lives of women, sometimes in unconventional settings.

Much like most of her collections, *"Massa" and Mina(h)* is a tribute to Bester and all domestics around the world. *"Massa" and Mina(h)* is about relationships between black and white women under apartheid from the perspective of the corporeal and the emotional. Multiple images make up the series, telling a story from the maid's perspective about a maid's private fantasies about her mistress. The pictures illuminate the intimacy of the relationship between maids and madams, who spend quiet moments together in a number of different scenarios. Whether it is the maid washing her madam's back or helping her dress, the women engage skin to skin in routine interactions, but also perhaps for one party or the other, these physical encounters translate into something more. In one image, the madam is in the bath, with the back of her head and torso shown to the camera and her buttocks and thighs obscured by Muholi's body. Muholi is on her knees with her hands in the water, but it is unclear what is she is doing since the madam is holding the washcloth in her hand. Muholi's face is turned toward the camera, almost as though she has been interrupted.

"Massa" and Mina(h) 2 presents Mina(h)'s perspective on the sexual tension between madam and mistress. Dressed in her cap and uniform, Mina(h) sits on her knees cleaning up children's toys, her eyes trained on her madam. Mina(h)'s head is positioned perfectly between the legs of her madam, who is represented by a pair of stockinged legs shrouded in a wedge of multicolored red skirt, her feet encased in a pair of green shoes. The woman is in mid-stride, walking away from Mina(h). The sexual undertones of this image are likely undetected by those unfamiliar with the American film *The Graduate* (1967) about a young man (Dustin Hoffman) who engages in an illicit affair with a mature married family acquaintance. The intertextual reference is observed by Brandon Edmonds, who notes, "Muholi has replaced the playful sexuality of *The Graduate*—its classic film poster has Mrs. Robinson's leg slicing Dustin Hoffman's Benjamin Braddock at the groin—with the raced reality of domestic work and South African economic power" (Edmonds). Here Mina(h)'s desire is discreet. Her invisibility gives her license to engage in her chores while at the same time mischievously taking a peek up her madam's skirt.

Mina(h)'s erotic desires are more clearly revealed in the first part of the *"Massa" and Mina(h)* series, which presents a sharp close-up of the black maid and her white madam boldly stealing a quiet, intimate moment together in the kitchen. At first glance, the image seems to convey a maid playing peek-a-boo with a child, but the madam's faint coral lipstick, large pink earrings, and tiny sliver of red-patterned dress reveal that the woman between Mina(h)'s hands is the madam. The maid's deep brown skin sharply contrasts with the alabaster skin of her employer. The maid's head is tilted down toward her mistress's head and her eyes are closed. The positionality of the women is important. The maid stands above her mistress, with her hands on the mistress's body. The image does not convey that either woman is distressed, for both women look relaxed. The subtle opening of the madam's lips within this sexual play connotes pleasure from being touched by the maid, whose body and breath are so close to her own. For this moment, the women are equals. It is only the maid's clothing that defines their difference. Matebeni remarks,

> Of the *Massa and Mina(h)* series, Ngcobo is convinced of an "emerging love affair" between the black maid and the white madam which intensifies with each image. It is, however, controlled by the dress codes, and in the maid's case, it is a blue uniform, which marks each woman's role. The uniform in this series acts as a way of maintaining the visual aesthetics of this contentious relationship. (411)

Despite the roles, in this frame it is the maid who assumes a position of power and control. Under the apartheid state, black women were only ever subservient to white women, so this portrait imagines what life might look like if these women were equals. Although Muholi appears in the portrait as a model, there's a real-life role-play happening as her lover, who poses as madam, appears alongside her in the image. In *Difficult Love*, Muholi spoke plainly about the difficulties of interracial dating when black women are assumed to be their white lover's maid. In this image, she recreates that sentiment. *"Massa" and Mina(h) 2* draws on a number of portraits featured in *Difficult Love*, which depict Muholi wearing a blonde wig, black dress, and gold jewelry. Muholi is served by a white maid wearing the typical light blue uniform and apron Muholi has worn in various portraits of herself as the maid. In one image, the white maid serves her black madam orange juice, kneeling in subservience to the madam, and in another image, she helps her put on her jewelry. Again, Muholi's subversion of the standard black maid and white madam transforms the black woman, so she is no longer other and invisible. Unlike *"Massa" and Mina(h)*, their relationship reveals no traces of mutual respect. Finally, *"Massa" and Mina(h) 3* presents Mina(h) naked—perhaps in a postsexual encounter with her madam. Her long dreadlocks are free from the maid's cap. The mistress does not appear in the frame—instead, she is replaced by a nonthreatening large white dog. Mina(h)'s nakedness demonstrates her freedom in this space, the permission to be herself. Although she is naked, there is nothing sexual about the picture; it is more a statement of stripping down bare to expose the essence of herself.

"Massa" and Mina(h) redefines what the relationship between blacks and whites can look like. While most relationships between madams and maids are purely platonic, it is highly likely that with time, some friendships grew into genuine romances. *"Massa" and Mina(h)* is an affront to the apartheid state. It is a testament to the failure of the effort to regulate the bodies of black and white men and women who were subject to miscegenation laws that denied black and white romantic relationships. Thinking only in heteronormative terms, the laws neglected to imagine the possibility of relationships between black and white women who in secrecy enjoyed each other's company. The African American poet Audre Lorde once wrote, "In the transformation of silence into language and action, it is vitally necessary for each one of us to establish or examine her function in that transformation and to recognize her role as vital within that transformation" (6). In a society where life is often challenging and indeed dangerous for LGBTQI+ individuals, the courageous activist work of Muholi, and others, transformed silence into action, resulting in a collection of artwork that demands the recognition of South African women in all of their complexity.

PART 2

We Wear the Mask

Servitude, an Art of Performance and Deception

5

A Sartorial Expression of Frenchness in Ousmane Sembène's *Black Girl*

A Francophone Revision of Jean Genet's The Maids

Genet's *The Maids* (*Les Bonnes*; 1947) is a one-act psychodrama about two sadistic, mentally unstable sisters who plot to kill their wealthy madame during a ritual game of dress-up.[1] This play, often interpreted as a critique of the economic divide between the working class and the French bourgeoisie, is a favorite of directors and writers who recognize the timelessness of the play, as it is malleable enough to suit (any) contemporary time. Over the years, a number of adaptations have grounded their representation of *The Maids* in the race and gender politics that undergird power struggles between black maids and their white madams.[2] Jaime Lloyd's 2015 production, for example, cast two black actresses as the sisters, who contextualize their oppression based on class and racism. Lloyd's version was deemed problematic by theater critics, who insist that literal interpretations of the play as commentary on social and political issues, or the oppression of labor, fail to understand Genet's script. In their view, the play is actually about the psychological torment experienced by two delusional sisters whose powerlessness and self-hatred are projected onto one another.[3] Matt Trueman opines,

> Lloyd's production . . . plugs the play into contemporary American politics, but loses the things that makes it so rich, potent and unsettling in the process. By thinking so strongly in sociopolitical terms, he underplays the script's psychological edge. That's where its charge lies: in the sister's totemic rituals.

In contrast to Lloyd, the writers and artists in this book whose work alludes to Genet's play—Mary Sibande, Renee Cox, Ousmane Sembène, and Vera Starks—treat the psychological dimensions of the characters' self-identities and their struggle for power relationships in tandem with social commentary about race, class, and gender. These writers and artists also reflect on the performative nature of the relationship between maids and employers, who each play a role in establishing their position and power within the household.

This chapter presents the first comparative analysis of Genet's *The Maids* with Ousmane Sembène's *Black Girl* (1966). Reading Genet's play against Sembène's postcolonial film about the power dynamics between maids and madams uncovers parallels between the way two men expose the interior lives of domestic workers, who wear masks of deference to shield their real identities as women who regard themselves as above their appointed place in society. Sembène's postcolonial and racialized approach to Genet's play is both a critique of the African subject's dependency on the colonial master for social, economic, and political empowerment and a metaphor for the power dynamics between the newly liberated African (maid) and the former colonial master (madame). Throughout the film, the maid and madame fight to establish their position within the domestic sphere. Diouana, the protagonist, who naively believes her migration to France and sartorial performance of Frenchness changes her status from lowly African girl to sophisticated French woman, refuses to accept the subaltern position that defines her as a black woman in French society. Conversely, Madame, a woman who wrestles with her own subjugation within the household, is threatened by Diouana's dogged determination to be her equal. Adamantly establishing their respective master/servant roles, Madame exploits and dehumanizes Diouana. In the end, Diouana is the victor in this power struggle; she achieves her independence from the colonizer by not submitting to Madame's psychological warfare and using her body as a site of resistance. Ultimately, she is liberated from oppression and forces the madame to become the maid.

Black Girl is one of the most important African films of the twentieth century. It was the first feature by an African filmmaker to chronicle the lives of migrant domestic laborers in Europe. The film was inspired by a woman Sembène read about in a newspaper as well as by his own experience as an immigrant dock worker in France, which he captured in his film debut *Borom Sarett* (1963). *Black Girl* was adapted from Sembène's short story of the same name, published in the collection *Volatïque* (1971), and like other francophone fictional works, it "explored immigrant motifs by deploying the classic plot of a centripetal flight from Africa" (Adesanmi 237).[4] The eighty-minute film, made in 1966 in twenty days for $20,000, was backed by French investors who mandated dubbing the film in French instead of using an African language like Wolof or even Arabic, thus compromising the essence of African storytelling (i.e., speaking in one's mother tongue).

The insistence of the French investors that Sembène distribute the film only in French mirrors the exegesis of the film's political commentary regarding Senegal's recent independence from France: as long as the Senegalese were bound to the French socioeconomically, politically, and culturally, they would remain captives of neocolonial domination and thus lack true independence. Coincidentally, despite his own politics, given the African government's lack of investment in filmmaking, Sembène was forced to do the very thing his film warns against: give up autonomy for colonial dependency. It is a contradiction he recognizes. In a 1969 interview with film historian Guy Hennebelle, he defended his decision to make the film with French backers, arguing that it was better to make the film with French financing than to not make the film at all (10). Thus for Sembène, bringing this important story about the dangers of neocolonialism and the plight of African migrant domestic workers in France to an international audience was more important than the inconvenience of releasing his film in the language of the colonizer. Yet again, the predicament serves the film well, for what the audience sees is the protagonist reduced to ventriloquism—a dub over of the African actress Mbissine Thérèse Diop's voice that renders her mute and reinforces the film's political message.

Situated shortly after Senegal gained independence from France in 1960, *Black Girl* raises poignant questions about gender and nation building: What role does the African woman play in the development of a postcolonial society? Diouana's gender and class restrict her ability to fully participate in the establishment of the political and economic infrastructure of the newly liberated nation. This is indicated when she is seeking employment in Dakar, the Senegalese capital where she lives, and overhears a group of young men musing about their plans to run for political office. While the men speak with confidence about their aspirations to participate in the construction of the civic life of the nation, Diouana can only listen to their excited talk. She has nothing to contribute to this new nation, and as an unskilled laborer, she still remains beholden to the colonizer for her survival. As media scholar Marcia Landy notes, "The economic and ideological structures of neo-colonialism and commodity capitalism are [were], according to Sembène, the newest historical expression of capitalist and imperialist domination over the masses of African men and women" (23). Diouana is not idle. She is proactive about seeking work and goes from house to house offering her services as a domestic to colonial families, who often slam the door in her face. Diouana's fortune changes after a young man takes her to a location where maids assemble and wait for white women to select them as day laborers.

Upon the arrival of a French madame, the African women clamor around, offering their services. The woman appraises her options, her imperial domination exercised through this act of selection. Interestingly, while the other women jockey to be seen by the French woman, Diouana remains seated. It is unclear if she thinks she is too dignified to plea for a job or unaware of the protocol for selling her labor, but Madame chooses her over the rest. Securing a job as a domestic gives Diouana self-worth. She takes pride in being able to support her family and, by extension, her community. Excitedly, she shares the news with her mother: "J'ai travaillé pour le blancs! J'ai travaillé pour le blancs! [I have a job with the white people, I have a job with the white people!]" (Sembène 16:43–16:48). As it is revealed later, Diouana's elation is not only pride in her ability to contribute financially to her household but rather related to access to the Frenchness she covets. When the colonial administration ends, so too does her job, but Diouana is fortunate—the family hires her to continue her duties in France. This arrangement should have been beneficial because the export of her labor would generate remittances that could bolster the Senegalese economy. Sociologist Saskia Sassen explains the relevance of remittances for unstable economies: "While the flows of remittances may be minor compared to the massive daily capital flows in various financial markets, they are often very significant for developing or struggling economies" (520). In Diouana's case, however, working overseas proves to be unfruitful. She is enslaved by her host family, who withholds her salary and the desperately needed remittances. Diouana's colonial dependency is illustrative of the gendered realities of women who could not advance without colonial intervention, and even then, they were reduced to a master/slave relationship, which counteracted their independence. Although Diouana's boyfriend warns her that the French will treat her like a slave and that she is foolhardy for migrating with the very people from whom she has recently been liberated, she fails to heed his advice. Diouana's motivation to be a French woman obfuscates rational thought and behavior; like the women in Genet's play, she finds herself participating in a performance that ends in tragedy.

Genet's play emphasizes the psychological breakdown of Claire and Solange, two depressives lacking self-worth and visibility in their society. These women are envious of Madame's wealth and jealous of Madame's relationship with Monsieur. In the afternoons, when Madame is away, the maids occupy Madame's boudoir and participate in an ongoing game of role-play. Each woman dresses up in Madame's luxurious fur coat and silk dresses and screams obscenities at the other. During this role-playing, their language is cruel and their treatment of one another is (depending on the director) sadomasochistic. The game is intended to simulate the murder of their mistress, with whom they have a love-hate relationship. The game is constantly interrupted by a bell indicating that they have run out of time. Eventually, Madame appears, and the women resume their roles as house servants. Despite their preparation to kill madame, they do not carry out their plan. Madame departs to see Monsieur (who has been released from jail), and Claire and Solange return to their game; this time, though, Solange-Madame, at Claire's insistence, poisons her sister, thus ending the game. The make-believe game—of playing Madame for the day—gives Claire and Solange an opportunity to be seen outside of themselves, independent of their mirrored image of servitude. Each has an opportunity to experience dominating the other, and they receive profound enjoyment in this role. Claire and Solange become so entrenched in their game that they begin disassociating from their true identities and lose the ability to distinguish reality from fantasy. The maids use melodramatic actions and bombastic language to keep the audience aware of the artificiality of their performance. Scholar Gary Day observes,

> What the audience is continually reminded of in this play, through the physical gestures as well as through the repetition of the word itself, is that what they are watching is indeed a play; gesture is both real and artificial, breaking down the distinction between those two terms, causing the same kind of confusion there is between ritual and reality every day. (153)

Solange and Claire's never-ending dress rehearsal to kill their madame reveals much about themselves and their hatred for Madame, which is really their hatred for each other and hatred for the systems of power that disenfranchise women like themselves. Olga Solovieva explains, "Their daily reenactments of a sadomasochistic master-servant relationship make it clear that the Madam is what each of them wants to be in relation to the other" (94). In the Lacanian sense of desire and fulfillment, their inability to satiate their quest for power keeps them locked in their rage and oppression.

In *Black Girl*, Diouana's psychological turmoil is a result of both her inherited colonial mentality and the dehumanizing behavior of her employers, who ultimately cause her mental breakdown. Like many colonial subjects, Diouana is a victim of cultural conditioning. As Frantz Fanon, Ngũgĩ wa Thiong'o, Aimé Césaire, and other postcolonial thinkers posit, women like Diouana are seduced into believing European language and culture is superior to their African heritage and thus begin mimicking the colonizer at the expense of their own cultural identity. Quoting Westmann, Fanon explains this process of acculturation: "The wearing of European clothes, whether rags or the most up-to-date style; using European furniture and European forms of social intercourse . . . writing a European language; all these contribute to a feeling of equality with the European and his achievements" (Westmann qtd. in Fanon 25). Diouana does not have access to French language, but she expresses her Frenchness through the Western clothes she begins wearing. Prior to her job, she wore mostly simple African attire, but over time her wardrobe changes. Sandals now cover her bare feet, and the plain African wrappers she wore daily are paired with European blouses. Even her natural hair is traded for a shiny wig. These outfits are a dress rehearsal for Diouana's migration to France, where her Frenchness will be validated.[5]

Diouana is giddy with excitement about her impending move to France. On an outing with her boyfriend, she discusses plans for a glamorous new life of shopping in French boutiques and visiting museums, a far cry from her dull existence in Senegal. She gullibly anticipates a life mirroring those of her mistress and the women she sees in French magazines. Her naive perception about her future as a migrant laborer is emphasized in the child-like song she sings to her boyfriend that life will be wonderful "en France, en France [in France, in France]" (Sembène 41:14–41:18).

Diouana's euphoria is typical of the colonial subject who is eager to strip themselves of their Africanness and trade their ancestral birthright for what Fanon calls the "magic vault of distance," where

> Paris, Marseille, Sorbonne, Pigalle becomes keys to the vault. He leaves for the pier, and the amputation of his being diminishes as the silhouette of his ship grows clearer. In the eyes of those who have come to see him off he can read the evidence of his own mutation, his power. Good-bye bandana, good-bye straw hat. (23)

Indeed, when Diouana leaves, she trades her African headdress for an elegant Western-style wig and the chic clothes of her mistress.

A Sartorial Expression of Frenchness

In typical African fashion, Sembène's narrative is nonlinear. The plotline develops through a series of flashbacks. Hence the film begins in medias res. When the audience is introduced to Diouana, she has just arrived in Antibes to report for work. What they see is a sophisticated woman elegantly dressed in a pencil skirt, black high heels, a beaded necklace and earrings, and a handbag; on her head, she wears a wig styled in a chic bouffant. Diouana knows that the verisimilitude of her performance is predicated on her ability to look and feel the part of a French woman, and the audience views Diouana according to her self-perception. Clothing, as Fred Davis asserts, "frame[s] much of what we see when we respond to one another and acquire thereby a special capacity to . . . say things . . . about ourselves" (338). Dressed in her stylish clothes, Diouana articulates the following statement: I am a French woman. While Diouana looks the part, as she will learn, she is not treated in kind. Some of her peers and relatives in Senegal might be impressed by what her clothes represent, but her French hosts fail to "speak her language." They do not regard Diouana as an equal or as a woman deserving of respect; they see her only as a maid, an African woman, and an inferior.

Diouana's skin tone is the only marker that distinguishes her from the many white Europeans passing through the port. Disembarking from a vessel, she is greeted by her employer's husband, who is charged with bringing her to the apartment. Wide shots from the camera capture the French Riviera with a long view of the ocean and the beach. Diouana drinks in the scenery that confirms her fantasies. When the man declares, "France est belle [France is beautiful]," she nods in agreement, seduced by the "magic" Fanon warned about (Sembène 03:06–03:08). There is a dreamlike quality to this scene that calls into question Diouana's ability to distinguish fantasy from reality. In fact, initially this opening scene was in color, shot using a pink filter—clearly an intertextual reference to F. Scott Fitzgerald's *The Great Gatsby* and the idealism of seeing life through "rose-colored" glasses. Soon the French landscape fades from view, and Diouana is taken to a less-than-glamorous apartment. Sembène establishes a contrast between the beauty and the expansiveness of the Riviera and the small drab apartment that eventually becomes Diouana's prison.

The home, decorated mostly in white, symbolizes Diouana's black (minority) status in this home and in the country in general. Fortunately, the apartment has a spectacular view of the French Riviera, which Madame is happy to show Diouana, but the gesture is tainted by her directive to also tour the kitchen: "Nice, Cannes, et Antibes, maintenant nous allons le cuisine [Nice, Cannes, and Antibes, now let's go to the kitchen]" (Sembène 04:59–05:12). This juxtaposition between the kitchen and the Riviera, which connotes luxury and leisure, is a symbolic marker of Diouana's life: she will never have access to the Riviera. Her place (as an African) is to be a slave to her French hosts, to cook and clean in the kitchen. The scholar Francoise Pfaff notes that the kitchen's decor further emphasizes Diouana's enslavement because the black-and-white design of the kitchen floor is reminiscent of bars on a jail cell. Thus for Diouana there will be no trips to French boutiques or cultural excursions to the museums she described to her boyfriend. The apartment is her only link to French culture.

Diouana's imprisonment is both physical and mental. As the days pass, she is shocked to learn the terms of her employment have changed. She is no longer solely the nursemaid, as she was in Dakar. In Antibes, she is required to work as the nanny *and* fulfill household duties such as cleaning and cooking. She is furious about the demotion that lowers her status from the au pair–type responsibilities she had in Dakar. She also recognizes the exploitation of her labor. Sembène uses her inner monologue to rant about her situation:

> Pour quoi suis-Je ici? Pourquoi suis-Je ici? La Salle de bain, la chambre, a couche le salon. C'est tout ce que je fais? Ce n'est pas ce pour quoi je suis venue en France? Je suis venu pour soigner des enfants. Je ne suis pas cuisiner. Je ne suis pas une femme de manage [Why am I here? Why am I here? The kitchen the bathroom the bedroom, the living room. That's all I do. That's not what I came to France for? I came to look after children. I'm no cook. I'm no cleaning woman]. (Sembène 06:22–06:55)

It is clear Diouana dares to think highly of herself. She certainly does not accept that she is inferior to the mistress, nor does she accept that she is a maid. Diouana's repetition of the same thought is reminiscent of Solange and Claire's nonsensical babbling about their envy for each other. Diouana channels her anger differently. Instead of emoting like Claire and Solange, who hiss and scream, she contains her rage. Landy notes, "The film's visual and verbal silences reinforce Diouana's own silence, seemingly giving us the servant's perspective rather than the filmmaker's, who might be tempted to speak more directly for her" (24). There are several factors accounting for her lack of histrionics. First, unlike the sisters, Diouana cannot speak French well, so even if she wanted to confront Madame, she would not be able to clearly articulate her thoughts. Moreover, she is in no position to be openly defiant. She is a woman alone in France with no family or identifiable allies to defend her circumstances, so she is forced to rail internally. Although Diouana does not directly confront the madam about her assigned role as the maid, she adamantly refuses to define herself in accord with this title. Diouana's verbal abilities may be restricted, but what she cannot say is expressed sartorially.

Clothing and accessories take a prominent role in Solange and Claire's ritualistic performance too. As long as they are dressed in Madame's clothes, makeup, and jewelry, they can perform their role with authenticity and authority. Sembène reworks Genet's text so that the ritual performance in the film is not the imagined scenario of two women who want to be maids for the day but the reality for Diouana, who is able to engage in her own ritual game of dress-up wearing her madam's castoffs. Diouana engages in what post-colonial scholar Homi Bhabha defines as colonial mimicry, reforming oneself into a "recognizable Other, as a subject of difference that is almost the same, but not quite. Which is to say, that the discourse of mimicry is constructed around an ambivalence; in order to be effective, mimicry must continually produce slippage, its excess, its difference" (122).

In *The Maids*, Claire and Solange can never simultaneously be dressed as Madam, for it would contradict the whole point of the game, which relies on props and clothing to distinguish the subordinate from the dominant. This is not the case in Sembène's film. Each day, much to her madam's chagrin, Diouana wears the madam's old clothes. Sometimes Diouana wears a makeshift apron to protect her clothes when she is cleaning or cooking, but typically she wears the same dress polka-dot dress.[6] These clothes are obviously inappropriate for the task, but they are Diouana's only way of establishing control and defining her identity. Thus, in her polka-dot dress, Diouana ascribes to Descartes's philosophy: "I think, therefore I am." Despite her race and class standing, her clothes establish a "sameness" with Madame that does not betray her occupation or social standing. Even though she gave Diouana her clothing, Madame takes offense to seeing Diouana dressed in her old belongings. If, as scholar Alison Laurie notes, "clothing is designed to show the social position of its wearer," then dressing identically to one's employer makes it difficult to establish the housewife from the help (207). Just as they do for Diouana, to the madam, her clothes symbolize Frenchness and civility, traits she is unwilling to share with Diouana.

The madam, fueled by a desire to undermine Diouana's efforts to play nursemaid, and desperate to affirm her own role in the house, chides Diouana for daring to think she is on equal footing. She tells Diouana to change her clothes because she's overdressed. Following this directive, Madame produces an apron that she fastens around Diouana's waist to ensure she knows her position both in the household and in French society. The apron's strings are a metonymic reference to chains that mark Diouana's body as enslaved. Donna McCormack argues, "The body is the site through which the colonial rule and national desires are played out" (283). This action by the madam supports McCormack's point. Placing the apron on Diouana's waist is a violation of Diouana's body and a direct statement about who controls her body in this space. Resentfully, Diouana wears the apron. Saidiya Hartman's polemic on the subversive strategies of African slaves argues "the reliance on masquerade, subterfuge, and indirections . . . obscured the small acts of resistance conducted by the enslaved" (8). Hence, like the slave, Diouana's small act of resistance is wearing the apron, but she resists Madame's attempt to debase her by refusing to remove Madame's clothing. She maintains her wardrobe under the apron.

One of the fundamental differences between *Black Girl* and *The Maids* is that beyond the game—that is, out of costume—Claire and Solange are equals. They are sisters who share the same socioeconomic background, and they are both unmarried women bound to lives as domestics. On the surface, Diouana and her madam are not equals. As noted, Diouana's race and class reaffirm her place within the household and French society in general, but on closer inspection, Diouana and the madam share parallel lives and a similar existence of subordination to male domination. Like Diouana, when Madame arrived in France, she lost the status she enjoyed in Senegal. In France, her pedestrian life is drastically altered from the lavish lifestyle she enjoyed as the housewife of a member of the colonial administration. No longer is she a well-kept woman who can lord over an army of staff at her beck and call. Interestingly, though, in some ways her life in Senegal was the reverse of Diouana's life in France. In Senegal, she was confined to her home, unable to speak the language of the locals, and she was an immigrant minority in a foreign land. The major difference for her was power and her freedom.[7] In France she maintains this power but little else. Her life is inconsequential. Her husband is a shadowy presence in the apartment; when he is not drinking cocktails, he is sleeping or out for the day, and her children (who appear to be in boarding school) are not even home to be nurtured.[8] Similar to Genet's maids, her frustrations and loathing of her own lowly predicament as a French housewife are projected onto Diouana. As the domestic, Diouana's existence in the household is not simply about reproductive labor. In her examination of the relationships between domestics and their employers, scholar Bridget Anderson explains,

> The domestic worker, whether "cleaner," "nanny," or "servant," is fulfilling a role, and crucial to that role is her reproduction of the female employer's status (middle-class, non-laborer, clean) in contrast to herself (worker, degraded, dirty). . . . it is the worker's "personhood," rather than her labor power, which the employer is attempting to buy. (31)

So here, Madame does not buy Diouana's "personhood"; instead, she attempts to claim it and destroy it in the process. Madame's verbal abuse, enforced uniform (apron), withholding of wages, and forced isolation in the apartment are tactics meant to disenfranchise Diouana, but they occur undetected by an audience in the home that can bear witness to her performance of subjugation. The verbal abuse and the apron are not enough to prove Diouana's inferiority. Like Solange and Claire, who are dependent on each other for an audience to watch their performance, Madame, like all oppressors, needs a captive audience of her own. Scholar James Scott maintains that the performance between the oppressed and subordinated is predicated on a "public performance" wherein both parties project an imagined scenario of dominance (4).[9]

To this end, the madam hosts a dinner party so she can perform her role as superior to the subordinate Diouana. During the dinner, Diouana's role is to be a subservient representation of the native African (i.e., an African souvenir of France's former conquest of Senegal). To reinforce her "Africanness," Diouana is forced for the first time to prepare African dishes. To the amusement of her guests, Diouana's subservience is on display as she acquiesces to Madame's request for more rice and black coffee. To the guests, Madame achieves her aim, and they take note of Diouana; one even fulfills their fetish of kissing a black woman and without permission kisses Diouana's cheeks. Throughout the evening, Madame barks orders at Diouana, whose scowl betrays her anger, and chastises Diouana for daring to show her displeasure. A telling moment occurs toward the end of the dinner, when a guest asks if Diouana speaks French. When Madame says she does not, the woman calls Diouana an animal, suggesting she is no different than a house pet who does not speak the language but responds to its owner's commands. Although Madame's public displays of domination are effective, in her own way, Diouana finds ways to resist, both with the clothing and through other tactics.

After weeks of abuse, Diouana recognizes that her dreams for an exciting life in Paris will never come to fruition and she finally begins taking control of her life. Diouana's isolation in the apartment and her detachment from other human beings beyond her madam and the children is unbearable. At one point, even the husband, who is mostly aloof about Diouana, intervenes with a proposal for Diouana to go out beyond the local store where she shops for the family, but this suggestion is rebuffed by Madame, who states that Diouana is lazy and underserving.

The Body as a Site of Resistance

Reflecting on her current life of drudgery and enslavement, Diouana admits to herself that in France, she is completely dislocated from her culture, and as a result she is suffering. The only representation of Africa is a mask she gifted to the family shortly after she was hired. Staring into the face of this mask, she comes face to face with her reality: she is like the mask, a decorative figure on display in a vast space of whiteness. The mask is also a signifier of her Africanness, the heritage she shunned in favor of the Frenchness, which compromised her autonomy. Self-reflection, which we do not see in Genet until the end, occurs when Diouana also looks out the window (which coincidentally also looks like prison bars) at the world beyond the apartment and realizes she will never attain any part of the world beyond the glass. She is also aware of her insignificance in this space as an invisible presence in France, much like many migrant workers who quietly slip and in out of neighborhoods undetected by community residents who are unaware their neighbors have enslaved individuals in their homes. Black British writer Zadie Smith writes about these invisible slaves in her novella *The Emperor of Cambodia* (2013), a story of a young live-in domestic from the Ivory Coast who is enslaved by a South Asian family. Fatou, like Diouana, is also unpaid, without her family, and dependent on her host family for survival. Fatou is free to leave the home, attend the local gym, and have lunch with friends, but this independence dupes her into believing she is free. Fatou does not even recognize she is enslaved until the family decides they no longer want her services and terminate her without warning. Smith demonstrates that in today's world, slaves cannot always be detected by the public. They may have jobs, they may be seen in social settings, and they may have no visible signs of enslavement, but much like Diouana, they can still be enslaved.

Finally, Diouana realizes her error in trying to mimic the colonizer and rejects the madam's Western clothing, which is symbolic of her oppressor and her psychological oppression. She states, "I will not wear your madam's clothes." Instead, she wears a plain cotton robe. Her rejection of the clothing is coupled with her decision to take back her power by resisting outwardly. Foucault wrote,

> A power relationship can only be articulated on the basis of two elements which are indispensable if it is really to be a power

> relationship: that "the other" (the one over whom power is exercised) be thoroughly recognized and maintained to the very end as a person who acts: and that, faced with a relationship of power, a whole field of responses, reactions, results, and possible interventions may open up. (789)

Diouana realizes her labor is her currency, so she refuses to work. Domestics have often used this method of passive resistance, calling out sick or refusing to work as an effective strategy to protest working conditions. When the maid asserts herself in this way, it is clear she wields some power in this relationship, especially one that is not defined by monetary exchange for her labor. Diouana goes to bed and refuses to work. Next, she takes off the wig, another marker of European standards of beauty. In place of the wig, she combs out her own hair. Diouana takes pride in her hair, and she spends a great deal of time in the bathroom combing and shaping it to her liking. Meanwhile, Madame is furious that Diouana has neglected her duties caring for the children. Diouana takes so much time primping in the mirror that Madame loses patience and bangs on the door, telling Diouana to commence her duties. Madame's fury evidences her realization that she is losing control over Diouana and, more importantly, her standing in the house. Once again, she relies on an audience to witness her authority—this time it is her son. Even the husband awakes from his slumber to see the show, but now it is Diouana who plays the leading role. She does not resume her duties, and the madam is left to prepare breakfast for her husband and children and clear the dishes.

When Diouana appears, she is wearing her own clothes, a striped dress from home that reminds her of happier times in Senegal. Scholar Vlad Dima suggests that this dress makes a statement about Diouana's enslavement: "We can see both the vertical lines on her dress and the horizontal ones on the floor, which brings together the two semiotic elements that suggest imprisonment" (65). Diouana is also wearing Madame's shoes. The shoes are not discarded because, in some respect, Diouana is still literally "walking in Madame's" shoes—she is still occupying the madam's role. Madame is incensed by her audacity and demands she remove the shoes. Diouana obliges and "steps out" of Madame's shoes, leaving them in the middle of the floor, as she walks to prepare her own breakfast in the kitchen. Diouana is essentially telling Madame that she can have the shoes, but she will have to pick up after Diouana.

Shortly after, the couple produce a note from Diouana's mother claiming disappointment at not receiving remittances. Diouana is anguished by the letter. Without the ability to write back to defend herself, she is powerless. Diouana turns to what Ayo Coly calls "internal self-exile" as a resistance strategy and retreats inward using her memories from home to escape from her reality (10).[10] Diouana's disassociation and "internal exile" is reminiscent of what happens to the character Nyasha in Tsitsi Dangarembga's *Nervous Conditions* (1988). In Dangarembga's novel, Nyasha spends her formative school years in England and returns to Rhodesia, Africa, with a new consciousness about the dangers of colonial education. Nyasha perceives her parents to be naive colonial subjects who are willfully blind to the way education is used to pacify colonial subjects. Unfortunately, Nyasha is an army of one in her household, and her crusade for intellectual freedom is rejected by her parents, mostly her father, who dismisses her political views as radical and insists she conform to the ways of the British. Recognizing the battle is lost, Nyasha retreats inward as a protective mechanism for survival, but in the end her feelings of worthlessness and isolation lead to a "nervous condition" and eventual breakdown. Diouana feels the same kind of alienation and despondency, which leads to her own mental break. In times of distress, flashbacks transport her back to happier times in Senegal. She recalls the day she met Madame, sharing the good news of her employment with her mother and her community, and preparing for her trip to France with her boyfriend. While these memories connote a happier time, Diouana fails to acknowledge the relationship between those memories and the colonizer, for her happiness was in part predicated on the colonizer's money and culture. Here in France, she has access to neither, and this realization prompts her to change her fate.

In *The Maids*, the women reach a point when they realize the game must end. The pain and anger that is consuming their lives becomes unbearable, and they believe they can achieve relief by killing Claire-Madame. At her request, Solange gives Claire-Madame the poisoned tea they have been using for their game. Once Claire-Madame drinks the tea, the role-playing ends, and Solange must face the consequences of her actions. Diouana too decides that the only way to change her plight and to not remain enslaved is to take her own life. In a final act of defiance, once again she refuses to clean the home or care for the children, leaving the responsibility for Madame. Moreover, in preparation for her departure, which could be read as a physical and spiritual flight, she packs up her belongings, including the African mask. Although Diouana gave the mask as a gift, the family is no longer deserving of Africa or its gifts, material or not. When Madame returns from an outing and sees the home in disarray, her child neglected, and a void on the wall where the mask was displayed, she confronts Diouana. She even strikes her. Not only has she once again lost her standing (again she has to finish the chores), but she has also lost her ownership and power over Diouana, as symbolized by the missing mask. Madame and Diouana fight over the mask, but after the husband's reminder to Madame that the mask belongs to Diouana, Madame relents. The husband negotiates for Diouana to keep the mask because he acknowledges that it does not belong in France any more than Diouana does. Obviously, his wife has more to lose; she is the one who will be left to do Diouana's job.

Sembène emphasizes this point when he has Diouana throw her apron at the husband's feet, not the wife's. One might read this action as a statement about patriarchy's role in the unrecognition of the housewife's reproductive labor, which necessitates the labor and the exploitation of migrant domestic workers like Diouana. After all, he is complicit in what happens to Diouana. He controls the finances that should have been used to pay

Diouana, which he only decides to pay once Diouana stops working. By this point, his payment is too late. Diouana enters the living room with the bills in her hand. The camera pans over the table and rests on the apron, now spread flat, perhaps in preparation for the next victim. Diouana stands in front of Madame and her husband and tears up the money they try to use to buy renewed productivity. But no amount of money can compensate for her dignity and humanity. She returns to her room to finish packing. As she does so, she makes a public declaration of her freedom and her refusal to work as a maid. In her final act of resistance, she symbolically returns to her African roots by braiding her hair and donning a white robe. After uttering her last words, "Elle ne me reverras plus jamais [She will never see me again]" (Sembène 48:03–48:04), she strips bare and enters the pristine white bathroom (cleaned by her own hands) and cuts her wrists, leaving a literal stain of her existence in the bathtub and in the minds of this family.

The political and social commentary in Sembène's didactic film makes a direct appeal to the formerly colonized to recognize the danger of colonial paternity. At the time of the film's release, countries such as Rwanda, Algeria, Uganda, and Kenya had recently become independent nations. Diouana's story is a warning that as long as they continued to blindly invest in the cultural hegemony of the former colonizer, they would continue to be exploited and oppressed. While Sembène's film was made fifty years ago, his ideas fit with contemporary discourse regarding globalization and transnational labor. Fifty years later, women (mostly from North Africa and sub-Saharan Africa) continue to migrate to France to work as maids for French families or African families who have relocated to France. Unfortunately, some situations are even more extreme than Diouana's. She consented to migration to France, but today, many young women are trafficked to Europe and forced into domestic service or prostitution. In 2013, for example, a fourteen-year-old girl from the Ivory Coast was sold to a French couple and forced to work as their maid. Like Diouana, she had no papers and was beaten and denied wages. There is hope for migrant domestic workers, those who enter countries legally or illegally. Human Rights Watch advocates, domestic workers' unions, and ordinary citizens are fighting to protect these women and training communities to be more vigilant about recognizing the invisible labor class who are subject to the oppression Sembène so powerfully captures in his film.

6

Maid in Hollywood

The Art of Performance in Theresa Harris's By the Way, Meet Vera Stark

From the 1920s to the 1940s, during Hollywood's Golden Era (1910–1960), many of the most successful grand dames of black Hollywood—such as actresses Hattie McDaniel and Louise Beavers and jazz singer Theresa Harris—were typecast as maids, a role that for some was all too familiar. Unknown to many, some black actresses finished a day of performing on set, then exchanged one apron for another and returned to the studio lots to work as domestics for white actresses or went to work as servants in private homes. The transition from literally working as a maid to playing a maid on-screen was seamless. Both jobs required the performance of deference and, as scholar Donald Bogle observes, a form of acting:

> On cue, you had to smile, nod, agree, acquiesce, soothe, reassure, comfort, and charm—often when you didn't want to. You also had to please people you frequently couldn't stand. Hollywood's colored domestics were like servants everywhere in the country, except that their role playing was far more intense, matching the dramatics of their employers. (46)

Unfortunately, most black actresses who made it to the big screen were given maid roles entrenched in denigrating stereotypes, but some actresses, such as Theresa Harris and others, managed to transform the maid into a dignified character.

This chapter explores how Lynn Nottage's satirical play, *By the Way, Meet Vera Stark* (2011), dramatizes the dilemmas and limitations imposed on black actresses in the film industry. Through her protagonist, Vera Stark, Nottage shows how some black actresses fought against the restrictive nature of maid roles by bringing depth to their performances, thereby forcing audiences to see the maid as more than a marginal figure in the background. Nottage also ruminates on the ambiguity of these double-voiced expressions of black actresses, whose performances conveyed multiple meanings and paradoxically reified and subverted socially constructed definitions of race and black womanhood.

In interviews, Nottage shares that it was the 1920s African American actress Harris who motivated her to create the character Vera Stark. Harris caught her attention in the 1933 film *Baby Face*, directed by Alfred E. Green. It is a racy drama about a woman, Lily Powers (Barbara Stanwyck), who is forced into prostitution by her father. After Lily's father dies, she takes control of her feminine wiles and uses the art of seduction to dupe men out of their possessions. Through it all, her best friend, Chico (Theresa Harris), is at her side. Nottage was struck by the relationship between Lily and Chico and the portrayal of the African American woman. For once, the black woman was not typecast as the mumbling maid confined to the domestic. Instead, she was in a part relevant to the story, with speaking lines and character development. As Nottage shows in the play, having lines meant all the difference to actresses, who hoped their appearances on-screen would make a memorable impression on the audience. Although Harris appeared in more than eighty films, she was an unsung talent in the industry. She was cast as a maid in so many films that she acquired the nickname "The Maid of Hollywood."[1] Harris played the maid alongside legendary white actresses like Ginger Rogers, Ruth Hussey, and Bette Davis, among others. During the 1920s, only white women were cast as leading ladies in mainstream productions. The black woman and other women of color were relegated to secondary and "othered" characters created to emphasize the superior qualities of the white character. Scholar Charlene Regester explains,

> In many early films, the black actresses' principal function was—by contrast in language, costume, and behavior—to illuminate or aggrandize the virtue, beauty, morality, sexuality, sophistication, and other qualities embedded in the "whiteness" of the white female actress and character. (2)

Despite efforts to dull the black characters, their beauty and wit often shined, but without storylines and character development, they rarely had the opportunity to prove they were as talented or as versatile as their white costars.[2] Harris was happy to be a working actress but was discontented with the parts she was offered. On September 11, 1952, Harris appeared in the cover story for *Jet*. Its title—"Theresa Harris: She Still Has Faith in Hollywood after 20 Years of Maid Roles"—confirmed Harris's status in the eyes of Hollywood. Later in her career, Harris expanded her repertoire with generic roles on radio: she plays a nondescript woman in the *Amos 'n' Andy* show and a housewife on *The Jack Benny Program*. Television, however, still typecast her as the maid.

Harris was frustrated with the lack of diverse parts and risked her reputation with studios and directors by speaking out about Hollywood's refusal to write roles for black women that were as complex as those given to whites. She seethed to interviewer Fay Jackson,

> I never felt the chance to rise above the role of maid in Hollywood movies. My color was against me. . . . The fact that I was not "hot" stamped me either as an uppity "Negress" or relegated me to the eternal role of stooge or servant. I can sing but so can hundreds of other girls. My ambitions are to be an actress. Hollywood had no parts for me. (qtd. in Bogle 126)

Harris was adamant that if she had to play the maid, she would take control over the portrayal of the role, opting to perform "without a maid's cap and us[ing] no dialect" ("Maid of Hollywood" 64). For Harris, these minor adjustments allowed her to reduce some of the racial stereotypes tied to plantation caricatures like the mammy. While she was not judged too harshly for playing the maid, over the years, others who played servant roles have been vilified for "holding back the race," an accusation that put actors in a precarious position. They could take roles and, like Harris, try to elevate the portrayal of domestic workers or ignore respectability politics, play their assigned role, and brace for sharp critique from the black community. This dilemma created a crisis of consciousness or double consciousness, as discussed by the African American sociologist W. E. B. Du Bois in his treatise, *Souls of Black Folk* (1903).[3] Thus, black performers wrestled with this conflict of how to portray themselves as African Americans on-screen.

As challenging as it was to play the maid, and as critical as some were of their decisions, women who played domestics were crucial to the legacy of black Hollywood because they paved the way for others to perform beyond racial and sexual stereotypes. This truth was recognized by actress/comedian Mo'Nique (Monique Angela Hicks), who in her 2010 Academy Award speech acknowledged Hattie McDaniel for "enduring all that she had to, so that I would not have to" (Kaltenback). In *By the Way*, Nottage likewise pays homage to those such as McDaniel and Harris, who enabled successive generations of black actresses to be cast in diverse roles, but she also examines the motivation for their decisions to play maids and the impact it had on their reputation.

By the Way premiered in May 2011 in New York City at Second Stage Theatre. The nonlinear hyperrealist play moves between temporalities, media, and genres. This satirical play is divided into two acts spanning seventy years: 1933 to 2003. The narrative follows Vera Stark's struggle to break into the film industry. The first act chronicles Vera's life as she and her friends compete to get casted in *The Belle of New Orleans*, a movie. In the second act, Vera is the subject for discussion at an academic symposium presented by a panel of African American scholars who share their observations about her career and controversial impact on blacks in film. As part of this discussion, there is a clip of Vera's appearance on a television show, where she reflects on her life in film and her relationship with her former friend, rival, and costar Gloria Mitchell. On the show, the two are reunited, and it is clear not much has changed: Gloria, who is in town to receive an award for her life's work, remains a star, while a drunk Vera is still "the maid" overshadowed by Gloria. Vera has a secret that might damage Gloria's career, but out of loyalty, she does not betray her, though she reminds her that her success is not due purely to talent. The secrets and deception of these characters, along with their double-voiced statements and actions, make the audience aware of the ambiguity of their utterances and the artificiality of their performances in and out of character.

Nottage shows that performance involves a constant negotiation in the slippage between reality and artifice. To achieve this ambiguity, Nottage uses in abundance double entendres, irony, the trope of racial passing, and minstrel performance to create what Mikhail Bakhtin refers to as a double-voiced discourse that allows characters to communicate one idea but mean something different. The performances occur in a number of spaces, such as film and television sets, including an auditorium where scholars engage in their own performances as they critique Stark's career. The performances of the actors and the characters are multilayered. *By the Way* demands that audiences note the fluidity between the characters' performances within performances—that is, as characters within the play but also as characters performing in the film that exists in the fictional world of the play. For some characters, their performances as actors begin and end when the camera stops and the costumes are removed. For others, their life is a continuous performance played out in life and on-screen. Ultimately, as Nottage reminds us, we are all performers on the world's stage, performing our identities, genders, sexualities, politics, and so on. Some, however, especially those who present a manufactured version of themselves, can find themselves trapped or liberated by their persona. There is also a metafictional quality to this play that enables Nottage to create a life for Vera beyond the physical play itself. To this end, Nottage creates a real website for Vera, *Finding Vera Stark*.[4] The page provides biographical details about Stark's life and career. Stark is actually one of two fictional African American actresses from the Golden Era of Hollywood to "live" beyond the text on social media. In 1996, writer/director Cheryl Duyne created a website and a real art exhibit for her character Fae Richards, a lesbian actress known as "The Watermelon Woman." Duyne plays one of the characters who imagines Richards's life as a black woman, as an actress, and as a lesbian woman in society performing her multiple identities.

Performance in *By the Way* is about the artistry of self-expression as well as about identity politics undergirding the racial and sexual hierarchies afforded to those who are *perceived* as authentic versions of the socially constructed categories they represent. Judith Butler's extensive work on gender and performance problematizes the rigid categorization of gender that tries to prescribe normative traits to bodies that perform "gendered" identities. Butler's concept of "performing" constructed identities has also been taken up by some critical race theorists who conflate Butler's feminist polemic with race.[5] In the same way gender is indeterminate, race also elides concrete definition. Nottage satirizes the notion of race with black female characters who subversively perform their raced and gendered identities.

The Irony of Racial Passing and Minstrel Performance

From the outset, *By the Way*'s audiences are required to pay close attention to the dual performances of the actors who transition in and out of character. Vera, for example, works as a maid in life and on-screen plays the role of Tilly the maid. Gloria, on the other hand, is Vera's madam in life and also her madam in the film. Thus at first it is not obvious that Vera and Gloria are performing. The play opens with a black woman dressed in a maid's uniform, mid-conversation with her white employer. Nothing betrays the fact that the two are "acting" until Gloria forgets her lines and Vera takes out the copy of the script tucked in her apron. Once the rehearsal is over and Gloria directs Vera to "fetch" a change of clothes, it is evident that the two are mirroring their roles in real life. This first scene sets the tone for the rest of the play: How do we distinguish between reality and fantasy?

While the two women maintain their respective roles, it is revealed that Vera and Gloria are actually cousins and childhood friends who began their careers on the black vaudeville (variety show) circuit. Vera moves to California in pursuit of her movie career and takes a job with Gloria to make ends meet. Gloria and Vera are both bidding for roles in *The Belle of New Orleans*, a melodrama about a biracial woman (Marie) who is set to marry a wealthy merchant until it is revealed that she is the daughter of a slave woman. Unable to bear the shame of her mixed-race heritage, she calls off the wedding, refuses to allow her fiancé to see her again, and suddenly dies, presumably from a broken heart. Vera, hoping to be considered for the role of Tilly (Marie's servant), hopes Gloria will put in a good word for her with the director, Maximillian von Oster. Nottage's fictional film cleverly alludes to *The Flame of New Orleans* (1941), a comedy starring Marlene Dietrich (Claire) as a woman who wins the affections of a wealthy banker by misrepresenting herself. When the banker learns from an acquaintance that Claire has a questionable reputation, he shows up at her home to call off their wedding. Unwilling to concede defeat, Claire presents herself as Lili, Claire's unsavory Russian cousin. For a while, she gets away with playing two separate women, but eventually her fraud is discovered. Many of the female characters in Nottage's play are similar to Claire (i.e., women who create dual personalities) except here they take on personas not for male attention but instead for survival and Hollywood success.

Throughout the play, the rehearsal scene between Vera and Gloria—along with added dialogue—is repeated, not as a live performance but as a reenactment captured on film for *The Belle of New Orleans*. Although this is somewhat different from the ritual performance in Genet's *The Maids*, the concept of masquerading (i.e., not literal dressing up per se but adopting a different identity) and the exaggerated performances of the women is similar. Based on their racial and class backgrounds, like Solange and Claire, Vera and Gloria should be women of equal standing, but the racial signifiers that define Vera as black and Gloria as white make their lives very different. Vera's costume and role remains consistent. She is a maid in real life, and she performs as a maid in the film. Unlike Solange and Claire, she never gets an opportunity to trade with Gloria. Gloria, on the other hand, were she darker, would be a maid too, but her fair skin enables her to engage in a racial performance predicated on the superficiality of her appearance—complexion, hair color and texture, and diction.

Nottage uses Gloria and other characters to address the history of racial performance as it relates to America's legacy of slavery and the institution of racism. Passing as white enabled slaves to flee from plantations and blend into white society, often marrying white to dilute the genes and remain undetected. Even after slavery, blacks continued passing for white. Some had contempt for their African blood and their inferior status in society; others passed for social mobility and the opportunity to be free of racial oppression. This phenomenon of racial passing has been well documented in a plethora of novels, such as James Weldon Johnson's *Autobiography of an Ex-Colored Man* (1912), Nella Larsen's *Quicksand and Passing* (1928), and more contemporarily, Danzy Senna's *Caucasia* (1998).

As a black woman light enough to pass in white society, Gloria does not have to return to her life as a black woman unless it is for the role she plays in *The Belle of New Orleans*. The irony of her role is the director's insistence that only a white woman can play the role of the biracial tragic heroine. Little does he know that she is indeed that tragic figure in real life. Gloria's believable passing performance as both a white woman and a biracial woman demonstrates the elusiveness of racial categorization. Moreover, Gloria is not the only character who is passing. As the character Anna Mae teases, everyone is masquerading. Anna Mae, however, is not light enough to pass as white but not so dark that she is presumed to be black. Her ambiguous appearance enables her to pass as an exotic other, in this case a Latina. Anna Mae exploits the stereotypes of the hypersexual Latina to attract the attention of von Oster and secures a role for herself in the film, not as a maid, but as Gloria's friend. Ultimately, Gloria and Anna Mae undermine socially constructed notions of racial identity, and Nottage shows us the baselessness of race. While Vera and her friend Lottie cannot pass as white or foreign, they do racially pass in their own way, by invoking tenets of the minstrel tradition and reinscribing stereotypical definitions of blackness.

Nottage shows that roles for black actresses were so limited, even the most talented, including those who were Broadway-trained, had to play servile roles. Vera's friend Lottie, for example, reveals that it has been seven years since she moved from New York to Los Angeles and she has yet to book a film. Back in New York, she had a thriving career as a Broadway actress, opening for big-name acts, but in Los Angeles, she has been unsuccessful even in getting the maid role she despises. In chapter two, the character Mildred commented on the typecasting of black female actors. In the story "About Those Colored Movies," Mildred bemoaned seeing black women playing the maid. Mildred's issue was not only about seeing blacks in servitude but also about the flatness of such characters, who were rarely seen as characters with their own lives apart from their jobs. Mildred's and Lottie's frustration with Hollywood's discrimination and lack of respect for black actors and actresses speaks to the invisibility of black women both in society and on-screen, in the 1920s and still today.

It should be noted that during the 1920s, there were a few black directors, such as William D. Foster, Noble Johnson, and Oscar Micheaux, who gave black actresses opportunities to showcase their range as trained performers and allowed them to play roles aside from the maid.[6] Some of these actresses had mild success, but they were not seen by broad audiences and did not get the exposure of mainstream productions. Black women have always struggled in Hollywood. Even highly popular and successful blues women like Ethel Waters and Hattie McDaniel, who after the Great Depression turned to acting, found themselves humbled by occupying "not a privileged but a subordinate space and articulated not the possibilities of black female power but the Yes Ma'ams of the black maid" (Carby 482). It has only been since the late 1990s to the 2010s that an ample number of black women have been cast as leads in films where they were not playing the mammy/nurturer, comic relief, or prostitute. Fortunately, African American directors like Kasi Lemmons (*Eve's Bayou*, 1997), Gina Prince-Blythewood (*Love and Basketball*, 2000), and Ava DuVernay (*Selma*, 2014) have changed the representation of black women on-screen so they can be seen apart from the controlling images of mammy, matriarch, and jezebel and instead be celebrated as high-powered attorneys, medical doctors, and political mavericks.

Nottage's play is a reminder that before writers like Lemmons and DuVernay existed, there were few roles for black women (in mainstream media) that were not the maid, so what were these actresses to do? Should they have caved to respectability politics and waited until casting agents and directors offered parts beyond plantation caricatures, or should they put their own moral standards aside and accept roles that would enable them to break into the industry and make changes from within? In Vera's case, she chooses to audition for a maid role. Thus, when she and Lottie hear news of a potential role in Gloria's film, they are excited about the prospect of being in a plantation movie, even if they will have to play slaves. Teasingly, Lottie reminds Vera she vowed never to play a servant, and Vera admits to saying this, but she also says this role could be life-changing for herself and for others. Vera feels no shame about her decision until she meets Leroy, a chauffeur by day and aspiring successful musician by night. Leroy, who is described as a black radical, shares Lottie's views about the antiquated representation of black women. Vera gets defensive about her decision to play Tilly and insists that playing the maid on a plantation is better than having to actually pick cotton on the plantation (as many people still did in the 1920s).

Eventually Vera gets the role of Tilly, but how she lands the role is troubling. When Maximillian von Oster takes a meeting with Gloria to discuss the film, Vera, who is serving in her authentic role as maid to Gloria, shows up ready to unofficially audition as a maid for von Oster. While Vera as the maid is typically in Gloria's shadow, during her audition she upstages Gloria and takes the spotlight. Similar to *The Maids*, where Solange and Claire compete for the attention of both the mailman and Madame's suitor, here, Vera and Gloria jockey for male attention, in this case the attention of the director, von Oster. Vera arrives at Gloria's party looking the part with an elaborate maid's uniform complete with a very large bandana. When Vera hears von Oster waxing poetic on his vision of *The Belle of New Orleans* as a real plantation-style drama capturing what he regards as an authentic representation of the past, she assumes her role. Well aware of his reductive view of black women, Vera exploits racial stereotypes from the minstrel tradition to exaggerate the mannerisms of African Americans as seen from the perspective of white audiences. Von Oster is clear he does not want actors but real negroes, "negroes of the earth" who know the exhaustion of toiling in the fields and the weight of their enslavement (Nottage 46). It is obvious to the audience that his definition of what is *real* and what is black is farcical. To von Oster, blackness is akin to how the slaves were misrepresented in Harriet Beecher Stowe's *Uncle Tom's Cabin* or with the character of Mammy from *Gone with the Wind*—passive black people, talking in thick slave dialects and lacking intelligence. As he speaks, Vera (and Lottie) become the visual representation of his manufactured perception of black identity. They hunch their bodies over, hum an old negro slave song, and mime behaviors synonymous with the deferential slave woman. Vera's act is bought by von Oster, who is certain in Vera he has discovered an authentic negro. He inquires about her "tragic" life story.

Vera knows what kind of story he wants to hear and what kind of performance of the plantation slave she must give. Speaking in slave dialect, she exploits Maximillian's ignorance by concocting a tragic story about being raised motherless and in poverty with her blues musician father. Struggling to survive, she was stripped of her innocence and turned to prostitution. Finally, to verify Vera's legitimacy, von Oster asks her to sing the blues. Gloria, who is envious of Vera's performance, taunts Vera and tells her to sing the blues she "knows so well." Vera of course does not live a blues life, but perhaps due to knowing the hardships of being a black woman, much to her own surprise, she is able to improvise. When she falters, she feigns being overcome with grief and unable to continue. Vera's behavior, as scholar David Krasner's examination of early black performers suggests, was not unusual. According to Krasner,

> Many black performers gained access to the theatre [and film] by imitating a misrepresentation of blackness constructed by whites. For a time, blacks imitated, to varying degrees, the caricatures preciously institutionalized by white minstrels in blackface. This created dual problems: African-American performers had to advertise themselves as "authentic" representatives, while simultaneously imitating the mannerisms and style conjured up by whites. (25)

Although Vera engaged in behavior she felt was necessary, later she acknowledges losing integrity by playing out the stereotype. Confiding in Lottie, she admits never thinking she would behave that way, but she had to do what was necessary to be cast as Tilly. Vera's act wins her the role, playing Tilly to Marie, the dying mistress played by Gloria. And, as we learn in act two, the part became the defining role that makes her famous.

Vera's scene in *The Belle of New Orleans* is quite short, but she, like Harris, uses the opportunity to showcase her talent and transform the maid from a passive, mumbling, insignificant character to a woman with deep emotion and depth. In the scene, just as in the rehearsal scene, Tilly (Vera) appeals to Marie (Gloria) to put her pride aside and receive her fiancé. Marie, however, is too overcome with grief and dies. Right before she dies, she proclaims that she is free of the burden of passing, and this tragic moment should be its end. It is at this moment, however, that Vera takes the opportunity for her character to have the same dramatic moment as Gloria's does. Recognizing the weight of the idea of freedom, for both the woman who passes and the enslaved maid, Tilly's eyes widen and she inaudibly echoes the word "free" (Nottage 61). In a calm voice, she appeals to Marie to hold on so they can conquer a new day tomorrow, but Marie is unwilling to fight. At first Tilly is inconsolable, but as the music reaches its crescendo, she moves to the window, parts the curtains, and looks out at the horizon, at the possibilities of life to come. The melodramatic action in this scene is amusing, and it would be easy to overlook the relevance of Vera's performance, but toward the end of the scene she makes a subtle shift in her language that allows her acting to shine through. In the first part of the scene, Vera relied on what scholar Jennifer Bloomquist calls "linguistic minstrelsy," a warped form of African American English (AAE) borne from Southern dialect (419). For example, Tilly says,

> I don't know what he know. But I do know dat he here.
> Mis', dat man out dere loves ya. And if you send him away
> Now it is gonna be a real shame. Ya can't keep hidin' from de
> Worl'. Talk to him, tell him how ya feel. Tell him ya love
> Him, cause ya and I know dere ain't no other man in ya heart but him. (Nottage 60)

Linguistically, Vera's speech shares many prominent speech patterns of AAE as it was employed by a number of minstrel performers who, according to Bloomquist, used "phonological patterns such as /th/ pronounced as /d/" in words such as *then* and *that* as *den* and *dat* and "syntactic features of negative concord" ("I ain't got no watch") to create backward-sounding speech used to promote racist views about black intellect and black inferiority (419).

In eleven of the twelve lines of dialogue, Vera speaks in a minstrel version of AAE. She gives her scenes all the affectations of the lowly slave woman expected from the director. Her final line, however, at the end of the film deviates as she switches to Standard American English (SAE). We learn, at the end of the play, that Vera negotiated with Gloria to let her have this last line: "Stay awake, and together we'll face a new day" (Nottage 60). Unlike the previous verbiage, where "we'll face a new day" might have read as "we's gonna face a new day," Vera does not deviate from standard subject-verb agreement. Switching languages in this moment, she aligns herself with the star of the film and makes her character at least linguistically equal. Adjusting her language at a pivotal moment in the film draws attention to her performance and allows the audience to take the character as seriously as the protagonist.

Respectability Politics

Nottage encourages us to think deeply about the decision made by women such as McDaniel and Harris, who opted to play characters thought of as racially problematic. Making the film was triumphant for Vera, but as Nottage shows, the court of public opinion has their own perspectives about characters such as Tilly. In act II, scholars on a panel at a colloquium dedicated to Vera's life and career in Hollywood gather to determine if Vera's performance was regarded as groundbreaking or a typical rendition of the mammy role. Here again Nottage presents another play on performance and satire. The panelists (Afua and Carmen) who assemble for the conference are characterized as a stereotypical feminist poet and an academic whose pontifications become about their own performance of eruditeness. Before hearing from the panel, Herb Boyd, the moderator, presents a jargon-laced opening salvo about Vera's performance in *The Belle of New Orleans*. Prior to hearing from the panelists, the audience is transported by a rare film clip of Vera's appearance on the 1970s Brad Donovan television show.

Vera is a sixty-year-old, bitter diva with a sharp wit. She shares the couch with a young British pop star whom she flirts with mercilessly. During the interview (interspersed with quick statements by the panelists), she reveals challenges in her life. While she went on to marry Leroy, his black nationalist rhetoric was too contentious for the industry, and his outspokenness cost her a film contract. Also, she was later caught up in controversy when she kissed a white man. Fortunately, she has not been totally forgotten by her fans and has a respectable residency at the Folies Bergère at the Tropicana in Las Vegas. Despite appearing in more than fifty-five films, *The Belle of New Orleans* eclipses all other accomplishments, and she is asked by Brad to recite the closing lines of the film that made her famous. Vera betrays annoyance that Tilly is the role for which she is most remembered. Vera wants her audience to know her life is bigger than acting. Juxtaposed against her roles of servitude is her radical life as a political activist. Not only did she march with Martin Luther King Jr., but she became a voice for black revolution before Malcolm X became the voice of black power. It is clear that accusations about selling out to play the maid or reciting lines from that first film are a sore point. After all, as she posits, would her critics have preferred if she worked as a maid in real life?

The scene switches back to the colloquium, where the scholars ruminate on Vera's success and her tragic ending. Boyd is the least impressed by Vera's career choices; he writes her off as a mammy who may have been in a lesbian relationship with Gloria before she died an alcoholic. Afua and Carmen are more sympathetic. In Afua's view, Vera understood the optics involved in playing the maid but tried to stretch the character beyond the stereotype. When it was apparent the industry would never allow Vera to grow as an artist, she stepped out of the spotlight. For Afua, Vera's most important legacy was not her acting but her radicalism and willingness to stand up to the industry and call them out for their racism and sexism. Carmen, on the other hand, does not let Vera off the hook so easily. While she recognizes Vera's struggle to find other roles, she maintains that Vera failed to transform her maid character. In a shocking revelation, she claims that Vera is not dead but alive, a bedraggled beggar living in a homeless shelter. While each panelist has a different interpretation of Vera's life, they can all agree: Vera's career was fraught with struggle, and her life ended tragically. The panelists return to the television video, where Gloria appears and finally publicly thanks Vera for her friendship. *The Belle of New Orleans* plays for the last time, and Vera once again gets to shine as she gets the honor of saying the last lines.

In Nottage's play, there are no accolades for Vera, and in the end, it is questionable if playing the maid was transformative. In the 1920s through to the 1980s, women like Vera had no choice but to play servants. In some cases, actresses were rewarded for their efforts. Hattie McDaniel, for example, mainly known for her part as Mammy in *Gone with the Wind*, earned an Oscar for her performance. Like Vera, though, McDaniel faced her own share of backlash from the black community. Even though she was praised by the *Amsterdam News* for playing Mammy, she was forced to defend her decision. In interviews, she explains that it was

> an opportunity to glorify Negro Womanhood. Not the modern, streamlined type of Negro woman, who attends teas and concerts in furs and silks, but the type of Negro of the period that gave us Harriet Tubman, Sojourner Truth, and Charity Still. . . . I knew the Mammy in the Civil War picture would have to wear a handkerchief on her head, to depict her people in slavery, but this would only serve to emphasizes the improved status of our race today. (qtd. in Regester 128)

Harris and McDaniel may well have hoped that seventy years after their performances, black women would have been free of playing the maid. Unfortunately, that was not the case. In 2012, Viola Davis and Octavia Spencer played maids in *The Help*. In fairness, they were not reduced to playing mammies on the plantation, but to some black women, they were still mischaracterized (as discussed in chapter 1). Like McDaniel, both women were nominated for an Academy Award. Davis was nominated for best actress but did not win. Over the years, she has repeatedly expressed regret for appearing in the film. (Her regret is in part due to the failure to allow the maids to actually tell their own stories.) Spencer, who won for best supporting actress, holds no misgivings about her role. After all, she did win an Oscar. Davis's remorse and Spencer's equanimity for performing as the maid speak to the underlying question Nottage raises in the play. Actresses want to act. As long as Hollywood has a narrow definition of black womanhood, actresses will continue to fight this battle. Ultimately, at the end, it is the actress who has to live with the consequences, good or bad.

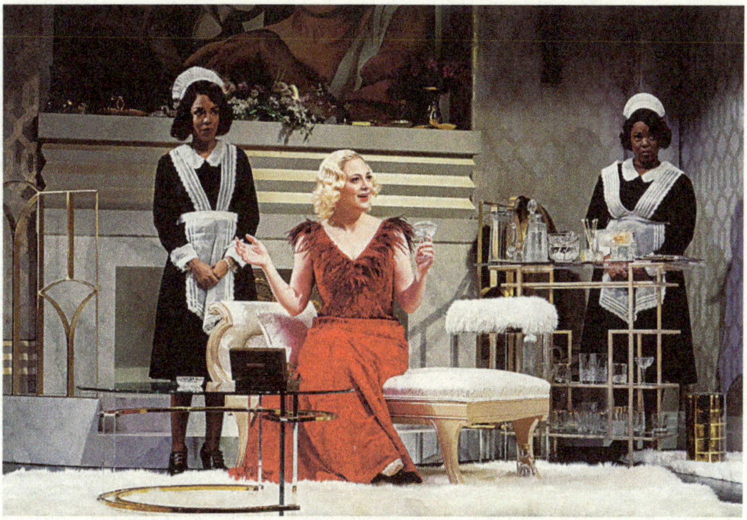

FIGURE 1. Photograph of Jessica Frances Dukes, Jenni Barber, and Heather Alicia Simms in Lynne Nottage's *By the Way, Meet Vera Stark*, 2018 by Joan Marcus.

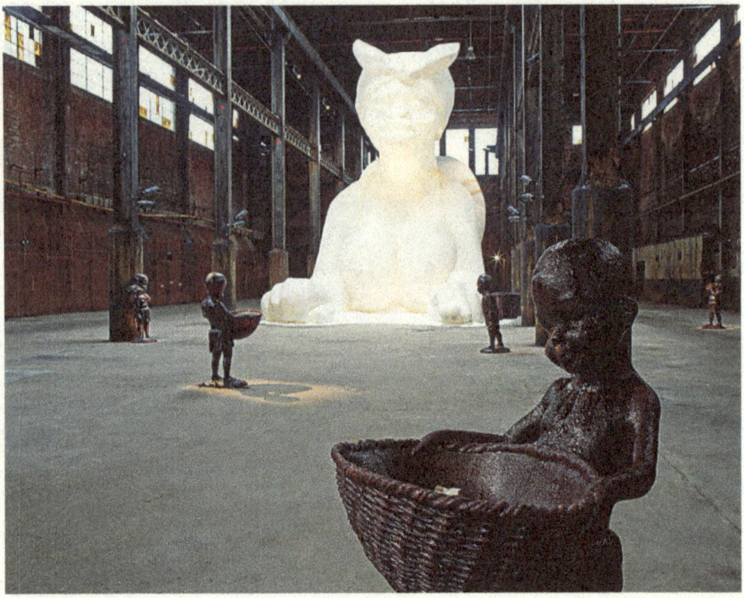

FIGURE 2. Kara Walker, *A Subtlety, or the Marvelous Sugar Baby, an Homage to the unpaid and overworked Artisans who have refined our Sweet tastes from the cane fields to the Kitchens of the New World on the Occasion of the demolition of the Domino Sugar Refining Plant*, 2014. Polystyrene foam, sugar. Approx. 35.5 x 26 x 75.5 feet (10.8 x 7.9 x 23 m). Installation view: Domino Sugar Refinery, a project of Creative Time, Brooklyn, NY, 2014. Photo: Jason Wyche.

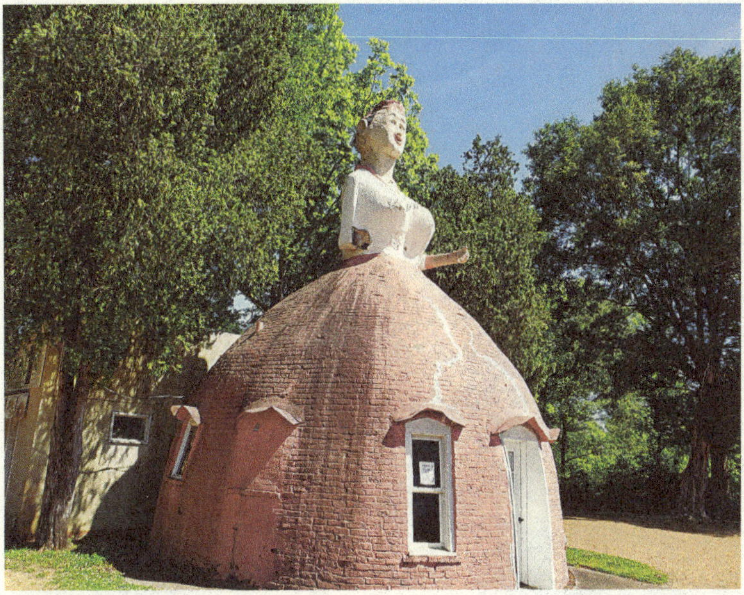

FIGURE 3. Photography of Mammy's Cupboard, Natchez, Mississippi. Photo: Tracee Loran 2019.

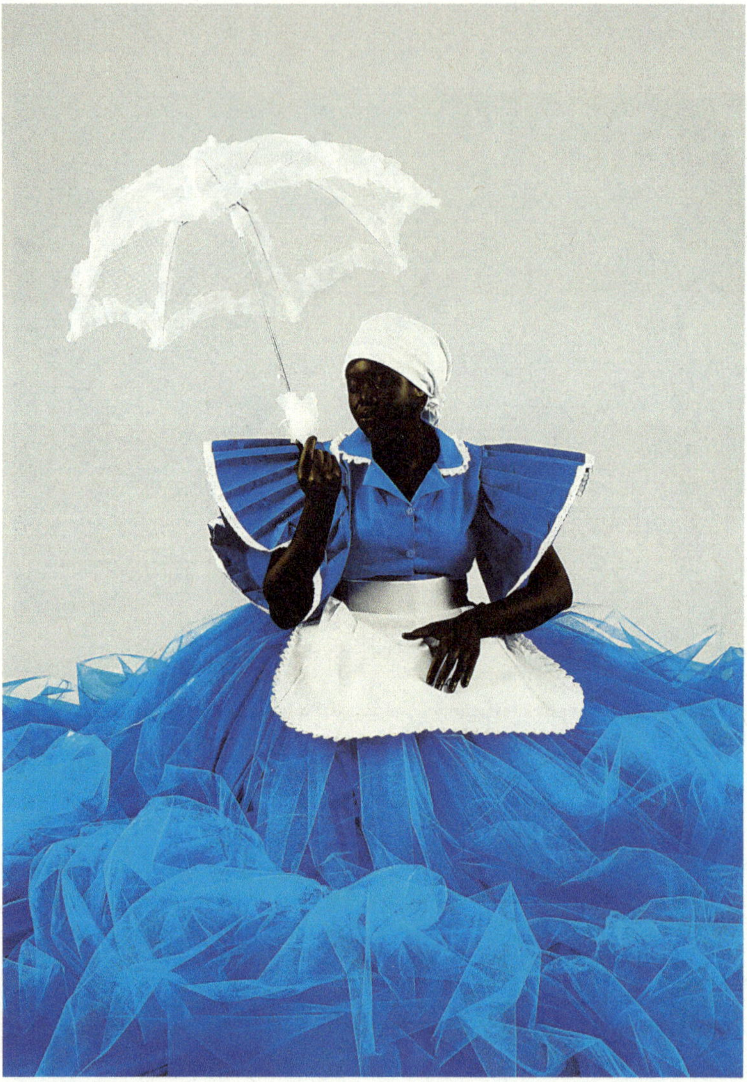

FIGURE 4. *I'm A Lady*, 2009. Image courtesy of SMAC Gallery, artwork copyright © Mary Sibande.

7

The Art of Dressing Up in Mary Sibande's *Long Live the Dead Queen*

> Hidden away in the homes and kitchens of suburbia, they are an open secret—such a normalized part of South African life that they are hardly noticed.
> —Shireen Ally, *From Servants to Workers*

In 2009, South African artist Mary Sibande was chosen by the Joburg Arts City project to display her photographic series, *Long Live the Dead Queen* (*LLDQ*), in an outdoor public gallery during the 2010 World Cup soccer tournament hosted by South Africa. Hanging at nineteen feet in the air, Sibande's captivating, vibrant prints featuring unconventional images of the black female domestic worker were mounted on billboards across Johannesburg in a feminist pictorial narrative. Sibande's photographs redefined the image of the black domestic and placed her on a global stage, moving her beyond the confines of the kitchen and into the public sphere.

LLDQ is a mixed-media exhibition of digital prints and fiberglass mannequins inspired by multiple generations of maids in Sibande's family. Sibande's public celebration of these women honored the strength and dignity of domestic workers in South Africa and across the globe. An analysis of the *LLDQ* series shows how Sibande produces an empowering portrait of the domestic worker, enabling her to be imagined outside of her marginalized station in society. In comparison to standard portrayals of domestics dressed in typical house dresses, white aprons, and headscarves while tending to the homes and children of white women, Sibande's ultraglamorous women, clad in both ball gown and apron, exemplify the unrealized potential of domestic workers. Moreover, her figures spotlight the intersectional oppression of black South African women who have been forced into decades of servitude and invisibility.

As noted in chapter 4, the prevalence of black South African women's employment in domestic labor has been directly linked to apartheid, a white supremacist legal and institutionalized system of racial segregation that from 1948 to 1994 oppressed and exploited native black men and women. For more than forty years, black men and women (along with other ethnic allies, including Indians and whites) fought against apartheid. On the frontlines were political organizations such as the African National Congress (ANC), of which Nelson Mandela was a member, and the Pan-African Congress, which fought relentlessly for the liberation of the indigenous population. These anti-apartheid freedom fighters courageously staged both nonviolent protests and violent guerilla attacks against the government, and those linked with these activities were jailed, tortured, and/or murdered. By the 1980s, the international community began acknowledging the human rights crises in South Africa, and nations began boycotting the government's racist regime.[1] As is well known, Nelson Mandela, who became South Africa's first black president, was imprisoned for twenty-seven years for his involvement with the ANC. In this turbulent time, black women toiled as domestic workers in the homes of their oppressors while secretly playing an active role in the liberation movement.

With so many generations of black women working in servitude, it became an accepted truth in the national imaginary that domesticity was the natural role for black women. Sibande's artwork chronicles the legacy of this occupation that was passed from one generation to another, with mothers training daughters to work as maids in the homes of white families who depended on cheap black labor. As was typical for most black families, three generations of women in Sibande's family worked as maids: her great-grandmother, grandmother, and mother. Mary Sibande, born in 1982, was the first woman in her family *not* to work as a maid. Unlike her foremothers, she had her mother, a maid turned beautician, as an inspirational figure to demonstrate that women could break the rule. Sibande was also fortunate to attend college. Initially, she hoped for a career in fashion design but missing a college application deadline necessitated a shift to fine art, which she studied at the University of Johannesburg. During her time at university, she honed her skills as a painter, sculptor, photographer, and performance artist and developed her first artistic project on domestic workers as part of a college assignment about her genealogy. Sibande created an ornate pair of shoes coveted by a black maid. In a 2013 lecture at the University of Michigan, Sibande explained that the shoes were heavily embellished, invoking luxury and wealth. The shoes symbolized the maid's desire to have more than just shoes—in effect, they were emblematic of the maid's desire to embody white wealth through stepping into the shoes of white women. Her grandmother's stories about her experience working as a maid served as the impetus for her first art piece, *My Madam's Things* (2006). Later, Sibande expanded *My Madam's Things* into a larger exhibit, this time figuratively and literally *stepping into* the shoes of her female relatives by using her body to make the mold of Sophie Ntombikayise, who is also a subject of *LLDQ*.

The *LLDQ* series is composed of multiple life-size mannequins molded from a cast of Sibande's body. As both artist and subject, Sibande uses her body to reincarnate her relatives and give them license to claim their own identities, similar to the work of Zanele Muholi.[2] Most importantly, she challenges the assumption that domestics are docile women, complicit in their oppression and content with their lives as domestics. In her discussion of South African art, scholar Marion Arnold notes, "In post-Apartheid society there is a growing consciousness that to be a woman is to understand womanhood on new terms, to be able to formulate new goals, utter previously secret aspirations, and use opportunities to transcend imposed limitations" (131). Sibande's mannequins expose the secret aspirations of domestics who outwardly express their desires through performance and imagination.

While Sibande uses her own body to cast the mold of Sophie, she is not to be perceived as a literal representation of the character. Rather, Sophie is Sibande's alter ego. Sibande explained to Percy Zvomuya, "Unlike them, I can choose to be a maid, to slip in and out of uniform, to be a superhero, anything I want to be." While Sibande's relatives did not have the freedom to "slip in and out of uniform," they did in the privacy of their imaginations suspend reality and take on alter egos that temporarily freed them from their drudgery. Sibande's exhibition features four maids who represent her great-grandmother (Sophie-Elsie), grandmother (Sophie-Merica), mother (Sophie-Velucia), and herself (Sophie Ntombikayise). The dual names signify the double identities, or alter egos, of the characters and also the denigrating naming practices of employers, who were often keen to infantilize and dehumanize their employees. During apartheid, white employers often claimed it was difficult to pronounce the African names of their maids, so they called them Shelia or, according to Sibande, Sophie (*Long Live the Dead Queen*). Insisting the African maid answer to an imposed "work" name forced on them an acceptance of Western cultural values. Renaming the maid based on convenience and familiarity undermined the maid's ancestry, stripped the maid of her identity, and resulted in the establishment of two identities: one African and one Western. In the presence of her white madam and her family, the maid's African identity was rendered invisible. In Sibande's exhibition, these African women all maintain the European name "Sophie" to designate the reality of their invisibleness and clone-like existence for employers, who did not distinguish one maid from another and devalued their individuality. At the same time, by adding the African names, Sibande subverts this naming practice and publicly reclaims the maids' African identities, thereby ensuring that audiences see domestics as individual women with their own cultural identities.

The renaming of African bodies is just one example of how employers establish their power and superiority over black women in South African society. Other tactics include

> having domestics wear uniforms, by having them address employers as "master" and "madam" while the employers use first names, and by the presence of some of the more demeaning aspects of paternalism (gift-giving, treating servants like children) with few of the traditional protections. (Rollins 47)

In the face of these actions, women often remained silent. In her seminal text on South African domestics, *Maids and Madams: Domestic Workers Under Apartheid* (1990), Jacklyn Cock argued that black women who maintain silence about the exploitative nature of their jobs are often mistaken for "deferential workers, which implies an acceptance of legitimacy of their own subordination" (Cock 85). The previous chapters, however, prove that such an assumption warrants reconsideration. It has been well documented by Cock and Ally that during and after apartheid, domestic workers vocalized the illegitimacy of their subordination as black women and fought against their exploitation by joining or establishing unions to protect the rights of domestic laborers and to advocate for fair labor conditions.

Like their African American counterparts, black women have played an integral role in the civil rights struggles of their nation. They have concurrently divided their loyalties to their race and their gender. Chapter 4 covered how domestic workers mobilized to form organizations such as SADWU and applied pressure on the government to make reforms for domestic laborers. According to a report from the International Labour Office in the 1990s, there were an estimated 780,000 women employed as domestics in South Africa (Budlender 5). Some of these workers were lending their efforts to the fight both to end apartheid and to release political prisoners (including eventual President Mandela) while also fighting for workers' rights. The work of these women was fruitful. In 1995, a year after Mandela became president, the Labour Relations Act covered domestic workers under its legislation. Unfortunately, concurrent with this new legislation, SADWU, with a membership of 350,000 workers, folded due to financial issues and the mobilization efforts of domestics was set back. Fortunately, in 2000, the organization regrouped and returned under the new name the South African Domestic Service and Allied Workers Union (SADSAWU). The group has been effective at advocating on behalf of workers who need assistance with collective bargaining or a labor inspector to follow up with grievances about mistreatment in the workplace.

Despite union representation, domestics continue to be exploited. Many are afraid to speak out for fear of losing their jobs or being subject to other retaliation, so, as Sibande illustrates, some maids expressed their discontent inwardly by adopting what Cock calls "a mask of deference" (103). In *LLDQ*, Sibande's mannequins reveal that behind their masks of deference is a silent rebellion against their subordination. The women conjure magnificent daydreams, allowing them to escape their lives in servitude where they are physically bound by their status as black maids. Ultimately, they transform themselves into prestigious women involved in occupations and activities much loftier than domestic service. Psychoanalysis suggests that most individuals possess both a real and an imagined self. These two identities shift back and forth to create multiple identities. Lacan describes this representation of the real and imagined self as the shifting of "the oscillation between a momentary ideal of self and other and external dynamic, creating multiple images of self and other and stimulating the 'fictional direction' of the developing ego" (Lacan 2). Sophie's multiple "selves" are presented visibly through her poses, props, accessories, and most importantly, clothes. In Sophie's imagined world, she can express her "secret aspirations" and become a new woman who engages in what scholar Patricia McFadden terms *crafting*, a black feminist practice that gives black women "the ability to . . . imagine and create something that is new; something that comes out of our collective desires to live lives of dignity and self-worth" (qtd. in Baderoon 898). Ultimately, Sibande enables her mannequins to *craft* a new narrative of womanhood that challenges the predetermined role given to black South African women.

Sophie Ntombikayise's Victorian Sartorial Liberation

The deferred dreams of Sibande's foremothers are visually articulated through their actions and attire. Each Sophie wears one of Sibande's meticulously hand-sewn gowns. The Victorian-era-inspired gowns are elaborately designed with pleats and bustles, adorned with lace, crinoline, and organza. The attention to detail, the buttons and puff sleeves, all highlight Sibande's effort to show her reverence for these women. The gowns are slightly reminiscent of the African-print Victorian gowns worn by the mannequins displayed in Nigerian artist Shinka Shonibare's installation *How to Blow Up Two Heads at Once (Ladies)* (2009), which also plays on themes of race and history. The colors and fabrics of Sophie's dresses have great meaning. The various shades of bright blue and purple jewel tones represent not only royalty but also the color of the Sunday uniforms of the Zionist South African church. Sibande explains,

> I use Victorian costumes as my starting point because of the colonial influence in South Africa. The costume is carefully replaced by a maid's fabric and pattern that is well known in South Africa while respecting the formal elements of the Victorian era. (Van der Walt)

The "well-known" indigo fabric she references is *isishweshwe*, a textile worn by both slaves and German women during the colonial period. Ultimately, both the textiles and the Victorian fashion serve as an appropriate metaphor for the confinement and oppressiveness of black women's lives under colonial rule and apartheid.

Victorian fashion was extremely restrictive for the women who were forced to wear it. The sheer volume of the dresses, weighted by hoop skirts and bound corsets, made it difficult for women to walk and breathe. Thus, while the dresses were beautiful in presentation, they were painful to wear. In Sophie's case, the dresses paradoxically symbolize the history of colonial oppression and, as art critic Percy Mabandu says, "liberation from gender, racial, and class constraints." Like Solange and Claire in Genet's *Maids* and Diouana in Sembène's *Black Girl*, enrobed in her dress, Sophie is deceptively free from her place in society. Unlike these other characters, Sophie isn't bold enough to actually wears the madam's clothes, but her active imagination gives her the same gratification. What is similar to Solange and Claire and Diouana is the repeated act of seeing Sophie dressing up in different outfits. Each Sophie dons her own costume, different in color and decorative elements. The uniqueness of each dress forces viewers to take notice of the individuality of these women who do not look or act like maids. In effect, the dresses contradict the black woman's perceived status in society, transforming her into a new and unrecognizable character. In her discussion of folk tales and metamorphoses, Carole Scott claims, "Clothing is also used to express in outward form the psyche's deepest desires and shadowy dreams, by enchantment bringing about a fantastical transmutation into our ultimate selves" (151–157). Sophie's dresses clearly express a range of different possibilities for her life if she could have had access to the privilege afforded to white women in South African society. In *The Maids*, the game of make-believe is dependent upon Claire or Solange switching roles. Here Sophie has no one with whom she can trade places, but the idea of playing both the maid and the madame is reflected in Sophie's dress.

The elaborate designs, bold colors, and voluminous size of the gowns distract viewers from noticing that on top of the elegant gown is the maid's apron and sometimes the headscarf (*doek*). Clothed in both gown and uniform, Sophie exists between worlds. The gown symbolizes her aspirations, but the maid's uniform is a reminder and marker of her oppression within the context of South African cultural and racial politics. Fashion scholar Jennifer Craik's research on uniforms shows that "one of the central features of uniforms is that their effectivity is dependent on a shared understanding of the meaning of their markers of distinction and difference" (Craik 41).

Wearing both the uniform and the gown, Sophie, like Solange and Claire (and Diouana), fights against her prescribed "role" in society and complicates the viewer's ability to "read" her uniform, resulting in the defamiliarization of her role as a maid.[3] To the viewer, Sophie is perceptibly both a maid and also a lady of social standing, and since the two are not mutually exclusive, her identity becomes indeterminate.

Dressed as Sophie Ntombikayise, Sibande joins the family tradition of working in domestic service. She explains,

> The issue of servitude within this family has been passed on from one generation to the next. . . . I will never be a maid, yet can dress like and perform as one. In this role I continue in a line of very strong women. By trying to capture some of their experiences, Sophie was created to be the next in line. (Wellershaus)

Although Sibande's education and class freed her from "being the next in line," her exhibit emphasizes the point that black women remain tied to roles of servitude as domestics and as women in a patriarchal society.

The title of the series—*Long Live the Dead Queen*—captures and pays homage to the continuation of this legacy of domestic service. Sibande explains that she was "playing with the idea of the dead queen. As soon as she dies, she's replaced with another one so the throne is forever occupied" (Cadwalladr). In the tradition of artist Jean-Michel Basquiat, who often used crowns in his artwork to honor heroes in African and African American iconography, Sibande clothes her queens in jewel tones of deep blue and purple, the colors of royalty, and even gives one a crown. The piece *Her Majesty Queen Sophie* (2010) depicts her grandmother, Sophie-Elsie, as a regal figure, clothed in a royal blue gown with light blue, green, orange, and pink ruffles peeking out from under the gathered material that cascades down the front of the garment.

The dress is accented by a spectacular, colorful neck plate of Maasai beads and multicolored ropes of material extending from the necklace and spilling onto the floor in mounds. Around Queen Sophie's head, red sunray-like beams are layered over the top of a white halo of light. Queen Sophie-Elsie is a commanding presence, and yet, interestingly, her eyes and the eyes of all the Sophies are closed. Sophie's retreat inward reflects an existential crisis. By closing her eyes, Sophie rejects her status as a racially and sexually inferior being, which black people often experience as a result of what Frantz Fanon refers to as being "fixed" by the "movements, the attitudes, [and] the glances of the Other" (109) that deem blacks as inferior. Once she opens her eyes, she must return to her reality, but her dual consciousness gives her agency and escapism. Her body and her labor might be under the control of her employer, but her mind is her own.

In her transformed state, Sophie takes on a variety of professions. She is a general, an orchestra conductor, a lady of leisure who loses her day in a shopping spree, and a hairdresser. Scholar Alison Laurie explains, "Dress enables people to identify themselves—socially, sexually, morally, aesthetically—to be recognized or to be misrecognized" (151). By dressing up in various elaborate costumes, Sibande outwardly expresses the aspirations of female relatives like her mother, who dreamed of becoming a hairstylist. *A Conversation with Madam CJ Walker* (2009) is probably one of the most personal pieces in the collection. The image channels the realized dream of her mother, who managed to leave her job as a housekeeper to become a hairdresser. Sophie-Velucia is featured, using synthetic hair to make a tapestry depicting the portrait of entrepreneur Madame C. J. Walker. Walker, one of America's first African American millionaires, amassed an impressive fortune from her creation and distribution of hair products for African Americans. Referencing this black, U.S.-born businesswoman in a work about South African domestics makes a profound connection to the global oppression of black women while demonstrating their potential to reach their goals and achieve success.

Sophie's dreams are so magnificent that they surpass even the status of her white female employer. In *The Reign* (2010), for example, she is a general seated on a rearing black stallion. Sophie holds her up her hand as if enacting the directive to charge the enemy. This particular piece resembles the artwork of African American artist Kehinde Wiley, who appropriates Old Masters portraits of European generals by substituting African American males in urban attire, and adorned in gold jewelry, for notable historical figures such as Napoleon. Like Wiley, Sibande plays with this conventional model of the iconic Eurocentric heroic figure, but in her version, the figure is black and female. As she sits upon the stallion, Sophie takes on the beast's symbolic characteristics of power and strength. The image is a visual feminist postcolonial statement about the potential for women to step into roles of leadership. Sibande is in effect examining the "herstories" of South Africa, the experiences of women who lived under the rule of colonists and who worked as servants (Ulldemolins).

This motif of featuring strong female leaders is repeated again in *Silent Symphony* (2010). Here Sophie is positioned behind a music stand, ready to conduct an orchestra. Her arms are raised in the air, her conductor's stick ready to direct the musicians. Again, Sophie looks stately as she occupies a position accessible to few women, especially black women, who before the end of apartheid had little access to concert halls and certainly could not expect admission into the male-dominated orchestra pit. In Sibande's photographic images and sculptures, Sophie's elaborate clothing and nontraditional activities create an unfamiliar image and a new postapartheid identity. Sophie's transformation is examined more fully in later works such as *A Reversed Retrogress Scene 1* (2013) and *A Terrible Beauty Is Born* (2013). In these pieces, Sibande metaphorically kills Sophie and allows her to enter the next phase of life. *A Reversed Retrogress Scene 1* (2013) depicts the old Sophie in her blue gown, arms sweeping the air in front of a purple-gowned doppelganger, who stands opposite holding the same pose. This purple-clad Sophie represents Sibande as she sees herself in the world today. As the title suggests, the mannequins represent Sophie's past and present life. Sibande explains, "They are the same image cut in half. . . . The new and the old are on the same stage literally, and there's this dance of happiness and also a silent violence that is happening" (Sibande, *A Reversed Retrogress*). The juxtaposition between happiness and violence represents the history of triumph and struggle. Sophie's joy comes from knowing she can escape her life of servitude, but she knows that new possibilities for her life did not happen without violence and struggle. In fact, the color of her dress matches the dye that was used by police to stain the clothes of anti-apartheid protesters, who were later arrested, in the "Purple March" (1989). Thus her purple dress is a reminder of this history of state violence. The new Sophie no longer has to lose herself in daydreams. In *A Terrible Beauty Is Born*, her transition is apparent by the apron falling from her waist. Her purple dress is constructed differently from the blue gowns; it is laden with heavy, bulbous strands of material that tangle around her ankles and extend above her head. This mass of material symbolizes a deconstruction and a regeneration of the self, as Sophie no longer relies on dressing up to escape from her life as a domestic. Instead, she has the freedom become whomever she wishes.

Conversely, in *LLDQ*, Sophie finds herself dependent on the performative act of putting on clothing to transform herself into a different woman. This dressing up easily associates her with cultural myths and fairy tales like *Cinderella*. Sibande, however, insists that Sophie should not been seen from this point of view because she has her own authentic African story unrelated to Western myth:

> I didn't want to relate my kind of dressing and dressmaking with the concept of Cinderella. That's a western narrative. I didn't want to take it there. You can say, well Cinderella's dress becomes this big ball gown, [but] I always reject the Cinderellas. . . . I think for me, telling the story about Sophie . . . my grandmother telling me about her past life and my mother, I take their stories and I make them fantastical, because at some point it was like a wish list. They wish to be this they wish to be that. (Sibande, interview with Tracey Walters)

Sibande does, however, appropriate the DC hero Superman. The hero is featured in pieces like *They Don't Make Them Like They Used To* (2008), an image depicting Sophie knitting a sweater decorated with the Superman insignia.

The Superman piece ironically plays to the notion of black women's perceived superhuman abilities, as Michele Wallace wrote about in her famous book *Black Macho and the Myth of the Black Superwoman* (1978) and as was captured in the Alicia Keyes hit song "Superwoman" (2008). Like Superman, who poses by day as ordinary journalist Clark Kent and by night as the mighty Superman, who saves the world, Sophie the maid has her own secret dual personalities. On the surface, she is an average maid carrying out her duties, but she is also this other persona, a superhuman character that endures all that comes to her as a heroic woman. Sophie can survive the demands of both motherhood and her arduous job as housekeeper, all while creating time to transport herself to a place where she can be free from her life of domesticity. As the maid, there are no quick changes, so she wears both dress and uniform. Sibande explains that the dresses Sophie wears are actually like a uniform. She says the idea was "to create something that would serve as a uniform within a uniform for her, an outfit that enabled her to express her desires" (Wellershaus). Sophie's superwoman finds time to be free of her domestic chores. We do not see the women tending to children, washing, ironing, or engaged in household duties. *I'm a Lady* (2009), for example, shows Sophie as a socialite, posing as though sitting for a portrait. She is outfitted in a magnificent dress, holding a lace parasol. The piece is whimsical and removes Sophie from the typical image of a dowdy housemaid and transforms her into an elegant lady. It is the kind of fantasy life Diouana dreams of in chapter 4. The same image carries through in "*. . . of Prosperity*" (2012). Here Sophie takes full advantage of retail therapy in a shopping spree. Large fabric shopping bags, made from the same material (and in the same color) as Sophie's dress, along with hundreds of cubes of material, almost engulf Sophie's body and suggest that her overindulgence is a response to what she lacks in real life. The notion of excess is also underscored by the monstrous size of the dresses. Simbao notes,

> The diameter of the dresses and the mounds of material used to make them suggest: something vaguely monstrous, however, about this world of excess. The billowing Victorian skirts take over the gallery floor, encroaching on the viewer's space, while the strings of beads seem to run on forever, piling up in heavy mounds. Through excess, Sibande alludes to the social stratification of both Victorian society and apartheid in South Africa, both of which emphasized position and place in social structure. The idea of "knowing your place" leaves little room to maneuver.

These gigantic dresses allow Sophie to create a space of her own and a rightful claim to space denied to black South Africans.

In South Africa, physical space is significant for many reasons. During apartheid, due to numerous laws such as the Land Rights Acts (1913) and the Native Trust and Land Act (1936), which prohibited residency and entrance in specific geographical areas, maids were often given small living quarters and personal space in white homes. South African artist David Koloane and Ivor Powell explain, "Apartheid was a politics of space more than anything. If you look at the 1913 and 1936 Land Acts they are all about space, and much of the apartheid legislation was denying people the right to move. It's all about space, restricting space. . . . Claiming art is also reclaiming space" (265). Sophie, via Sibande, takes ownership of spaces typically unreserved for black women, in galleries and on billboards. The exaggerated sizes of the dresses worn by Sibande's sculptures also mimic the grand scale of Sophie's dreams; in the same way epics are appropriated and used to tell stories about lowly figures, Sophie is given status unreserved for such women.

The Public Response

More than twenty prints from the *LLDQ* series were selected by the Central Johannesburg Partnership Project, Art at Work (AAW), to be mounted on billboards throughout the city. According to Lesley Perkes, a former director of the AAW program, Sibande's art was chosen because it presented a powerful, iconic image that was recognizable to most members of the public. As Sibande told scholar Mary Corrigall, "If people are not raised by a domestic worker then their mother or auntie has worked as one. This is why Sophie always hits home, she always evokes the familiar"—and in this case, the unfamiliar (Sibande, interview with Mary Corrigall). As a readily identifiable national mother figure, Sophie is a haunting reminder of apartheid. The billboards depicting Sophie were strategically placed across Johannesburg so that they were highly visible to neighborhood residents and motorists on the expressway. The prints, magnificent in size and highly visible, were wrapped around churches, hotels, and apartment buildings. Perkes says it was important to feature the prints specifically in the inner city because they wanted the art to be experienced by "people who work and live in the city. We wanted there to be an exhibition for them, and also those who pass the city on their way to something else to also see it. It was strategic—we wanted people to see it on the North, South, West, East . . . where many live and work." Perkes's sentiment was echoed by Sibande, who felt it was important that the images not remain confined to the gallery space. "African art is not accessible for all South Africans," Perkes lamented. She added that if her images were only in private galleries, they wouldn't be seen by the very women she captured in the paintings and sculptures.

Mounting the prints across the city and in the townships, and thus making them accessible to a broad audience, was just the first task for the organizers. As Perkes explains, it was not enough for people to *see* the images amidst a landscape of billboards advertising typical products or public service announcements; they also wanted viewers to understand the intentionality of the artwork. In an effort to educate the public about the images and the AAW program, organizers released a two-minute advertisement that introduced Sibande and explained who and what Sophie represented. The pictures also had an advertising quality that Sibande says was deliberate: "I intentionally use[d] the language of advertising. . . . Without the advertisement, I don't know if people would have known what it [art] was" (Sibande, interview with Tracey Walters). Unfortunately, even with this instructional video but with no tagline explaining what was being sold, some found the images perplexing. As the maid figure, Sophie is symbolic of the commodification of black women's labor, a point noted by Sibande, who asserts, "From the day we put up the pictures she became a product" (Sibande, interview with Tracey Walters). Some passersby actually mistook the art as an advertisement for a maid service or even a domestic product. Sophie, however, is not solely selling a product. She is also advertising the black woman's place in South Africa's history. For the more astute viewer, the signifier (cap and apron) and its correlate signified (servitude, class, and race) symbolized much more than domesticity. In essence, taking into consideration the fantastical element of the images, some viewers might have concluded that Sibande was trying to tell a very complex story about the past or the future possibilities for black women's lives. These different interpretations of the billboards fulfilled Sibande's agenda: to deconstruct the reading of the black maid to show that Sophie should not be defined by her apron.

The general public's response to Sophie was mixed. While some liked the images, others were baffled, especially by the Victorian garb. Those who overlooked the gown and saw a black female figure in a cap and gown were still unclear about what they were seeing. One woman said she understood that Sibande was telling a story but could not explain what story she was telling. Another woman claimed that she identified with the image of the maid but had difficulty deciphering the meaning of the props. Admitting her confusion, she stated, "We ask ourselves many questions, what is this ad for, because I can see it is me, with the apron and with the umbrella, [but] it's not. . . . The umbrella, I don't know" (van Wyk). Conversely, journalist Nechama Brodie reported seeing Sibande's art with friends on a building the day after it was mounted but noted how few people actually saw it. She recalls it taking a long time before "a man in khaki overalls and a woolen hat follows our eyes up, up, up to the side of the building. He stops, with an awkward stumble mid-stride, and at last he sees. He is the only one. And then he carries on walking" (Brodie). Journalist Lisa van Wyk was also struck by the public's obliviousness or lack of understanding about the artwork. Van Wyk reports that one woman exclaimed, "It doesn't have the message, I don't understand it!" (van Wyk). Perhaps for Sibande, this was precisely the point of the piece; it forces viewers who actually see it to wrestle with the image and to not know immediately how to interpret its meaning.

While the billboards made a strong statement about black women in South Africa, equally as relevant is the physical space inhabited by the billboards. Returning to Simbao and Koloane's earlier comments about the importance of space in South Africa, Sophie takes ownership of multiple spaces formally closed off to indigenous Africans. Sibande's art takes advantage of the "public" space that is rightfully hers and in turn makes a significant political statement about the African woman's right to claim space. Thus, with Sophie's images located on buildings across Johannesburg, Sibande reclaims the space for the maid and all indigenous South Africans. In his discussion of what he calls "visual colonialism," cultural critic Nicholas Mirzoeff observes that "the visual culture of colonialism had a significant role to play in both explaining and defining the colonial order" (282). In the case of early South African art, for example, white artists objectified black men and women and denied them a sense of humanity and multidimensionality. Sibande's art responds to this visual colonialism with a visual postcolonial narrative that indicts and exposes the colonial order's elitism, racism, and sexism during and after apartheid. Finally, the artwork Sibande produces is not just about politics; it is also about aesthetics—an experimentation in style, technique, color, and texture. Arnold questions if the powerful image of the maid detracts from appreciating the artwork itself:

> Images of black female servitude cannot be viewed with innocence: personal experience is bound to influence the ways which

> perceptions are generated. Several issues then become paramount. Can visual language and aesthetic factors make their presence felt when subject matter is socially provocative? (96)

In Sibande's case, the aesthetics of her work are not compromised by the political. The regal, beautiful statues in their colorful dresses stimulate the imaginations of those who are drawn into the various figures displayed in the photographs or gallery space. The magnificence of Sibande's work, the scale, the attention to detail, and the uniqueness of her approach to this subject are not eclipsed by the political nature of the work. Rather, it is aesthetics that lead South Africans (and the rest of the world) to see the beauty of her artwork and engage with the long history of a once oppressive government and the second-class status of women.

PART 3

Representing for Laure

African American / Caribbean Women's Reimaginings of Édouard Manet's Olympia

8

From the Margin to the Center

The Maid in Édouard Manet's Olympia *and the Politics of Recognition in the Artwork of Mickalene Thomas and Renee Cox*

For more than two hundred years, the nameless black maid in Édouard Manet's masterpiece *Olympia* (1863) has been eclipsed by Olympia herself, the flaming red-haired iconic figure of sexual agency or (depending on interpretation) sexual deviancy. To many art historians, the nameless odalisque (female slave / chambermaid) in Manet's painting was an inconsequential prop, an object used to accentuate Olympia's body. The easy dismissal of the black maid's role as secondary to Olympia is emblematic of the invisibility of black women in general. Victorine Meurent, who posed as Olympia, and Laure, the woman who posed as Olympia's maid, were both well known to Manet. He had painted each woman (separately) on many occasions.[1] In this famed painting, which put the two together, Meurent reclines on a mass of white and cream bed linens. Her naked body is accessorized with a pink flower in her hair, a black ribbon tied around her neck, and a dainty pair of shoes on her feet. The cream flesh tones of her skin blend with the flower-patterned duvet beneath her body and fade into the garment worn by Laure. While Meurent's hand covers her pubic area, she appears uninhibited in her nudity and meets the viewer's gaze confidently. Laure stands alongside Meurent holding a large, colorful bouquet of flowers that obscure her torso. Long, red earrings bring life to Laure's dark complexion, which mutes her features. Her eyes are fixed squarely on Meurent's face, patiently awaiting acknowledgment of the gift she is ready to hand over. To Laure's left, a black cat, a prop no different than Laure, perches at the end of the bed.

Through the decades, Laure has captured the imagination of countless black artists who redirect the viewer's gaze onto her so that she is not an accessory to Olympia but instead a subject in her own right, deserving of subjectivity. Olympia, on the other hand, is often phased out of the reworking of Manet's painting and at times represented in name only. Many of the black artists who reimagine Olympia make Laure more than a dull figure in the backdrop of the original. The artists highlight aspects of the character Manet neglects: a strong composition of her features, clearly defined contours of her nude body, and (in some cases) a brazen display of her sexuality. Laure is brought to life through colorful backdrops that compliment her brown skin and make the pieces more visually arresting. Multimedia artists Mickalene Thomas and Renee Cox give Laure among the most radical makeovers. Thomas's *Left Behind #2* (2014) and *Marie Femme Noire Nue: Couchée #2* (2014) and Cox's *Olympia's Boyz* (2001) and *Missy at Home* (2008) defamiliarize *Olympia*. These reworkings draw upon earlier discussions about performance, sexuality, inverted power relationships, and class to illuminate how their twenty-first-century appropriation of *Olympia* elevates Laure from simple handmaid to empowered black woman.

In 2018, Laure was thrust into the spotlight when art historian Denise Murrell curated a groundbreaking exhibition that forced the art world to acknowledge the absence of substantive critical engagement with the presence of the black model in French and American art. Although art historians have produced scholarship charting the trajectory of how black figures in paintings by artists such as Manet, Henri Matisse, Edgar Degas, et al. are represented, Murrell's exhibition was the first to convince the art establishment to grant these models visual representation. The show, *Posing*

Modernity: The Black Model from Manet and Matisse to Today, spotlighted the relevance of black models who appeared in countless French and American paintings (oftentimes with white figures) but were disregarded by the art establishment. Murrell adapted the show from her dissertation, "Seeing Laure: Race Modernity from Manet's Olympia to Matisse, Bearden and Beyond." She partnered with her alma mater, Columbia University, to mount the show—first at the Wallach Art Gallery at Columbia University and later in France at the Musée d'Orsay.

Murrell's exhibition of more than one hundred pieces shifted focus from the white subjects in the paintings to the black subjects that were, in the eighteenth and nineteenth century, status symbols used to showcase the wealth of the white figures who commissioned the paintings. Unlike the white figures who were given subjectivity, black models were stripped of humanity, treated as accessories or props, and thus indistinguishable from jewelry or pets in the paintings (Dunne). In fact, in English art, "images of dogs and black servants were introduced, sometimes interchangeably, to insinuate a patrician subject's ability to command loyalty" (O'Leary 21). Murrell's show gives the black figures humanity by "restoring the names of models whose official identities have been lost" (des Cars qtd. in Murrell xiii). Laure was given the honor of having *Olympia* retitled *Laure*, and Madeline, the model who sat for Marie Guillemine-Benoist's *Portrait of a Negress Woman* (1800), is now recognized in the painting's new permanent title: *Portrait of Madeline* (1800). Naming these black women and learning about their histories allows for a more complex understanding of the positionality of black women in nineteenth-century Western society. Ultimately, these black women are redefined beyond their generic characterization as either slaves or sexual oddities. Murrell asserts,

> These significations open up the suggestion that, by the 1870s, the image of the black Parisian woman no longer carried a single signification. As the eroticized black woman is transformed from the Other who exists wholly outside French society

> to a free working woman within the metropolis, art begins to represent this new figure in differing the roles comparable to her European counterparts. (80)

Acknowledging the diversity in nineteenth-century black women's experiences is also important because it opens up a series of questions about who these women were and how they survived in this society.

Laure is probably one of the most appropriated figures from the exhibit's impressionist-era canon. Laure is featured in several of Manet's paintings, including *Children in the Tuileries* (1861–1862), *La Négresse* (also known as *Portrait of Laure*; 1862–1865), and *Olympia* (1863). Again, although the title of Manet's painting points to the maid as the subject, Olympia's nakedness consumes most interpretations of the work. For its time, Olympia's nakedness was a scandalous display of deviant sexuality. Despite being fully clothed, Laure's alterity as an African woman becomes the symbolic representation of sexual immorality—her own and Olympia's. The mischaracterization of a black woman's sexual deviancy was a combination of social mythology and scientific experimentation.[2]

During slavery, white slaveholders not only forced enslaved black women to bear children outside the sanctity of marriage, which was immoral, but they concocted stories about the powers of their seduction to account for the predatory behavior of plantation masters who routinely had sex with and impregnated slave women. To save face and absolve their husbands of wrongdoing, plantation mistresses helped perpetuate the myth of hypersexuality. Furthermore, scientists who were determined to prove the inferiority of African people used black bodies as specimens to identify physiological differences that would account for their otherness. The size and shape of black women's sex organs made them scientific anomalies, as in the case of the Venus Hottentot discussed in chapters 1 and 9. In his study of the Venus Hottentot and the fetishization of the black body, Sander Gilman maintains,

> One of the central functions of the black servant in the visual arts of the eighteenth and nineteenth centuries was as a marker of the sexualization of the society in which he or she was found. . . . By the nineteenth century, as in *Olympia* . . . the central white female figure is associated with a black female in such a way as to imply a similarity between the sexuality of the two. (119)[3]

Gilman's statement illustrates how white society protected the integrity of white women's sexuality at the expense of black women's morality.

Despite the hypersexualization of black women's bodies, feminist critic Lorraine O'Grady bemoans the absence of Laure's sexuality. In O'Grady's view, because Laure's sexuality is concealed by a bouquet of flowers, Manet "excises" her sexuality to preserve the "femininity" of the white prostitute's body (3). Art historian Darcy Grimaldo Grigsby, on the other hand, offers an entirely different reading. She redirects the focus from Laure's servility and sexualized body to Laure's earning power as a "newly enfranchised member of the working class" (432), which Murrell observes as well. In discussing Laure's transactional dealings with Manet as a model contracting her services rather than as a slave being forced to perform sexually, Grigsby remakes the image of Laure. Artists Mickalene Thomas and Renee Cox have created artworks that seem to be a combination of O'Grady's and Grigsby's portrayal of Laure, which ultimately claim "the body as a site of black female subjectivity" (O'Grady 5). Thomas and Cox focus exclusively on Laure, often omitting Olympia from their reworkings of Manet's masterpiece.

Laure: Out of the Shadows

Before turning attention to Thomas and Cox, it is important to discuss early renditions of Manet's *Olympia* by African American male painters William H. Johnson and Romare Bearden, two artists who influenced Thomas's and Cox's renditions of *Olympia*.

Johnson's *Nude* (1939; oil on burlap) is one of the earliest intertextual references to *Olympia*. He portrays a nude woman on a pristine white sheet that is juxtaposed against her nut-brown skin. The sheet is like a canvas exhibiting the model's body. Her bedroom is drenched in color: green, red, yellow, and blue hues are incorporated throughout the room, on the bed linens, the fruit bowl, the vase and flowers, and the coffee table. The vibrancy in the room matches her demeanor. She is relaxed and unguarded, one arm bent at the elbow and supporting her head, the other gently cupping her waist. Whereas Olympia's hand covers her pelvis, Johnson's nude is not inhibited by social mores. She is in a contemplative state. Her eyes, bright and white, are looking up toward the ceiling, as though she is oblivious to the viewer's gaze. What is most noticeable about Johnson's image in comparison to Manet's is Johnson's use of space. The fullness of the body in Johnson's painting takes up much more of the canvas than the model in *Olympia*. Also, the fleshy contours of Johnson's black nude are antithetical to Manet's lithe model. In *Nude*, the woman's wide hips and soft paunch indicate that she is a woman whose body has succumbed to middle age.[4]

A coffee table displaying a colorful bowl of fruit sits in front of her recliner. A wine bottle and glass are positioned next to the bowl. These elements in the room give Laure's character a story. Her bedroom's decor—the flowers and coordinating bed linens—indicate that she is a working woman who can afford these simple luxuries, while her casual pose on the couch and the single wineglass suggests she is not waiting for the company of a man (or a woman), nor does she need their company to be entertained. Olympia is omitted from the scene altogether, so Laure's nakedness is hers alone. Johnson's image does not read as pornographic. His female figure is bare, but her pose is not provocative.

Outside art circles, Johnson's paintings may not be as well known as *Olympia*, but the painting had an indelible impact on African American artists. Since 1970, subsequent versions of *Olympia* have been a conflation of *Olympia* and *Nude*. Romare Bearden's *Patchwork Quilt* (1970; paper and cloth collage), for example, picks up on Johnson's use of bright colors to accentuate Laure's body. According to curator Ruth Fine, Bearden cited "the beauty of the black woman as a subject of immense importance to him, and over the years it provided one of his abiding motifs" (92). As part of his collection of images of black women, Bearden made compositions featuring women in all aspects of everyday life, including at the brothel, so it is unsurprising that he would have been inspired by Manet's *Olympia* as well as by Henri Matisse's odalisques.[5]

Bearden's approach to *Olympia* is much more restrained than Johnson's. In lieu of fresh flowers and a colorful fruit display is a busy multicolored patchwork quilt composed of mismatched floral patterns, mini polka dots, and striped swatches of fabric, all of which sharply contrast against the inky blackness of the model's body. Here space is constrained. No other decorations are present. Laure wears a pink head scarf with a light pink sash draped around her waist. She lays facedown on the patchwork quilt, unwilling to engage with the viewer. Although her head is facedown, her side profile is visible, and there is a rigidity to her body that, in comparison to Johnson's figure, appears statue-like. One arm is held stiffly, parallel to her body, pointing downward, and her hand is tautly elevated above her hip. Her feet, positioned one in front of the other, are similar to the way figures are painted in Egyptian hieroglyphics. The cubist style of this collage flattens the figure's form until she almost blends with the textile she lays upon. Although the figure appears to be naked, her body is fragmented in different shades (jet black for the face, waist, and legs, with different shades of brown for the arms and breast) and in sharp angles, denying any reference to overt sexuality. Bearden is uninterested in portraying his version of Laure as exhibitionist prostitute or passive servant. Instead, he imagines a woman who, in this moment, is blocking out the world. The hardness of this body is reflective of the protective armor worn by black women, especially for women in urban centers like Harlem, a popular setting for Bearden's paintings. Like Johnson's *Nude*, she is an average woman with an ordinary life, free to exist without any imposed definition, much like the other women he depicted in his artwork. *Patchwork Quilt* is one of the most recognized pieces of African American art ascribed to Manet, but often compositions of Laure indicate a direct reference to Johnson as well.

American-born multimedia artist Thomas is one such artist influenced by African American artists Johnson, Bearden, and Carrie Mae Weems along with European masters Matisse, Manet, and Gustave Courbet. Thomas, who went to Pratt for undergraduate school, was a graduate student at Yale when she learned about how Matisse and Manet featured black women in their art. In an interview with journalist Julie Belcove, Thomas said that, like Murrell, she endeavored to make black women visible in art and in the discourse related to these particular works in question. To create her collages/paintings and photographic images of black women, Thomas draws from her own life, history, pop culture, and politics (e.g., Lauryn Hill, Solange Knowles, Michelle Obama, and Whoopi Goldberg). Like so many black women in this study, Thomas is committed to ensuring that artistic representations of black women are adequately represented in spaces where they have historically been excluded, that their experiences are validated, and that they are afforded the same respect as those in the dominant culture. For continuity and the effort to tell her own story through art, Thomas appears in her artwork alone and with her lovers. She often uses the same models, one of whom is her late mother, who is featured in pieces like *Ain't I a Woman (Sandra)* (2009) and *Mama Bush: I'm Waiting Baby* (2010). For more than ten years, Thomas has reworked Manet's Laure, and other Manet-inspired interpretations, in a never-ending twenty-first-century makeover. Similar to other artists in this study, her mother is one of her biggest inspirations. Her mother's inner confidence, sensuality, and glamorous style are often a reference point for Thomas, who composes images of bold black women. Thomas creates art with a black feminist agenda that removes Laure from Olympia's shadow and exonerates her from passivity and sexual otherness. Alone in her boudoir, she is a strong, confident woman who can display her body on her own terms.

Similar to Johnson and Bearden, Thomas often uses textiles and rhinestones to accentuate Laure's figure. The luxe fabrics, both on the bed and on her body, are used to reinforce the glamour and dignity of her subjects, who are as flamboyant as the patterns on their bed linens. Thomas pays homage to her Laure-inspired figures through African American cultural markers like Afro hairstyles and 1970s fashion (makeup, clothing, and jewelry). Thomas's attention to their makeup and hair is meant to highlight their femininity and features as a celebration of African American beauty in spaces where their beauty has historically been undermined. Even the names of paintings like *Qusuquzah Lounging with Pink + Black Flower* (2016) suggest the range of complexions, body types, shapes, and sizes. In most of the earlier works, the clothing in the images (though mostly seventies inspired) has a timeless quality that allows the figures to be read as women of yesterday and today. In the majority of the images, Laure gazes out at the viewer. Her gaze is not one that allows them to be objectified. Instead, given Laure's invisibility (and her failure to observe the viewer), Thomas allows her figure to see and be seen. As a female artist, Thomas disrupts the conventional meaning of the gaze. As she says in an interview with artist Sean Landers, while the dominant (male) influences the gaze, "the fact that the gaze in question is from one woman to another is more powerful to me than the male" (Thomas, "Artist Mickalene Thomas" 36).

Sometimes, Thomas's subject is depicted naked with groups of girlfriends together in representations of Old Masters fully dressed in images where they were disrobed (see Manet's *Le déjeuner sur L'herbe* [*Luncheon on the Grass*; 1863]) or lounging on her bed resting after a full day's work; at other times, she is naked but owning her sexuality. In *A Little Taste Outside of Love* (2007), for example, her Laure figure reclines with her back away from the viewer. Her side profile reveals one bare breast and an ample thigh but not much else. This woman's sexuality is not for public consumption; her body is not for sale. Her head is turned as though she were interrupted. The expression on her face shows mild interest in the intruder but not enough to create any crease of her forehead or expression in her eyes. Like Bearden's piece, the room is sparsely furnished, making the body the primary subject. Beyond the swamp-green walls accented with black-and-white art-deco-like furnishings, rhinestones adorn everything (throw pillows, wallpaper), and most importantly, they outline the model's figure, underscoring her radiance. This woman is the complete antithesis of Manet's portrayal of Laure, shrouded from head to toe in fabric.

In *Left Behind #2* (2014) and *Marie Femme Noire Nue: Couchée #2* (2014), Laure is less coy than she is in *A Little Taste Outside of Love*. *Marie Femme Noire* has Bearden's cubist style. The body is composed as disparate pieces, with different shades of brown and one arm disproportionate to the rest of the body. The main feature here is a single black-and-white Picassoesque printed eye engulfing the top of her face. There is an android quality to this piece, perhaps a futuristic version of Laure ready for the next century. Unlike Manet's Laure, who does not make direct eye contact with anyone, this woman has the self-awareness of being watched, and she returns the gaze, projecting it back on the viewer. In *Left Behind #2*, the model, instead of reclining, sits up on the bed with legs tucked to the side. In this image, Thomas plays on the idea of identity, our own dual personas—the one shown in public and the other revealed in private. Black women have often described their experience of putting on a mask and concealing their true selves as a mode of survival, especially in corporate America, where they are often one of a few and are at times subject to microaggressions related to their physical appearance and culture. One beige layer of skin zips off to reveal another lighter brown body, her slightly drooping breasts and pubic hair on display. Again, the collage includes screen-printed eyes staring out at the viewer. The subject conveys the idea that you are looking at me, but I am looking right back at you. In the privacy of her own home, this woman can display who she is inside and out.

Finally, in *Sleep: Deux Femme Noires* (2012), the subject moves out of the boudoir and into the public. Patterned wall-hangings and pillows are traded for a lush, green imagery of foliage in an idyllic woodland, set against the jet-black skin of one woman and the almost neon yellow hue of another. The darker of the two women intertwines her sinewy legs around her partner's. This modern take on Laure, disrobed and laying with another woman (perhaps even Olympia), takes us back to Muholi's portraits of homoerotic desire. The women's public display of affection is observed by the viewer, but the couple are unconcerned with the audience's gaze. The couple's ability to have their intimate moment uninterrupted, without fear of retribution, calls into question the lack of security for and scarce representation of the black queer body, as was discussed in chapter 4 with Muholi's portraits. While the viewer can enjoy Thomas's image of these two women, the everyday realities of hate crimes against lesbians and the trans community make it difficult for many women to openly share this kind of affection in public spaces. Perhaps this is wishful thinking for Thomas, but it is an important way to reframe the way we think about Olympia and Laure and their daily interactions. Jamaican-born photographer Cox also takes up this challenge of rethinking the relationship between Laure and Olympia.

Olympia's Maid Made Over: A Performance of the Black Housewife

Renee Cox is an American-based performance artist who has a penchant for distorting the familiar. She is well known for her playful revisions of images that challenge and create new readings of history. Working in the tradition of other black female artists such as Lorna Simpson, Kara Walker, Sibande, and Muholi, Cox uses herself as a model in these self-portraits to challenge Western hegemonic representations of the black female body. Cox's aesthetic is also similar to Thomas's in that her artwork often inserts black figures from print and pop culture in spaces traditionally occupied by white bodies. In the piece *Rajae for President* (1998), for example, a black female superhero is created to address the absence of black female superheroes in pop culture. In a very controversial work, *Yo Mama's Last Summer* (1999), Cox reconfigures Leonardo da Vinci's iconic painting of *The Last Supper* with a cast of mostly African American males, with herself featured as a naked Jesus Christ. Cox's nude, full-frontal female body dared spectators to reimagine the biblical story of Jesus's last supper from a black female perspective. The controversial series drew criticism from many, including Rudolph Giuliani, the former mayor of New York City, who perceived the images as "disgusting" and "anti-Catholic" and proposed the city create a commission to regulate "decency standards" to keep such work out of publicly funded museums (Bumiller). While some were offended by *Yo Mama*, Cox's supporters defended the artwork on the basis of freedom of speech and artistic expression. While Cox's more controversial works generate a lot of attention, lesser-known pieces are equally as powerful, especially her playful revisions of Renaissance artwork and nineteenth-century portraiture—in particular, her take on Manet's *Olympia*. Cox, like other black artists, knew it was incumbent upon her to help change the predominant image of black servants as props in Western portraiture. In a 2015 interview with French artist Christine Parravicini, Cox recounts being frustrated by the lack of representation and the singular image of black people as servants in the Renaissance art she saw while visiting Florence, Italy. Her disappointment inspired her to appropriate the Renaissance style.

Her reworking of Renaissance art forms is evident in pieces from *American Family* (2002), where Cox creates an alternative to the typical European landscapes and Renaissance garb. Instead, she creates an African setting with characters dressed in African prints. Within this highly stylized collection, we find the piece *Olympia's Boyz*, a direct allusion to Manet's painting. Like other pieces in the *American Family* collection, through language, clothing, hairstyles, and other props, there is a concerted effort to ensure that black culture is both represented and juxtaposed against European culture that is traditionally on display in portraiture. Like Johnson, Bearden, and Thomas, Cox defamiliarizes Manet's portrait racially, culturally, and geographically. To begin with, the title *Olympia's Boyz* invokes African American Vernacular English

(AAVE); the *s* in *Boys* is replaced by a *z* (*Boyz*) to emphasize the cultural ethnicity of the black characters in the photograph. Thomas, as Laure, takes Olympia's place on the bed. In her distinctly Africanized version, Laure reclines on the bed wearing a pair of gold shoes. Her long dreadlocks cover her left breast, and on her arms and neck she wears simple African jewelry. In place of the cream-colored cloth sheets and flower-embossed slipcover on Olympia's bed is a bold, black-and-white checkered African textile. Standing beside Laure are two young boys on guard in African head wraps, covered from the waist down in bright cloth. Each boy holds a spear in his hand.

As noted, other artists have erased the white model from the picture and made Laure and her sexuality the focal point of the portrait, but Cox's inclusion of the two "boyz" adds a different dimension to the image. In *Olympia's Boyz*, Laure is granted sexual agency, but the inclusion of her two boys highlights the importance of her body not simply as a sexual object but also as a mother. Given the history of slavery, which often separated mothers from their children—and even when it did not, affected black women's ability to parent their children as they wished—it is important for Laure to claim her children as her own. This ownership is reinforced in the title itself: *Olympia's Boyz*. As scholars Eversley and Morgan observe,

> Cox's appropriation of family for herself and her sons is a challenge to centuries-old assumptions that the black female body can only produce children that are commodities and will only nurture children who will be slave owners. There is, of course, a subversive pleasure here for Cox as she meets the viewers' gaze with a satisfaction borne in the depiction of her sexual pleasure. (13–14)

And finally there is the gaze. It is combative, steely. It is the look of a fearless woman, a mother protective of her children. She is intent on meeting the viewer's gaze. Like the figures in Thomas's portrait, she demands to be seen and to look right back.

Cox's focus on black life carries over to *The Discreet Charm of the Bougies* (2008), a photographic collection of digital prints that takes its name from the Luis Buñuel film *The Discreet Charm of the Bourgeoisie* (1972). Buñuel's surrealist film is about a group of wealthy friends who make a number of attempts to meet for dinner but find their plans foiled by a series of bizarre events, including misunderstandings, sexual trysts, and espionage. Ten images make up Cox's collection, which was first exhibited at the Galerie Nordine Zidoun in Paris from November 1 to December 20, 2008. Art historian and curator Deborah Willis maintains that "photographers employ the visual language of testifying" about their individual and collective experience, constructing images that depict a new, privileged status for their own black female bodies (187). The photographic prints of the affluent black housewife in *The Discreet Charm of the Bougies* present a refreshing new image for the black woman that is antithetical to the racist and sexist portrayals of black women from Manet's era until today.

Women such as Bester and Sophie, who have been discussed in previous chapters of this book, could once only dream of having access to the kinds of wealth and opportunity afforded to their white employers. In chapter 7, Sophie had to close her eyes and dream of trading places with her madam, and in chapter 4, wearing the secondhand clothes of her madam was the closest Diouana could get to living a day in the life of her employer. In both cases, the women resisted the rigid definition of womanhood designed for their lives and gave themselves permission to walk in the shoes of their white madams. The protagonist of Cox's semiautobiographical visual narrative is also given license to participate in a similar reverse role-play in her rendition of *Olympia*, where she switches places with Olympia and becomes the mistress. This changing of roles between madam and servant (discussed in chapters 5 and 7) is once again reminiscent of the role-playing in Genet's *The Maids*. In comparison to the characters in Sembène and Sibande's works, though, here the transference of roles is permanent. Cox's black housewife is not merely playing dress up. Instead, she defamiliarizes the familiar binary of the white mistress and black female help, which is the image most consistent in Western iconography in media.

Cox's *The Discreet Charm of the Bougies* is in part based on her experience living as a housewife in Scarsdale, a wealthy suburb of upstate New York. In interviews she recalls feeling unenthused with the mundane rituals of her life and used a pictorial narrative to record an ironic account of her experiences as a well-kept suburbanite. Cox's performance of a high society housewife is channeled through the character Missy, who is placed in a variety of staged scenarios exhibiting her conspicuous consumption, boredom, and social isolation in suburbia. Like carefully staged Instagram or Facebook posts, Missy's daily activities, jet-setting to Beijing and Ghana for shopping, lounging by the pool, or picking up children from the school bus, are recorded in a digital diary. In one of the few in-depth studies of this collection, scholar Jacqueline Smith suggests the superficiality of the character (i.e., her shallow existence of shopping, drinking, and lounging) brings to mind housewives from reality television shows. Like these TV shows, there is an artificiality that comes through in the images of this self-indulged housewife. Despite the frequent shopping trips and leisurely days, unhappiness is revealed by images of Missy disoriented by alcohol and the prescription medications she abuses. In *Missy by the Pool*, for example, she is relaxing in a hot tub. Her hair is wrapped in a fluffy white towel and she is wearing white-rimmed sunglasses. As she leans back against the rim of the hot tub, enjoying an afternoon cocktail, a haze of cigarette smoke billows from her lips. To her right, a bottle of alcohol is positioned next to a glass half filled with amber liquid. The alcohol is perhaps to ameliorate her solitude, for she is mostly alone except for the piece *Black Housewife* (2008). *Black Housewife*, also known as *Missy at Home*, finds Cox sitting in her drawing room with a white maid who is preparing her afternoon cocktail.

Few have considered *Missy at Home* as an intertextual reference to *Olympia*, but there are a number of recognizable similarities between the two works. Cox's defamiliarized version of *Olympia* disrupts the typical portrait of the black madam with her white maid. Similar to Larry Rivers's (painting/sculpture) *I like Olympia in Black Face* (1970), and in the vein of Genet's *The Maids*, Cox juxtaposes the original painting with a new version that switches the roles between the women so that Laure is recast as Olympia and Olympia models as the servant. In contrast to Rivers, Cox avoids an exact transfer of roles from prostitute to handmaiden because the image of the black prostitute / stereotypical jezebel is one that is already ingrained in Western iconography. Cox's representation of the nude black body is transformed from sexualized object to the sublime. Stylistically, Cox's photograph captures several elements of the typical nineteenth-century portrait also known as the "conversation piece."

In *Missy at Home*, a full-bodied view of an impeccably dressed Cox performs as Missy/Laure. Here Laure is repositioned in the photograph so that she is in the foreground, and she is given a complete makeover. Laure's shapeless cream dress is replaced by a sharply tailored black hooded dress, accessorized with white pearls, black stockings, and high heels. Laure's lips are accentuated by deep red lipstick, and her eyes are rimmed with black makeup. In comparison to Olympia, who casually reclines on her bed of rumpled ivory-colored sheets, Missy/Laure sits erect in her low chaise lounge decorated with white accent pillows. Moreover, unlike Bearden's and Thomas's versions, her portrait shows restraint, the bold patterns are muted. The somber colors in Cox's piece suggest this woman has succumbed to respectability politics, which adheres to nineteenth-century African American ideals of asexuality. Her heavy black clothing betrays no hints of her sexuality. One hand rests on the furniture. Missy/Laure regains her subjectivity as she looks at the camera with an unreadable expression. To her right, a sour-faced Olympia, dressed in a starched black-and-white maid's uniform serves Missy her afternoon cocktail from a silver tray. The bouquet Laure presents to Olympia is reduced here to a small arrangement of flowers just visible above Missy/Laure's head. There is a tension in the maid's face. Her tight jaw suggests resentment at having to serve this black woman, while in *Olympia* there is familiarity between the two women: Laure stands close to the bed as she presents the flowers to Olympia. Here there is a noticeable distance between Missy and her maid that is established by the positioning of a large wooly-haired, cream-colored dog (replacing Manet's black cat) sitting between them.

Throughout the room, there is a contrast of black and white. The walls, molding, decorative pillows, and rug are decorated in shades of white and cream that sharply contrasts with the black clothing and dark skin of the madam. In Manet's painting, the light is reserved for Victorine and the linens that blend with the skin of her body. Laure is so deprived of light it is difficult to see her features. In *Things of Darkness: Economies of Race and Gender in Early Modern England* (1995), Kim Hall says, "Portraits of black slaves . . . are specifically shaped by the contrast between dark and light skins, which links the representation of black and white to the organization of property and gender" (227). Cox adopts this artistic device through her use of black and white to emphasize her race and her power. Her skin is black and the maid's uniform is partially black, while her possessions and the things she controls are white: the plush white rug, the decorative pillows, the dog, and her maid. Just as white artists used black bodies to showcase their wealth, the same is true here, except the idea of a white woman serving a black woman is a novelty.

As noted previously, clothing is essential in the formation of identity or social role. In *Olympia*, Laure does not have to wear a maid's uniform for the viewer to read her status. Conversely, Cox does not have the luxury of making the same assumptions about how her maid will be perceived by the viewer. Uniforms, as Mary Romero explains, are worn to distinguish the maid from other help as "visible signs" of class and racial hierarchy (143). Similar to Diouana in *Black Girl*, the uniform worn by Cox's white maid is essential for the denotation of her social station. Furthermore, this black housewife's performance of wealth and superiority must display the requisite features: a lavish home, elegant clothes, jewels, and a maid. Given that a black maid is the expected laborer for the white woman, Cox relieves the black woman from this duty. Cox's refashioning of Manet's painting makes an important statement about visual representations and the power dynamics between black and white women. Historically, due to slavery, racism, and patriarchy, black women have always (at least publicly) been treated as subordinate to white women. Images of black women serving white women are familiar to our visual lexicon, but to see this relationship in the reverse disrupts the "natural" order of things. Here Cox invites an alternative possibility for the visual representation of the power relations between black and white women. Muholi draws on this idea as well in *Difficult Love*, with a portrait of herself as madam with a white maid serving her tea. Muholi experiments with this role reversal to imagine what life might have been like (postapartheid) if blacks were served by whites. In reality, white women are employed as maids to black women, but this is not an image seen often enough. In essence, Cox debunks the idea that black women must only be maids to white women. In this way, she uses a "a new visual language" to talk about race, power, and class (Kariim).

Cox's wealthy housewife also performs a new version of black womanhood that subverts the controlling image of the black woman as mammy or jezebel so often portrayed in media. Cox's upper-class status and respectability demands modesty from Laure. Here Missy is in heavy garments that prevent the viewer from projecting the image of the hypersexualized body onto her figure. Feminist critic Lisa Collins observes,

> Édouard Manet's *Olympia* demonstrated to the French Salon of 1865 that the Black female body need not be undressed to evoke the erotic. Drawing from an established visual legacy of the Black figure as servant in the shadows, laboring for white people and often attending to white women, Manet employed a fully dressed West Indian maid to imbue his painting with illicit sexuality. Laure, the barely visible Black woman, serves as a contrast to the stark white female beauty of the wealthy prostitute. (104–105)

Cox's heavily clothed body redirects the focus of the image to the well-dressed woman's class, which contradicts the standard imagery of the black sexual deviant. However, even these images of respectability can be problematic, for as Collins says, the "black lady" is yet another controlling image of black womanhood used to reconcile the negative images of promiscuity or bitchiness: "To achieve middle-class status, African American women must reject this gender-specific version of authenticity in favor of a politics of respectability" (139).

This politics of respectability is one that denies a black woman the opportunity to express herself sexually. Cox does not deny Laure her full womanhood. Instead, she cleverly projects her sexuality onto the portrait that hangs on the wall opposite the couch. The photograph portrays her naked, toned body holding her baby boy in her arms. In the lower right-hand corner of the image, a mirror picks up a reflection of the maid, thus also equating her with the picture's display of overt sexuality. Whereas Olympia's sexuality is the most prominent feature of Manet's painting, here it is secondary.

Historically, there have been few examples of black womanhood in media that have been portrayed like Cox's housewife. In the 1980s, there was Claire Huxtable from *The Cosby Show*, while recently Michelle Obama and Kamala Harris are "acceptable" representations. Cox is not simply performing an aspirational portrayal of the middle-class black woman. She actually draws on her own lifestyle and autobiographical experience living as an upper-class Jamaican in the United States (i.e., comfortable enough to have very well have hired a white maid). Few black women prior to the twenty-first century have experienced the luxury of white women serving as maids. When one considers the growth of a burgeoning black middle class, especially in places like North Carolina and Georgia, meccas for successful entrepreneurs, the reality of a white woman serving a black woman is a testament to the progress made by this community. Thus Cox's portrait serves as an important cultural and historical marker that counters the prevailing image of black servility and entertains the possibility of black people being catered to by their former oppressors.

Ultimately, Cox's portraits allow for new conversations about the representation of black women in art and society. Like Thomas, she challenges traditional images of Manet's Laure and transforms her into a highly stylized strong and confident woman who steals Olympia's spotlight and earns the right to be mentioned by name.

9

Kara Walker's "Marvelous Sugar Baby 'Sphinx'"

A Satirical Rendition of the Mammy

On U.S. Route 61 in Natchez, Mississippi, stands Mammy's Cupboard, a seventy-nine-year-old, twenty-eight-foot-tall stone restaurant constructed and painted in mammy's image: an African American woman of darker complexion, wearing her trademark bandana and a broad red skirt. In her hands, she holds a tray ready to serve guests.[1] Mammy's Cupboard was the brainchild of Henry Gaude, a businessman, who built the establishment in 1940 to steer patrons to his service station. Today Gaude's monument, still in operation, remains a landmark restaurant and a significant marker of southern culture. While some visitors who dine there are intrigued by its southern charm, others view Mammy's Cupboard as an agonizing reminder of slavery.[2] In recent years, debate about the existence of establishments such as Mammy's Cupboard, Confederate monuments, the Confederate flag, and black memorabilia have intensified. Ideological differences over how to preserve history and culture has led to fierce disputes and conflicts resulting in fatalities. Even President Donald J. Trump weighed in on the controversy over a statue in Charlottesville, Virginia.[3] In several states, monuments have been removed, Confederate flags are no longer displayed on public buildings, and increasingly, African Americans buy racist memorabilia as a way to destigmatize this debasement of black identity. For African American artists such as Kara Walker, there is inherent value in revisiting plantation caricatures, such as the mammy, and exploiting the glorification of the antebellum period. Rather than create counterimages to expunge denigrating racial stereotypes or historical untruths, Walker has steadily produced a body of artwork ironically drawing on these stereotypes and whimsical musing on the old South. This final chapter discusses how works like *A Subtlety*, also known as the *Marvelous Sugar Baby*—subtitled "an Homage to the unpaid and overworked Artisans who have refined our Sweet tastes from the cane fields to the Kitchens of the New World on the Occasion of the demolition of the Domino Sugar Refining Plant" (2014)—enable Walker to paradoxically use humor and horror to confront the abhorrent histories and myths borne of the institution of slavery.

The *Marvelous Sugar Baby* was conceived in 2013 after Walker was approached by the art agency Creative Time to create a public installation to commemorate the demolition of the one-hundred-thirty-two-year-old Domino Sugar refining plant in Brooklyn, New York. At almost twice the size of Mammy's Cupboard, the structure was 75.5 feet long and 35.5 feet high. Walker and her team molded this enormous mammy figure using polystyrene, resin, and bleached sugar donated by Domino. The *Marvelous Sugar Baby*, which portrays a satirical "whiteface" mammy, gave audiences much to debate as they took in the profile of a magnificent, naked, black slave woman sculpted out of sugar. The sheer size of the mammy's buttocks, and her pendulous breasts and exposed vagina, demanded a close inspection of the form. As with all of Walker's pieces, audiences were invited to project their gaze onto the body of this black female nude and perhaps move beyond the obvious to extract a more complex interpretation. The corporeality of Walker's architectural incarnation of the mammy was designed to showcase the black woman's body as a repository of history. Mapped onto the body of her mammy was a meditation on the sugar industry as a global financial monopoly, its fortune amassed through the enslavement and the commodification of black women's bodies. Linked to this history of slavery is the interconnected legacy of the exhibitionism and stereotyping of black bodies that marked black women as inferior oddities to be objectified in the market square. Walker attempts to reclaim the black body and, like Cox and others, reveres it.

Walker's mammy figure was grandiose and mythical: half human and half beast, much like the way black women have been mischaracterized by the dominant society. The top half of the structure was an incarnation of the mammy figure with features closely identified with individuals of African descent: high cheekbones, broad nose, and full lips. The sculpture was adorned with the metonymic bandana knotted at the front, symbolizing her association with the mammy. Below her neck, mountainous breasts sat between her zoomorphic form. Like Egypt's Great Sphinx of Giza, the lower half of the figure sits on her haunches, her bottom tilted in the air and her vulva on full display. The Sphinx's characteristics further link to her Africanness and inspire reverence. Despite its size, Walker's mammy was effectively a piece of black memorabilia put on display. It was a powerful reminder of how black women were subjected to the "thingification" Martin Luther King Jr. warned about when he said that black people who remained politically and socially enslaved would be reduced to objects.[4]

In media and in the collectibles industry, the black woman as mammy has been mass-produced as a tchotchke or knickknack—that is, a small decorative item to be bought and sold. In the documentary *Black Memorabilia* (2019), filmmaker Chico Colvard examines the role of black memorabilia (or Sambo art) contemporaneously. In addition to showing the production plants manned by Chinese workers who mass produce these items for a global market, he includes the perspectives of the buyers and sellers (i.e., those who defend their ownership of black memorabilia and claim their affinity for these collectibles is not about antiblackness but rather a nostalgic connection to the past). For others, regardless of how painful it is to see and own the pieces, their didactic value—as artifacts of this nation's history—is most important. In this vein, Walker's sugared mammy sculpture offers a history lesson on the interlinked relationship of slavery, race, sugar, and the black woman's body, all consistent themes in her oeuvre.

America's legacy of slavery has been consistent in Walker's work. Prior to *A Subtlety*, Walker perfected the craft of making black-and-white, hand-cut, paper silhouettes and watercolor paintings on fifty-foot panoramic tableaus. These antebellum cycloramas were reminiscent of metafictional neoslave narratives (i.e., a contemporary narrative set in the time of slavery, in the tradition of writers such as Bernadine Evaristo).[5] Walker's intense, cartoonish style, juxtaposed against perverse images of slavery—graphic sexual scenes, scatology, and physical violence—create visceral reactions and are thus designed to provoke emotion and raise consciousness about the histories being witnessed. *Rise Up Ye Mighty Race!* (2012), a homoerotic shadow-puppet film, for example, features a male slave owner performing fellatio and other sexual acts with a black male slave resulting in the slave's impregnation. One of Walker's best-known works, *Gone: An Historical Romance of a Civil War as It Occurred b'tween the Dusky Thighs of One Young Negress and Her Heart* (1994), is a dystopian riff on Margaret Mitchell's *Gone with the Wind* (1936). Walker's appropriation of Mitchell's novel parodies the sentimentality of the romance between the maiden (Scarlett O'Hara) and her suitor (Rhett Butler). In Walker's rendition, told from the perspective of "one young negress" (who Walker has identified as an alter ego), the terror and violence done to African American slaves, who were raped and tortured, are no longer pushed to the periphery. Instead they take center stage in her narrative about life during and after the Civil War. *Gone: An Historical Romance* depicts slaves subjected to rape and other kinds of physical abuse at the hands of their slavers. Walker's artwork certainly has shock value that is intended to elicit empathy, but as historian Saidiya Hartman points out, reproducing voyeuristic scenes of black pain can be as sadistic as the violence reenacted, especially if the viewer is desensitized to the violence:

> Only more obscene than the brutality unleashed at the whipping post is the demand that this suffering be materialized and

evidenced by the display of the tortured body or endless recitations of the ghastly and the terrible. (7)

Furthermore, Hartman contends, it is problematic for viewers to encounter such brutality because they are forced into a position as either spectator or witness. Much like the writers and artists she admires (Toni Morrison, bell hooks, and Glenn Ligon), Walker is dedicated to showcasing the atrocities of life for blacks in America (and beyond), no matter how difficult they are to digest.[6] Hartman's statement articulates the concerns of many in the art community who question the motivation of artists such as Walker who produce such titillating artwork.

Unsurprisingly, Walker's works are considered repugnant by some and have elicited anger from the black community in general and from other African American artists who accuse her of using art to exploit black pain. In fact, in 1997, African American artists Betye Saar and Howardena Pindell both wrote letters decrying Walker's representation of African Americans. While Saar called Walker's work "revolting" and created a petition for her MacArthur Genius Award to be rescinded, Pindell said in a speech at the Johannesburg Biennale, "Walker consciously or unconsciously seems to be catering to the bestial fantasies about blacks created by white supremacy and racism" (qtd. in Als). African American scholar Henry Louis Gates Jr. was one of few who came to Walker's defense, explaining, "Only the visually illiterate could mistake post-modern critiques for realistic portrayals. . . . That is the difference between the racist original and the post-modern, signifying, anti-racist parody that characterizes this genre of artistic expression" (Gates qtd. in Als).

Gates clearly recognizes the subversive strategies Walker employs to confront the legacy of abuse experienced by black people, but the satirist always has to bear in mind that slippage can occur; parody can easily be lost on audiences who fail to appreciate that topics like slavery or police brutality can be treated humorously. In his essay "Post-Black Art and the Resurrection of African American Satire," scholar Derek Conrad Murray explains the risks involved with using satire because it requires being self-critical and critiquing the dominant culture's perception of black people as Other (9–10). Thus satire has been a minefield for Walker, who is aware of the animus her artwork creates but gravitates to the form because it is the genre that allows her to most clearly express herself and contribute to the discourse on race, power, and sexuality.

In interviews, Walker has responded to the attacks on her work:

> I thought a lot over the years since my work got a lot of positive attention, a lot of negative attention because I was getting negative attention from artists who were of my father's generation . . . who really took issue with my work but took issue with my work in a lot of different ways, some of it was quite personal, some of it was quite critical . . . of the mechanism of the art world and the art market; who's looking at the work, who is buying, what kind of images or negative representations might get supported by the establishment, so . . . I can understand where they were coming from. (interview by Anna McNay)

Despite the criticism, Walker is undeterred by the respectability politics of an older generation of artists and does not allow them to dictate how she should create artwork about race, oppression, and gender.

Sweet Mammy: The Consumption of the Black Body: Mammy/Jemima

When it came time for Walker to work on the Domino project, she chose to work with sugar as a primary material. It might be an obvious choice of material for an exhibit honoring the sugar industry, but Walker's use of sugar defamiliarizes this household staple. Rather than present a piece glorifying Domino's prominence as a successful supplier of one of the world's most desired products, Walker focuses on the more sinister aspect: the sugar industry as a whole. Essentially, she critiques its role in the denigration of black women through the use of the mammy / Aunt Jemima figure to market sugar and other products. To gain a clear understanding about sugar as a commodity and its global geopolitical and social value in the Western industrial world, Walker consulted Sidney Mintz's *Sweetness and Power: The Place of Sugar in Modern History* (1985), among other works. Sugar became one of the most valued commodities in the American colonies, and America invested millions of dollars in the sugar trade; by the turn of the twentieth century, the United States had monopolized much of the industry.[7] Domino Sugar, which built its Williamsburg sugar factory in 1856, was one of the largest refineries, responsible for making half the sugar in the United States. During slavery, sugar (also known as "black gold") was a major source of revenue for plantation holders in the Caribbean colonies and in America, and because of it the nation prospered. American plantations thrived off the labor of black slaves and indentured servants who worked in the field and in the refineries under deplorable conditions. Sugar was, as Walker says, "blood sugar" (i.e., it was tainted red by the blood of the workers): "Like we talk about blood diamonds today, there were pamphlets saying this sugar has blood on its hands" (Walker, "Artist Kara Walker"). The desire for sugar to sell as well as to consume was so great that people went to great lengths to harvest it, regardless of the impact on human lives, most especially the lives of enslaved Africans. The *Marvelous Sugar Baby* exhibit, completed in 2014, captures the Domino factory's inheritance of this legacy of global capitalism.

Walker emphasizes the insidious nature of sugar production and slavery in the New World and, as the artist's statement indicated, pays homage to the "unpaid and overworked Artisans who have refined our Sweet tastes from the cane fields to the Kitchens of the New World on the Occasion of the demolition of the Domino Sugar Refining Plant." Thus, Walker's exhibit is not actually a celebration of the Domino company and its contribution to the marketplace. It is rather an homage to slaves, and especially the black woman whose image was mischaracterized and then marketed to sell sugar products.

While learning about the commercial history of sugar certainly motivated Walker to use sugar as one of the primary materials for the installation, equally as important in this decision was her new awareness of the medieval practice of making subtleties—that is, confectionary sculptures made for both decorative and edible purposes. Subtleties were a feast for the eyes and the stomach made from mostly edible objects and presented at medieval banquets as a spectacle to entertain guests. The sheer intricacy and scale of the delicacies commanded the attention of guests, who marveled at the craftsmanship and the sometimes ironic qualities of the creations. Food sculpture "marked the end (or start) of a course" and could be "made in the shape of anything. From castles to ships and birds" ("Famous Trends"). This concept of making a large-scale exhibition out of sugar resonated with Walker, who built her career on making gigantic kitsch pieces that were by definition literal visual "spectacles." Moreover, the subtlety gave Walker a clear vision about how to articulate a narrative about sugar and its relationship to the history of the racial and sexual politics of black womanhood. In essence, Walker's subtlety becomes a not-so-subtle metaphor for the commodification, consumption, and exhibition of black womanhood and, more succinctly, the black woman as mammy / Aunt Jemima, past and present.

The corporeality of Walker's *Marvelous Sugar Baby* was a reminder of how the black woman's body has been consumed and commodified literally and figuratively, which a number of black feminist critics have discussed ad infinitum.[8] First, as slaves, black women were commodities routinely bought and sold as goods, assessed for both for their labor (the ability to work in the fields) and their sexuality (the ability to bear children). The commodification of black women's bodies did not only occur on the auction block. Later, the creation of the mammy stereotype allowed industrious white male entrepreneurs to box and bottle her image as a marketing ploy to sell sugar, pancakes, and syrup.

Out of all the plantation stereotypes, the mammy is the most recognizable. Mammy, a stout woman of dark complexion with a broad smile, wears a standard uniform: a brightly colored bandana, a necktie, and an apron resting over a voluminous skirt. For more than 150 years, this portrait of the mammy has been immortalized in media (television shows, art, and literature), in commerce (retail and memorabilia), and in architecture (monuments and buildings). As noted in the introduction, the mammy is what Patricia Hill Collins defines as a "controlling image of black womanhood," a pernicious creation of southern mythology used to propagate a narrative embedded in historical amnesia that mischaracterized white supremacist slave owners as affable employers of contented black laborers. The utopian portrait of antebellum life with mammy as the devoted surrogate mother of the plantation house who chose the family of her slaveholders over her own relatives conveniently overlooked the reality of the brutal dehumanization of chattel slavery. Mammy was so beloved by members of the white community that from the 1890s into the early twentieth century, mammies featured on bas relief carvings and stone tableaus (alongside other slaves who were allegedly loyal to their white masters) and on monuments erected to honor the heroism of Confederate soldiers. According to Kimberly Wallace-Sanders, "loyal slave" monuments were used as part of the "reification of the Confederacy" (94). Mammies also appeared in monuments housed in several Confederate parks, including Confederate Park in Fort Mill, South Carolina, and the Confederate Monument at Arlington National Cemetery.[9]

Efforts to preserve the myth of mammy were so fervent that even members of the federal government fought to have her enshrined. In 1923, Senator John Williams of Mississippi brought a bill to the U.S. Senate to erect a mammy monument. The bill, which had full support of the United Daughters of the Confederacy, was passed by the Senate, but after public outcry from the black press and the black community that perceived the mammy as an affront to the dignity of black women, the bill was aborted.[10] Although endeavors to build a national monument failed, in 1940, Gaude's mammy restaurant served as an informal monument.

During the post-Reconstruction era, the maternal mammy figure who cared for the plantation's children and family morphed into the Aunt Jemima caricature. Dressed in the same outfit as the mammy, Aunt Jemima was the quintessential image of domesticity whose legendary cooking and secret recipes could be bought and sold. Aunt Jemima's outfit was updated with a festive patterned head scarf (often red-and-white polka dots) with a check-patterned dress. Her dark skin gleamed against pearly white teeth on view in her broad smile. The literal marketing of Aunt Jemima as "the unpaid artisan" was developed as a strategy to sell a new ready-mix pancake mixture that supposedly tasted like the pancakes slave women made on the plantation (Walker, *A Subtlety*). The Jemima character, whose image was popularized in folklore, lent authenticity to the product. In 1890, Bert Underwood of the Aunt Jemima Manufacturing Company trademarked the Aunt Jemima image and name.[11] In 1893, the physical manifestation of Aunt Jemima was introduced at the World's Columbian Exhibition when R. T. Davis (who purchased the company in 1990) hired "Nancy Green, a formerly enslaved woman from Kentucky to wear a maid's costume while making pancakes, singing songs, and telling stories about life on the plantation to mostly white audiences" (Wallace-Sanders 61).[12] Later, at the second Chicago's World Fair (1933), Anna Robinson toured the country as Aunt Jemima. Green and Robinson effectively helped sell both pancakes and a caricature of black womanhood.[13]

The success of Aunt Jemima pancakes led to the marketing of additional products such as molasses and cane syrup. These products have a direct relationship to Walker's deliberation on the relationship between sugar and the commodification of the black female form. Stereotypical portrayals of Aunt Jemima used in the marketing campaigns of companies who sold sugar (and products related to sugar) made millions from an image synonymous with slavery. In 1906, for example, the Brooklyn-based Rigney and Co. used the Aunt Jemima caricature to sell their "rock candy drip and maple syrup" product. As per usual, a smiling Aunt Jemima is depicted in uniform, ready to serve. In the 1930s, Aunt Jemima appeared on the packaging for Longwood Plantation's Pure Cane Syrup. In this label, a smiling Aunt Jemima set against a yellow backdrop holds out a plate of steaming pancakes drizzled in Longwood syrup. Other companies such as Penick & Ford, Ltd., created a new character, Aunt Dinah. Aunt Dinah was most likely a textual reference to Old Aunt Dinah from Harriet Beecher Stowe's famed plantation novel *Uncle Tom's Cabin* (1852). On the Penick & Ford blackstrap molasses canister, the servile figure is recast as a woman lighter in complexion. Her pursed lips and steady gaze make her countenance far more composed than Aunt Jemima's. In fact, the portrait looks as though a real model might have posed for the artist. Interestingly, this dignified representation of Aunt Dinah is a sharp contrast to the figures on the company's corn syrup tins, which portray two jet black "Sambo"-like figures standing under the heading "Sho' Is Fine."[14] Taken together, the Aunt Jemima images on sugar packaging help endorse the image of blacks as servile and inferior to whites.

Unfortunately, Aunt Jemima continues to reign, although she has been made over—first in 1968, when she slimmed down and lost her headscarf for a headband, and again in 1989 to commemorate her hundredth birthday, when she was given earrings and permed hair. In 1994, R&B singer Gladys Knight reincarnated Green and Robinson's roles when she became the national spokeswoman for the Quaker Oats Company. According to journalist Brent Staples, Knight received criticism for her decision to front the brand. Finally, in June 2020, in response to a national reckoning with racial bias and social injustice, Quaker Oats Company announced plans to change the brand name, marketing, and packaging. Long before the Quaker Oats decision, others took their own initiative to make over Aunt Jemima's image. In the 1970s, a number of black artists defamiliarized the passive Aunt Jemima image with satirical versions of a radicalized woman. Artist Jon Onye Lockard's painting "No More" (1972), for example, recreates the Aunt Jemima pancake box and syrup bottle, portraying an enraged Aunt Jemima wearing a bandana representing the colors of the Black Liberation flag. Unlike the typical Aunt Jemima, Lockard's figure is unsmiling, and one of her fists busts through the pancake box, raised in the black power salute. Lockard's position is clear: Aunt Jemima has gone rogue; she is a revolutionary no longer willing to be a slave to racist marketing of the happy servant. Betye Saar's "The Liberation of Aunt Jemima" (1972) figurine takes on the same radical tone. Her blackface Aunt Jemima holds a broom in one hand and a rifle in the other. An image inset on the figurine's skirt features another Aunt Jemima (this time not in stereotypical blackface) holding a white baby. The message in Saar's piece is explicit: while society might see the black woman as the plantation "darkie," underneath that exterior is a woman with her charge, performing her assigned duties.

Interestingly, the Domino Sugar factory's understated yellow boxes, sometimes decorated with a red masquerade mask and domino bricks, opted to use a white maid instead of the typical mammy / Aunt Jemima. In 1912, a promotional booklet for the Domino Sugar company, published by the American Sugar Refining Company, used an illustration of a white scullery maid for the cover art. The girl, sporting springy, pre-Shirley-Temple ringlets, holds a silver tray with an opened box of Domino sugar placed next to a mug and teaspoon. The girl is cute, free of Aunt Jemima's sass and deferential smile. Although Domino might not have been directly complicit in promoting the plantation stereotypes, the company, founded in the nineteenth century by the Havemeyer family, most certainly profited from the Caribbean slave trade, which made New York one of the most powerful sugar manufacturers in the nation. It is this rich history about the sugar industry that Walker tries to capture in her piece about sugar and its relationship to the oppression of black women.

Walker's appropriation of the subtlety very cleverly establishes the semiotic relationship between sugar and blackness. From the auction block to fairs, mammy / Aunt Jemima was a commodity that traveled the nation selling pancake mixes and syrup and stories about the good old days on the plantation. Others made money selling mammy as a scientific abnormality, such was the case with Joice Heth, a performer who was marketed as George Washington's 161-year-old mammy. She was exhibited at fairs (including P. T. Barnum's) and placed on display in a cage alongside other "freaks of nature." Marketing Heth's advanced age as an oddity was financially exploitative, and Heth, like many black women, was treated as a spectacle to reinforce stereotypes about the otherness/abnormality of the black body. This notion of the otherness of black women's bodies that has reduced black women to public spectacle stands at the heart of Walker's exhibit. In satirical fashion, Walker exaggerates the otherness of black women's bodies. If, as bell hooks argues, "in the sexual iconography of the traditional black pornographic imagination, the protruding butt is seen as an indication of a heightened sexuality," then *Marvelous Sugar Baby* was sex personified (hooks, *Black Looks* 63). Walker explains,

> It's what I do because I'm interested . . . in the narrative of the narrative, I'm sort of interested in the stereotypes that I've already received that already preexist in the world before I came to them and they are exaggerated because they were already exaggerated they are exaggerated because of the history of violence that comes with racism that are so absurd and outrageous you read these accounts . . . people being victimized because of race and the extremes that perpetrators will go to in order to banish this very physical idea of a person . . . it's absurd so why not be completely outrageous and pull that kind of sensibility out of myself and out of the viewer. (Interview by Anna McNay)

The dehumanization of black women along with their fetishization and exhibitionism draws an obvious intertextual reference to Sandra Baartman (the Venus Hottentot), who was discussed in chapters 1 and 8.[15] Just as Venus's body was fetishized and commodified, the same is true for the *Marvelous Sugar Baby*, which does not simply represent the past but also bears on the present and encourages us to think about the way black women continue to be exploited. Currently, for example, stereotypical images of the black woman—mammy, jezebel, angry black woman—remain as pervasive archetypes in pop culture that are promoted on reality shows, music videos, and social media. The debasement of the slave woman was another way to profit from black women as they were placed in cages and exhibited before spectators who visually cannibalized their bodies. At the Domino Sugar factory, here again the black woman's body was subject to fetishization and visual consumption by audiences who were just as eager to participate in witnessing the highly sexually objectified body of Walker's *Marvelous Sugar Baby*.[16]

So Why Mammy?

Lisa Farrington argues that black artists have worked hard to dismantle myths of black womanhood, noting the following:

> The false paradigms that portray Black women as physically unattractive and sexually promiscuous, passive and aggressive, good caregivers to white children and bad mothers to their own children, have all been challenged by black artists. The efforts of women artists of color, in conjunction with those of Black male artists, have resulted in a partial dismantling of these myths. ("Faith Ringgold's *Slave Rape* Series" 132)

For Walker, dismantling myths about black womanhood does not mean removing them from the denigrating images that have debased their personhood, for she likes to play with the contradictions. She uses the myth as a subversive strategy to draw attention to their fatuous nature and at the same think critically about the myths, including their origins and their damage. The *Marvelous Sugar Baby*, for example, is defamiliarized beyond the asexual spinster stereotype so she can lay claim to her sexuality and humanity. Some feminist critics maintain the mammy was defined by her creators as asexual. Her uniform of large skirts, headscarf, and necktie was meant to make her undesirable and was intended to tone down her sexuality so she would not compromise the sexual morality of the slave master. Conversely, others point out, despite efforts to hide mammy's sexuality, her body, hips, bottom, and breasts made her sexual. Walker's denuding of mammy allows her to reclaim her sexuality. As Patterson-Faye suggests, "Behind her wide grin, underneath her headscarf, and covered by her long skirt, lies the truth about 'mammy'" (927). It is this truth that is perhaps the Sphinx's secret: under the clothing, detached from the myth of mammy, is a fat black woman's body, a body she can claim without shame. By disrobing mammy, Walker peels off the layers of history that have falsely defined black women. The victimization of black women's sexuality has grave consequences for how black women have governed their bodies.[17] Walker's Sugar Baby is not to be held captive by the stereotype; rather, she hearkens back to African American versions of *Olympia* that allow black women the opportunity to flaunt their body unapologetically. As Hilton Als wrote of Walker, "She's taken the black servant in Manet's *Olympia*—exhibited the same year black American slaves were 'emancipated'—and plunked her down from the art-historical skies into Brooklyn, where she finally gets to show her regal head and body as an alternative to Manet's invention."

Walker's version of *Olympia* reclaims not only the black body but a particular kind of black body, one that rejects Western standards of beauty. For her part, Walker is committed to showing the body, in Barbara Christian's words, as "sensuous and funky," the antithesis of the sublime, chaste, white woman's body. The voluptuous body of her black woman is to be celebrated for her curves, not hidden and swathed. To see mammy in this new way liberates her from dowdy nursemaid. It also raises questions about the lack of representation of nude shapely figures such as Walker's *Marvelous Sugar Baby* in media and in Western art. It is a conversation reminiscent of Denise Murrell's exposition discussed in the previous chapter. African American sculptors such as Augusta Savage, Saar, Wangechi Mutu, and now Walker, among others, have sculpted black female nudes that stand in juxtaposition to countless European nude female figures in Western art; outside the African artistic canon, the representation of black female nudes in Western museums and galleries is scant. This lack of representation is problematic, for as the Rastafarian poet Faybiene Miranda points out in her 1987 poem, "I Am That I Am" (qtd. in Hepner and Hepner 344), black women do not fit into the paradigm of

Western beauty equated with the Venus de Milo. Indeed, the Sugar Baby is not Venus de Milo, a slender figure, the epitome of white beauty; instead she is a voluptuous African queen. Walker's piece raises questions about not only the lack of black nude bodies in art but culture in general, and people are beginning to take note. In 2019, African American recording artist Lizzo posed nude in the cover art of her debut album *Cuz I Love You.* Unlike many mainstream artists, Lizzo is the antithesis of a svelte woman, but she is a woman who embraces her full being. The response on social media to Lizzo's album cover was overwhelmingly positive. Lizzo was praised for her body positivity, which is helping efforts to broaden the concept of black beauty and shattering antiquated definitions of beauty manufactured by advertising firms and reality stars.

Walker's sculpture also takes on this discourse about body politics. *Marvelous Sugar Baby* is a physical manifestation of how white standards of beauty set by the dominant society are transmuted onto the black body. This concept is presented through the materials Walker selected for the sculpture. Sugar Baby is white. Certainly, for artistic reasons, the white sugar might simply have been more visually stimulating or malleable. However, given that Walker's sugared mammy signifies black womanhood, it is interesting that she opts not to use brown sugar. Arguably, brown sugar might not have been an ideal material to work with for the creation of a giant sculpture, but Walker is playing on the notion of "refinement" to talk about the transformation of the black body. In essence, if the raw brown sugar represents the black body in an unrefined and "othered" state of womanhood, the refined version signifies the ideal or cultivated representation of white womanhood. However, what is presented instead is a sort of reverse whiteface. Scholar Evelyn Hammonds's description of the female body in the West is helpful for this discussion of the female body in racialized binary terms. She asserts,

> The female body in the West is not a unitary sign. Rather, like a coin, it has an obverse and a reverse: on the one side, it is white; on the other, not-white or, prototypically, black. The two

bodies cannot be separated, nor can one body be understood in isolation from the other in the West's metaphoric construction of "woman." White is what woman is; not-white (and the stereotypes not-white gathers in) is what she had better not be. (Hammonds)

Walker's exhibit presents the binary as a sort of reverse whiteface. As the white, refined mammy figure, the "real" black woman's body is rendered invisible and transformed into a false image of black womanhood constructed by the white psyche, and yet with the proportion of her body, she cannot fully adhere to tenets of white beauty. In a way, it is a play on sociologist W. E. B. Du Bois's notion of double consciousness, whereby blacks are made to feel inferior as a result of social conditioning that forces them to see themselves through the eyes of a dominant society. Except Walker is suggesting that it is not how they see themselves, but it is how they are seen by whites. By employing the figure of both the mythical Sphinx and the mammy / Aunt Jemima, Walker's Sugar Baby serves as an example of this effort to debunk myths about black women and their mythical qualities and redirects them onto those who create them in the first place.

While Walker's *Marvelous Sugar Baby* could not be ingested by the guests who gathered to see the Sugar Baby, they were no less impressed with the massive confection on display at the abandoned sugar factory. The *Marvelous Sugar Baby* was widely publicized on social media and in cultural magazines such as *Time Out*. During its run, crowds of people a mile long snaked around the warehouse, patiently waiting to see Walker's creation. Audiences were invited to interact with the piece through social media. First, #KaraWalkerDomino encouraged visitors to take pictures and selfies to post with the hashtag. There was also a Digital *Marvelous Sugar Baby* that enabled "viewers to use their cursors to turn and position a 3-D model of the sculpture, bring it to a pause at any point within a full rotational circle" (Peabody 157).[18] The dank, dilapidated Domino factory was the ideal space for Walker's artistic representation of the rottenness of the sugar industry's history and its oppression of the laborers (especially enslaved Africans) who toiled in the fields and factories. Once audiences visited the exhibit, all of their senses were engaged. The floor was sticky with black and dark brown globules of crystallized sugar, the air smelled acrid, and the lighting was dim. Close to the entrance of the main exhibit, five figurines of young boys with baskets strapped on their backs or carrying sacks were placed around the warehouse. The contrast of their black bodies against the white sculpture was reminiscent of the shadows and contrasts between black and white employed in Walker's silhouette tableaus. The boys positioned around the Sphinx in their own way called to mind Cox's *Olympia's Boyz* watching over their mother. These baby-faced boys, also made of sugar, were brown and black and in various states of deterioration, their decay symbolic of the sense of loss. Walker says she wanted to reflect the harsh, dangerous working conditions that resulted in severed limbs and severe burns. The crumbling, melting figures were also a reminder that the profitability of sugar came at a cost to human life. Positioned in the far corner of the warehouse-turned-gallery near the exit sat the *Marvelous Sugar Baby* in all her glory, caged between steel bars with bright lighting accentuating her body.

The nakedness of the *Marvelous Sugar Baby* alludes to the stripped bodies of black women on the auction block. Perhaps unsurprisingly, many attendees behaved remarkably similar to the British and European crowds gathered to see Baartman on exhibition. While some quietly gazed at the spectacle before them, a number of individuals reportedly laughed and jeered at the Sugar Baby and made rude gestures in front of the figure, such as pretending to put their tongues on her vagina or pinching her nipples, actions all caught on camera and posted to social media sites. In an interview conducted by filmmaker Ava DuVernay, Walker had difficulty responding to a question about the objectification of the body by spectators and how the violation made her feel. Walker did not have to defend herself, however. Show attendees who saw others reducing the *Marvelous Sugar Baby* to a sex object did the work for her by chastising those who were dishonoring the body.

Many were alarmed by the offensive behavior that, in their minds, undermined the solemnity warranted for such commentary on the enslavement of black women. To combat such callousness, groups such as The Kara Walker Experience: WE ARE HERE used Facebook to organize a trip to the exhibit and educate viewers. The group gave stickers "to remind white visitors that the descendants of slaves were in the room, present and watching the whites pose in front of their history like tourists." They promoted the event as follows: "A gathering for people of color at Kara Walker art installation in the Domino Sugar factory. Invite your friends . . . so that we can experience this space as a minority."

African American professor Nicholas Powers took matters further. He chastised visitors for their lack of empathy and respect for his history. In his blog post entitled "Why I Yelled at the Kara Walker Exhibit," Powers explains that "I feared the mostly white visitors would not see me or the violent history that the art reflected." Disappointed at white visitors' vulgarity, he continues,

> I caught the eye of a few people of color, we talked and shook our heads at the jokey antics. . . . We felt invisible, and our history was too. . . . As I watched their joking, my thoughts spun and I walked into the crowd, turned to face them and began yelling. . . . You are creating the very racism this art is supposed to critique. (Powers)

There is much to consider about Powell's policing of the patrons. Did he have the right to tell audiences how they should interact with the artwork? To chastise them? The polarizing reactions to the piece were not unusual for visitors to Walker's exhibitions, and by videotaping her guests, Walker probably wanted to know how individuals would behave. Social media also allowed for debates about her sculpture to continue long after patrons left the exhibit. Answers to these questions played out in retweets and responses to Powell's blog post (which ranged from objective meaningful discussions to rantings and hostile statements by trolls). Reporter Kristin Iversen suspected Walker anticipated such volatile reactions:

> This type of despicable behavior by white patrons is undoubtedly something that Walker knew would happen and is part of what makes her work so effective. The not so subtle message in Walker's work is that not all that much has really changed in our society; we are still collectively invested in the objectification and diminishment of minorities—black women in particular.

Indeed, Walker was curious and amused and secretly taped visitors. In interviews, she insists she was not really spying, just watching out of curiosity, interested in seeing how people reacted, especially black families. In fact, on the last day, people were allowed to touch the sculpture. Walker's voyeurism served as what hooks calls an "oppositional gaze," where she was able to participate in a broad range of looking relations (hooks, *Black Looks* 16). Yes, the *Marvelous Sugar Mammy* was a spectacle, but so were the attendees. Their childish behavior was being observed by the mighty creator, who was recording responses to be used for a new project. Medieval guests who were privy to feasting their eyes on the spectacle of the subtlety had had the bragging rights to have been in attendance when the master craftsman presented their spectacle. Only those who were there can attest to its brilliance, for the rest of the pieces were legend, fictionalized accounts about the greatness of a large-scale confectionary. The same is true for the *Marvelous Sugar Baby*. By the end of July, the *Marvelous Sugar Baby* was demolished. In the end, Walker's sugared mammy was like any other piece of black memorabilia. Some understood the historical relevance and the value of confronting (and correcting) our painful history, and others were disaffected. Either way, Walker allows us to claim it, reject it, to do with it what we will.

Conclusion

I have spent ten years of my life writing this book about domestic workers. Initially, I conceived of writing an ethnographic study on Caribbean domestics in Brooklyn, New York, but with time the project evolved into a multidisciplinary critical analysis of the global domestic worker in media. I never foresaw writing this book. The project began percolating back in the 1980s when I arrived in the United States from Hertfordshire, England. I was startled by the number of black women pushing strollers with babies who were not their own, and I was perplexed to see black women still engaged in an occupation that I equated with servitude. At the time, I lacked sufficient knowledge about the history of slavery and institutional racism in the United States, and I was unaware of how colonialism and economic recession in the Caribbean led to systematic oppression and workforce discrimination, which limited employment options for black women. More importantly, I didn't know that many women in my family (including my mother) had migrated to the United States from the Caribbean and worked for years as domestics (and in related fields) as a way to gain permanent residency for themselves and their children.

Later, when I had my own children, I was forced to reconcile my conflicted thoughts about nannies. I questioned if it made a difference that I was a woman of color hiring another woman of color to care for my children. During the 2000s, there were so many black women in Brooklyn working as babysitters that on any given day picking up a child from school, a library, or the playground, one saw more nannies than parents. One day while picking up my daughter from nursery school, even I was mistaken for a nanny. As my daughter lined up with the other children waiting to be released for the day, an unknowing classmate pointed to me and (much to my daughter's dismay) declared, "Your nanny is here!"

There were moments while writing the book when I questioned if my approach of using media to engage in a discussion about household workers, laborers' rights, immigration, and representation was impactful. As I neared the finish line, two important cultural moments occurred that validated my project. First, the #MeToo and #TimesUp movements—with some prodding—drew attention to the vulnerability of pink-collar workers and put domestic workers squarely in the middle of a national and global discussion about systemic sexual harassment and sexism. In the early phases of the movements, the media focused mainly on white and privileged, high-profile women in the entertainment and corporate industries who demanded a cultural shift in social and legal attitudes that propagate patriarchal oppression. Using their prestige, Hollywood actresses told stories of being sexually harassed and assaulted by men in the entertainment industry and forced the hand of legislators to hold sexual predators accountable for their assault upon women's (and men's) bodies. They, along with corporate professionals, vowed to pressure industries to examine equity, inclusion, and sexism in the workforce. The clarion call of these women had a ripple effect in other industries in the private and public sector. Companies that were previously lax in their responses to allegations of sexual misconduct took reports more seriously, while others held trainings and revised workplace conduct policies. In regard to the issue of pay equity, companies engaged in self-assessments to determine how to address the pay inequity in their workforce.

At the nadir of the #MeToo and #TimesUp movements, those at the forefront who were given license to speak for all women often failed to recognize the voices and experiences of women of color, especially black women, whose sexual assault cases are prosecuted at lower rates than white women's are and whose salaries are also considerably less than those of their white counterparts. The point here is not to privilege one group's suffering over another. Rather, my objective is to illustrate how women of color have been fighting to address these central issues spotlighted by these movements, but they have not had the same traction. Consider the origins of the #MeToo movement. Discourse around sexual assault linked to the term *MeToo* began in 2006 by Tarana Burke, a civil rights activist who started MeToo as a grassroots movement to help young girls (and boys) of color who were victims of sexual violence and exploitation. It wasn't until 2017, when actress Alyssa Milano used the term *MeToo* in a social media post as a way for women to personally acknowledge their experience with sexual harassment or sexual assault that #MeToo became an international phenomenon recognizing survivors and Burke's work on behalf of girls of color.

Even as the movements attempted to be more inclusive, they also fell short of acknowledging women who were not in Hollywood or corporate America. In news coverage, women who stand at the margins of society, such as service workers and domestic workers like those discussed in Childress's *Like One of the Family* and Brown's *Minding Ben*, many of whom are immigrants and many of whom happen to be black, were denied representation. These women, who barely making a living wage and experience verbal and sexual assault in the workplace, had their own stories tell. Finally, in December 2017, *Time* magazine published its "Silence Breakers" issue that recognized the importance of including the voices of these domestics as part of a photographic story representing survivors from all walks of life.

The timing of the #MeToo and #TimesUp movements, along with the release of Alfonso Cuarón's Academy Award–winning *Roma*, created a sustained discussion about domestics that moved beyond the academy and the picket line. Although *Roma* was not about domestics in America, black women, or migrant domestics in America, it resonated with Americans more than *The Help*, another contemporary movie about household workers. While *The Help* was popular—mostly for women of a certain generation or regional location—*Roma* presented a powerful narrative about domestic workers that made the public more empathetic than usual about domestics in general. Hollywood used its platform to bring visibility to domestics beyond the movie by supporting a number of events honoring and supporting domestics. They worked in tandem with the NDWA to leverage the media coverage of the film into an opportunity not only to spotlight the need for national legislation to improve workers' rights and fair wages but also to enable the workers to be heard. Jess Morales Rocketto, political director of NDWA, said,

> Putting the domestic worker on the screen is a huge win for us. . . . We're gonna take the momentum of this big moment and work to pass the Federal Domestic worker bill of rights; historic legislation that would finally give domestic workers the dignity and respect they deserve on the job.

Her efforts were not in vain. In 2019, Kamala D. Harris (D-CA) and Pramila Jayapal (D-CA) proposed a Domestic Workers' Bill of Rights Act (H.R. 3760) and pushed for the same kind of worker's protection Keyi highlighted in *The True Nanny Diaries*. Coincidentally, in addition to Netflix making a donation to NDWA for every *Roma* ticket bought in a theater in February 2019, producers of the movie, as well as Cuarón, worked in tandem with NDWA to bring together domestics, actors, and activists to screen the movie. On February 24, 2019, they hosted a red-carpet event "Honoring the Heroines of Our Homes" that included guests such as activist Tarana Burke and actresses Laura Dern, Natalie Portman, Rashida Jones, and Eva Longoria. At this event, domestics (who were gifted gala attire from Rent the Runway) spoke of their experiences throughout the night.

Roma proved the public is eager to learn about the daily experiences of women who are finally having their say but in large measure remain invisible. Hopefully, the success of *Roma* will convince studio executives to support many more films about domestic workers, potentially featuring black women who, as this study shows, have their own unique stories to tell. If media mogul Lena Waithe has her way, this could soon become a reality. According to news outlets, the Emmy winner acquired the rights to Kiley

Wright's highly celebrated novel *Such a Fun Age* (2019), yet again a novel by a nanny-turned-writer who, like Childress, Keyi, and Brown, creates a strong voice for the working-class black woman. Moreover, in the tradition of these women, Wright uses her novel to address the vulnerabilities of black domestic workers who not only struggle with workplace abuse and economic insecurity but also lack access to health care or social security benefits. It's been almost seventy years since Childress published *Like One of the Family*. In this time, black women have traveled to space, served as surgeon general, and run for president, but as Wright's novel reminds us, they continue to labor in other women's kitchens. We can only hope that seventy years from now, they are telling a different story.

Acknowledgments

This book has been many years in the making. Although the process has been long, it has been worthwhile, and I am grateful for all the individuals who have supported me along the way. First, I give thanks to my beautiful daughters, Amouri and Tori. Girls, I appreciate your patience and understanding my need for space to finish this manuscript. To my loving husband, Dean, as always, thanks for believing in me. To my mother, whose sacrifice and hard work enabled me to have a career, with this book I honor you. To my brothers and sisters, thanks for your unwavering support. And to my mother-in-law, thanks for your enthusiasm about my work.

Sandra, thanks for traveling to South Africa with me so I could sow the seeds for this project. To Dr. Anne Klein Kelly, I could not have finished this book without you. Nancy Vescovo, thanks for the frank chats about domestics (of all backgrounds). I would like to also thank all the women who enabled me to interview them, whose names have been withheld. To Laura, a fellow writer Who understands the pain and solitude of writing, I am grateful to have had you on my side. Norma Stanton, you have always been a great cheerleader. I'm glad you can finally purchase the book. Tracee Loran, I can't thank you enough (and your mum) for going to Natchez, Mississippi, to take the picture of Mammy's Cupboard. The book just wouldn't have been right without this image.

A special thanks to my Stony Brook crew. Daniela, Mary Jo, and Stacey, thanks for reading early drafts and proposals. Dani, although it took us eight years to coteach our course on domestics, it was so worth the wait! Michelle, I appreciate your sincere interest in my book project. A special shout-out to Shobana, a fantastic colleague who always motivates me to achieve far more than I can imagine. To Natasha, thank you for taking the time to read my chapters at a moment's notice. Michelle and Max, I appreciate your nonjudgmental encouragement.

A shout-out to Mary Sibande for allowing me to use her artwork for the book jacket. I am also grateful to Kara Walker and Jason Wyche for allowing me to include an image of the Sugar Baby, free of charge. To my editor, Karen Adams, it's been great working together and thanks for taking me on. To the Rutgers University Press staff, specifically Kimberly Guinta and Jasper Chang, thank you for your support and patience. Finally, I would like to acknowledge all the domestic workers who toil night and day to provide for their families. This book is in honor of your strength and dignity.

Notes

Introduction

1 See Pauline Hopkins, *Contending Forces: A Romance Illustrative of Negro Life North and South* (1900; repr., New York: Oxford UP, 1988).

2 Roxane Gay famously challenged hooks's argument in "Beyoncé's Control of Her Own Image Belies the bell hooks 'Slave' Critique," *Guardian*, May 2014, www.theguardian.com/commentisfree/2014/may/12/beyonce-bell-hooks-slave-terrrorist.

3 For more on the mammy in advertising, see Lorraine Fuller, "Are We Seeing Things? The Pine-Sol Lady and the Ghost of Aunt Jemima," *Journal of Black Studies* 31, no. 1 (2001): 120–131.

4 See Daniel Geary, "The Moynihan Report: An Annotated Edition," *Atlantic*, September 2015, https://www.theatlantic.com/politics/archive/2015/09/the-moynihan-report-an-annotated-edition/404632/.

1. Overview

1 See Vanessa May, *Unprotected Labor: Household Workers, Politics, and Middle-Class Reform in New York, 1870–1940* (Chapel Hill: U of North Carolina P, 2011), 113.

2 See Premilla Nadasen, *Household Workers Unite: The Untold Story of African American Women Who Built a Movement* (Boston: Beacon, 2015), 11.

3 Cooke went undercover and worked at the market to get a more in-depth understanding of the women's challenges. See Marvel Cooke, "I Was Part of the Bronx Slave Market: Where Men Prowl and Women Prey on Needy Job-Seekers," *Daily Compass*, 8 Jan. 1950.

4 The 1913 Land Act had similar objectives.

5 See Pierrette Hondagneu-Sotelo, *Domestica: Immigrant Workers Cleaning and Caring in the Shadows of Influence* (Berkeley: U of Carolina P, 2001), 20.

6 According to Kasinitz, the highest profession for Caribbean women was nurse's aide (12,640), followed by administrative employment (10,640), nursing (7,900), and domestic work (7,460). See Philip Kasinitz, *Caribbean New York: Black Immigrants and the Politics of Race* (Ithaca: Cornell UP, 1992), 104.

7 See Scales-Trent for more on African women in France: Judy Scales-Trent, "African Women in France: Citizenship, Family, and Work," *Brooklyn Journal of International Law* 24, no. 3 (1999): 705–737.

8 For a deeper analysis, consult Encarnación Gutiérrez Rodríguez, "The Hidden State of the New Economy: On Transnational Migration, Domestic Work, and Unprecedented Intimacy," *Frontiers: A Journal of Women's Studies* 28, no. 3 (2007): 60–83.

9 See www.bbc.com/news/uk-25048307.

10 For more on Britain's slavery, see www.antislavery.org/slavery-today/slavery-uk/.

11 See www.kalayaan.org.uk/for-workers/employment-rights/.

2. Let's Hear It from the Maid

1 Many articles on *The Help* referenced *Like One of the Family*. See www.washingtonpost.com/blogs/blogpost/post/the-help-is-it-jim-crow-lite-or-a-story-needing-to-be-told/2011/08/15/gIQAIRPJJJ_blog.html and www.msmagazine.com/2011/08/10/why-im-not-looking-forward-to-the-help/.

There are a plethora of articles and blog posts decrying *The Help*'s representation of black women, including www.andsoitbeginsfilms.com/2012/02/why-i-hate-help.html, acriticalreviewofthehelp.wordpress.com/should-not-be-in-the-help/, and www.theatlantic.com/entertainment/archive/2011/08/the-help-softening-segregation-for-a-feel-good-flick/243395/.

2 *Freedom* was a left-wing Harlem, New York–based publication.

3 Rosa Parks's defiant act was inspired by Claudette Colvin, who had also refused to give up her seat on the bus.

4 Gore observed that Childress, Jones, and Cooke used their work to call out white supremacy (3). See Dayo F. Gore, *Radicalism at the Crossroads: African American Women Activists in the Cold War* (New York: NYU Press, 2011).

5 Harris reports that on Childress's last day as a domestic, she threw keys at her employer's head: Trudier Harris, *From Mammies to Militants: Domestics in Black American Literature*. (Philadelphia: Temple UP, 1982), xxii.

6 For more on black humor, see Lawrence Levine, *Black Culture and Black Consciousness: Afro American Folk Thought from Slavery to Freedom* (Oxford: Oxford UP, 2007), 344.

7 For more on health ordinances, see May 167.

8 Disturbingly, the incident is supposed to be amusing.

9 See Mariarosa Dalla Costa and Selma James's *The Power of Women and the Subversion of the Community* (Bristol: Falling Wall Press, 1975).

3. Dirty Work

1 An exception is Jennifer Lopez's film *Maid in Manhattan* (2002), a film about a Latina domestic who was released five years earlier and sought to add diversity to the filmic portrayal of domestics. It was the only one among the many other *Mary Poppins*–like films. (The film version of *The Help* did not appear until 2011.)

2 Seven years earlier, Poo founded DWU, a multiethnic group of nannies from Asia, the Caribbean, and Latin America who recognized the advantage of fighting together and ensuring all workers had an opportunity to be seen and participate in their agenda.

3 Domestic workers were excluded from protections under the 1935 National Labor Relations Act.

4 New York State Domestic Worker's Bill of Rights: www.labor.ny.gov/legal/domestic-workers-bill-of-rights.shtm. Since 2014, California also has its own Domestic Worker's Bill of Rights.

5 See June Barrett and Mily Treviño-Sauceda, "#MeToo Is Creating a 'Ripple Effect' for Domestic and Farm Workers," *Vice*, May 2018, www.vice.com/en_us/article/9kgp7y/metoo-domestic-workers-farm-workers-organizing.

6 For further information on wages for domestic workers, see www.workingnowandthen.com/new-york-domestic-workers/.

7 *The Help* is an exception but is also very problematic. See chapter 2.

4. Forbidden Kinship

1 This encounter is well documented by Gabi Ngcobo in "It's Work as Usual: Framing Race, Class, Gender through a South African Lens," *AFRICAVENIR International*, 2014, www.africavenir.org/publications/e-dossiers/revisions/gabi-ngcobo.html.

2 *Madam & Eve* is a cartoon strip created by Stephen Francis and Rico Schacherl in 1992. Eve is a trickster figure who constantly outwits her gullible madam.

5. A Sartorial Expression of Frenchness in Ousmane Sembène's *Black Girl*

1 *The Maids* (*Les Bonnes*) is based on the 1933 murder of an employer by her two French servants (sisters Christine and Lea Papin).

2 For more on racialized and gendered casting of *The Maids*, see Rachel Shteir's article, "Interpreting 'The Maids' Through a Shifting Societal Lens," *New York Times*, July 31, 2014.

3 The Papin sisters' crime was also heavily debated. Some suggested the murder was not simply rooted in pathology but rather their social circumstances: their poverty and abuse by their own relatives caused their hatred and violent murder of their madame.

4 In 2015, the film was revived and shown at the Cannes Film Festival. In honor of its fiftieth anniversary in 2017, it was rereleased, restored, and remastered by the Criterion Collection.

5 Diouana is seduced by what Ngũgi wa Thiong'o calls the "cultural bomb," a self-hatred act of seduction that "annihilates a people's belief in their names, in their languages, in their environment, in their heritage of struggle. . . . It makes them want to identify with that which is decadent and reactionary." Ngũgĩ wa Thiong'o, *Decolonizing the Mind: The Politics of Language in African Literature* (Portsmouth: Heinemann Studies in African Literature, 1986), 3.

6 For more on the symbolism of the polka dots on Diouana's dress, see Vlad Dima, "Ousmane Sembène's 'Noire de . . .' Melancholia in Photo, Text, and Film," *Journal of African Studies* 26, no. 1 (2014), 60.

7 For more on this interpretation, see Marcia Landy, "Politics and Style in *Black Girl*," *Jumpcut* 27 (1982): 23–25.

8 Conner says Madame expects Diouana to "deny her complexities in order to appease Madame's warped views about Blackness and servitude; it is a reversal of Conrad's *Heart of Darkness* wherein barbarity is found within the domestic sphere." Allison Conner, "*Black Girl* Unmasks the Phantoms of Colonialism," review of *Black Girl*, directed by Ousmane Sembène, *Bitch Media*, 1 Sept 2017, 69, www.bitchmedia.org/article/black-girl/director-ousmane-semb%C3%A8ne.

9 For more on performance and domination, see Carole Scott, "Magical Dress: Clothing and Transformation in Folk Tales," *Children's Literary Association Quarterly* 21, no. 4 (1998): 4–5.

10 For more a more in-depth discussion of internal exile, see Ayo Coly, *The Pull of Postcolonial Nationhood: Gender and Migration in Francophone African Literatures* (Maryland: Lanham Lexington Books, 2010).

6. Maid in Hollywood

1 See the cover story for *Jet*, September 11, 1952.

2 For more on Harris's career, see Dargis, "Just a Maid in Movies, But Not Forgotten," *New York Times*, April 24, 2011.

3 In his psychoanalytic interrogation of the African American psyche, Du Bois theorized about the dual consciousness of African Americans who struggle to define the self as they view themselves through the eyes of the dominant society. W. E. B. Du Bois, *Souls of Black Folk* (Chicago: McClurge, 1903).

4 For the website, see *Finding Vera Stark*, bythewaymeetverastark.com/vera-stark-bio/.

5 For more on the theory of performativity, see Judith Butler, *Gender Trouble: Feminism and Subversion of Identity* (New York: Routledge), xvi–xvii.

6 See S. Torriano Berry and Venise Berry, *The 50 Most Influential Black Films: A Celebration of African-American Talent, Determination, and Creativity* (New York: Citadel, 2000).

7. The Art of Dressing Up in Mary Sibande's *Long Live the Dead Queen*

1 For more on the boycotts, see Jonathan Hyslop, Salim Vally, and Shireen Hassim, "South African Boycott Experience," *Academe* 92, no. 5 (September–October 2006): 59–70.

2 A similar concept is taken up by Muholi in her portrait series, *Somnyama Ngonyama, Hail the Dark Lioness* (2017).

3 Wearing both a maid uniform and the madame's outfits is reminiscent of Diouana's efforts to subvert her reality.

8. From the Margin to the Center

1 Laure's surname is unknown.

2 For more on Laure's sexuality being projected onto the white body, see Jessica Dallow, "Reclaiming Histories: Betye and Alison Saar: Feminism and the Representation of Black Womanhood," *Feminist Studies* 30, no. 1 (2004): 77.

3 Sandra Baartman's body becomes the quintessential representation of sexual deviancy.

4 The softness of the body is reminiscent of Elizabeth Catlett's *Reclining Woman*, a mahogany sculpture of a woman reclining on her side, her physique similarly lean but with a muscular body.

5 See *The Apprenticeship of Jelly Roll Morton* (1971), collage on paper with ink and graphite, and *Reclining Nude* (1970), paper with ink and graphite.

9. Kara Walker's "Marvelous Sugar Baby 'Sphinx'"

1 According to Pattern, "Under mammy's brick skirts, punched with arched windows, Mrs. Henry Gaiety operated a small restaurant. . . . Gaiety catered to visitors drawn by the Natchez Pilgrimage of Homes—a tour of the town's grand old houses and an affective celebration of the plantation myth," 78. Pattern also notes that over time, "mammy's skin was lightened in an effort to make her less culturally offensive." Phil Pattern, "Mammy, Her Life and Times," *American Heritage* 44, no. 5 (1993): 78.

2 Several reviewers on the social media site *Yelp.com* call the establishment racist.

3 In 2017, a rally held by the KKK in protest of the removal of Confederate statues in Charlottesville, Virginia, led to the murder of Heather Heyer, an antiracism protester, by a Klan member who used his car as a weapon to attack opponents. After the tragedy, President Trump caused controversy when he defended the instigators and implied both sides were culpable for the attack.

4 See Martin Luther King Jr., "Where Do We Go From Here?," August 1967, www.kinginstitute.stanford.edu/king-papers/documents/where-do-we-go-here-address-delivered-eleventh-annual-sclc-convention.

5 See Bernadine Evaristo, *The Emperor's Babe* (London: Penguin, 2004), a contemporary narrative set during the Roman Empire.

6 Journalist Hilton Als reports Walker is deeply influenced by the aforementioned writers and artists.

7 For a historical overview of the sugar industry, see Marc Aronson and Marina Budhos, *Sugar Changed the World: A Story of Magic, Spice, Slavery, Freedom, and Science* (New York: Clarion Books, 2017); and James Walvin, *Sugar: The World Corrupted: From Slavery to Obesity* (New York: Pegasus, 2017).

8 For a more in-depth analysis on the commodification of black woman's bodies, see bell hooks "Selling Hot Pussy: Representations of Black Women's Sexuality in the Cultural Marketplace," in *Black Looks Race and Representation* (Boston: South End Press, 2010).

9 Mammy is featured in Samuel White's 1896 slave monument. Wallace-Sanders reports the United Daughters of the Confederacy financed a monument featuring mammy on a stone obelisk in 1914 (Wallace-Sanders 97).

10 Wallace-Sanders and others discuss how the United Daughters of the Confederacy were willing to raise funds for the mammy statue, which was to be erected near the Lincoln Memorial. Kimberly Wallace-Sanders, *Mammy: A Century of Race, Gender, and Southern Memory* (Ann Arbor: U of Michigan P, 2011), 60.

11 Quaker Oats bought the company in the 1920s.

12 Black people were not permitted to attend the fair.

13 Both maple syrup and molasses are viscous substances made with boiling water. Maple syrup, which is extracted from maple trees, is a combination of water and syrup, while molasses is a by-product of the sugar refining process. See www.sugar.org/sugar/refining-processing/.

14 Interestingly, a smiling white boy appears on the Penick corn syrup label. Aunt Jemima and Aunt Dinah's images were an alternative to more denigrating images of black people who were used to sell dusting clothes, soap, and tobacco.

15 Peabody suggests, "Walker is preoccupied with the dominant problems in Baartman's historical record: the overbearing presence of her genitalia, and the complete absence of her voice." Rebecca Peabody, *Consuming Stories: Kara Walker and the Imaging of American Race* (Berkeley: U of California P, 2016), 67.

16 In a strange turn, physical attributes of black women are now commodified. Larger buttocks and fuller lips—formerly antithetical to white standards of beauty—are, with the assistance of cosmetic surgery, available for a price.

17 Until the nineteenth century, black women went to great lengths to adhere to respectability politics that made black women asexual, and this is reflected in music, literature, and art. The naked body of Walker's Marvelous Sugar Baby defies all efforts to deem the black female body as sexually invisible.

18 See Peabody for more on Walker's Digital Marvelous Sugar Baby database (158).

Works Cited

Adesanmi, Pius. "Of Postcolonial Entanglement and Durée: Reflections on the Francophone African Novel." *Comparative Literature*, vol. 56, no. 3, Summer 2004, pp. 227–242.

Ally, Shireen. *From Servants to Workers: South African Domestic Workers and the Democratic State*. Ithaca, Cornell UP, 2009.

Als, Hilton. "The Sugar Sphinx." *New Yorker*, 8 May 2014, www.newyorker.com/culture/culture-desk/the-sugar-sphinx. Accessed 28 Aug. 2019.

Anderson, Bridget. *Doing the Dirty Work: The Global Politics of Domestic Labour*. London, Zed Books, 2000.

Arnold, Marion. *Women and Art in South Africa*. New York, St. Martin's Press, 1996.

Aronson, Marc, and Marina Budhos. *Sugar Changed the World: A Story of Magic, Spice, Slavery Freedom, and Science*. Clarion, New York, 2017.

Association of Black Women Historians. "An Open Statement to the Fans of *The Help*." *AALBC*. aalbc.com/reviews/the_help_historical_context.html. Accessed 5 Feb. 2017.

Baderoon, Gabeba. "'I Compose Myself': Lesbian Muslim Autobiographies and the Craft of Self-Writing in South Africa." *Journal of the American Academy of Religion*, vol. 83, no. 4, 2015, pp. 897–915.

Bakhtin, Mikhail. *The Dialogic Imagination: Four Essays*. Translated by Michael Holquist et al., Austin, U of Texas P, 1982.

Bearden, Romare. *Patchwork Quilt*. 1970. Cloth, paper and acrylic. Museum of Modern Art, New York.

Berman Springer, Shari, director. *The Nanny Diaries*. Film Colony, 2007.

Bethlehem, Louise. "By/way of Passage." *JWTC Blog*, 29 July 2010, jhbwtc.blogspot.com/2010/07/byway-of-passage.html. Accessed 19 Sept. 2019.

Bhabha, Homi. *The Location of Culture*. New York, Routledge, 1994.

Bishop, Claire. *Artificial Hells: Participatory Art and the Politics of Spectatorship*. London, Verso, 2012.

Bloomquist, Jennifer, "The Minstrel Legacy: African American English and the Historical Construction of 'Black' Identities in Entertainment." *Journal of African American Studies*, vol. 19, no. 4, 2015, pp. 410–425.

Bogle, Donald. *Bright Boulevards, Bold Dreams: The Story of Black Hollywood*. London, One World Publications, 2006.

Brand, Dionne. "No rinsed blue sky, no red flower fences." *Sans Souci and Other Stories*. Ithaca, Firebrand Books, 1989, pp. 178–182.

Brodie, Nechama. "Look up, up, up." *Mail and Guardian*, 9 July 2010, mg.co.za/article/2010-07-09-look-up. Accessed 22 Sept. 2014.

Brown, Tamara Mose. *Raising Brooklyn: Nannies, Childcare, and Caribbeans, Creating Community*. New York, New York UP, 2011.

Brown, Victoria. *Minding Ben*. New York, Hyperion, 2011.

Budlender, Debbie. *The Introduction of a Minimum Wage for Domestic Workers in South Africa*. Geneva, International Labour Organization, 2016, www.ilo.org/wcmsp5/groups/public/---ed_protect/---protrav/---travail/documents/publication/wcms_465069.pdf. Accessed 3 Sept. 2014.

Bumiller, Elisabeth. "Affronted by Nude 'Last Supper,' Giuliani Calls for Decency Panel." *New York Times*, 16 Feb. 2001, www.nytimes.com/2001/02/16/nyregion/affronted-by-nude-last-supper-giuliani-calls-for-decency-panel.html. Accessed 15 Sept. 2015.

Buñuel, Luis, director. *The Discreet Charm of the Bourgeoisie*. Twentieth Century Fox, 1972.

Butler, Judith. *Gender Trouble: Feminism and Subversion of Identity*. New York, Routledge, 1990, pp. vi–xvii.

Cadwalladr, Carole. "New Africa: The South African Artist Addressing Her Family's Past." *Guardian*, 25 Aug. 2012, www.theguardian.com/artanddesign/2012/aug/26/new-africa-south-african-artist. Accessed 2 Oct. 2014.

Carby, Hazel V. "'It Jus Be's Dat Way Sometime': The Sexual Politics of Women's Blues." *The Jazz Cadence of American Culture*, edited by Robert O'Meally, New York, Columbia UP, 1998, pp. 469–482.

Childress, Alice. *Like One of the Family: Conversations from a Domestic's Life.* Rev. ed., Boston, Beacon Press, 1986.

———. Professional Papers. 1940–1994. Archives and Manuscripts, Schomburg, New York Public Library ScMG 649 box 1.

Christian, Barbara. *Black Feminist Criticism: Perspectives on Black Women Writers.* Ann Arbor, U of Michigan P, 1985.

Clare, Rene, director. *The Flame of New Orleans.* Universal Pictures, 1941.

Clark-Lewis, Elizabeth. *Living In and Living Out: African American Domestics in Washington, D.C., 1910–1940.* Washington, D.C., Smithsonian Books, 2010.

Cock, Jacklyn. *Maids & Madams: Domestic Workers under Apartheid.* London, Women's Press, 1989.

Colen, Shellee. *"Like a Mother to Them": Stratified Reproduction and West Indian Childcare Workers and Employers in New York.* Berkeley, U of California P, 1995.

Collins, Lisa. "Economies of the Flesh: Representing the Black Female Body in Art." *Skin Deep, Spirit Strong*, edited by Kimberly Wallace-Sanders, Ann Arbor, U of Michigan P, 2002, pp. 104–105.

Collins, Patricia Hill. *Black Feminist Thought: Knowledge, Consciousness, and the Politics of Empowerment.* Rev. 2nd ed., New York, Routledge, 1999.

Colvard, Chico, director. *Black Memorabilia.* C-LINEFILMS, 2018.

Coly, Ayo. *The Pull of Postcolonial Nationhood: Gender and Migration in Francophone African Literateurs.* E-book, Lanham, Lexington Books, 2010.

Conner, Allison. "*Black Girl* Unmasks the Phantoms of Colonialism." Review of *Black Girl*, directed by Ousmane Sembène. *Bitch Media*, 1 Sept. 2017, www.bitchmedia.org/article/black-girl/director-ousmane-semb%C3%A8ne. Accessed 2 Jan. 2019.

Cooke, Marvel. "I Was Part of the Bronx Slave Market: Where Men Prowl and Women Prey on Needy Job-Seekers." *Daily Compass*, 8 Jan. 1950, viewpointmag.com/2015/10/31/the-bronx-slave-market-1950/. Accessed 11 Nov. 2016.

Cox, Renee. *American Family.* 2010. www.reneecox.org/american-family-statement. Photograph. Accessed 17 Aug. 2016.

———. *Black Housewife* (*Missy at Home*). 2008. www.reneecox.org/discreet-charm-of-the-bougie?lightbox=i0158w. Photograph. Accessed 17 Aug. 2016.

———. *The Discreet Charm of the Bougies*. 2008. www.reneecox.org/discreet-charm-of-the-bougie. Photograph. Accessed 17 Aug. 2016.

———. Interview with Adelaide Damoah. "Art Success: Adelaide Damoah in Conversation with Rene Cox." AD. 2 Feb. 2013, adelaidedamoahart.com/2013/02/art-success-adelaide-damoah-in-conversation-with-renee-cox/. Accessed 31 May 2019.

———. Interview with Christinerose Parravicini. "*Renee Cox.*" *UnDo.Net*, 14 Nov. 1998. Accessed 4 Oct. 2015.

———. Interview with Nicole Plett. *Never Has She Ever: Renee Cox Solo Show*, 21 Oct. 2008, www.libraries.rutgers.edu/sites/default/files/dwas/pdfs/Cox_interview_by_Plett_Oct_2008.pdf. Accessed 21 Mar. 2015.

———. *Missy by the Pool*. 2008. www.reneecox.org/discreet-charm-of-the-bougie?lightbox=i2eu7. Photograph. Accessed 14 Aug. 2016.

———. *Olympia's Boyz*. 2001. www.reneecox.org/american-family?lightbox=i11ctt. Photograph. Accessed 14 Aug. 2016.

———. *Rajae for President*. 1998. www.reneecox.org/raje?lightbox=i25ve. Photograph. Accessed 14 Aug. 2016.

———. *Yo Mama's Last Supper*. 1999, Brooklyn Museum, New York.

Craik, Jennifer. *Uniforms Exposed: From Conformity to Transgression*. Oxford, Berg, 2005.

Cuarón, Alfonso, director. *Roma*. Spectaculos Filmicos El Coyul, 2018.

Dalla Costa, Mariarosa, and Selma James. *The Power of Women and the Subversion of the Community*. 3rd ed., Bristol, Falling Wall, 1975.

Dallow, Jessica. "Reclaiming Histories: Betye and Alison Saar: Feminism and the Representation of Black Womanhood." *Feminist Studies*, vol. 30, no. 1, 2004, pp. 74–113.

Dangarembga, Tsitsi. *Nervous Conditions*. Washington, D.C., Seal Press, 1988.

Dargis, Manohla. "Just a Maid in Movies, but Not Forgotten." *New York Times*, 21 Apr. 2011, www.nytimes.com/2011/04/24/theater/theresa-harris-a-black-actress-who-left-an-impression.html. Accessed 9 Mar. 2018.

Davis, Angela Y. *Women, Race, and Class*. New York, Vintage Books, 1991.

Davis, Fred. "Of Maids' Uniforms and Blue Jeans." *Qualitative Sociology*, vol. 12, no. 4, 1 Dec. 1989, pp. 338–349.

Day, Gary. "Artaud and Genet's *The Maids*: Like Father, Like Son?" *Twentieth Century European Drama*, edited by Brian Docherty, London, Palgrave Macmillan, 1994, pp. 146–161.

Dennis, Nicole Benn. *Patsy*. New York, Liveright, 2019.

Dima, Vlad. "Ousmane Sembène's '*La Noire de . . .*' Melancholia in Photo, Text, and Film." *Journal of African Studies*, vol. 26, no. 1, 2014, pp. 56–68.

Dozier, Raine. "The Declining Relative Status of Black Women Workers 1980–2002." *Social Forces*, vol. 88, no. 4, 2010, pp. 18–34.

Dresner, Zita A. "Alice Childress's *Like One of the Family*: Domestic and Undomesticated Humor." *Look Who's Laughing: Gender and Comedy*, edited by Gail Finney, New York, Gordon and Breach, 1994, pp. 221–229.

Du Bois, W. E. B. *Souls of Black Folk*. Chicago, McClurge, 1903.

Dunne, Susan. "Portraits of British Aristocrats and Their Servants at Yale Museum." *Hartford Courant*, 16 Oct. 2014, https://www.courant.com/ctnow/arts-theater/hc-arts-column-dunne-yale-1019-20141016-story.html. Accessed 28 June 2015.

Duyne, Cheryl, director. *The Watermelon Woman*. First Run Features, 1996.

Edmonds, Brandon. "Two-by-Two by Various Artists at Irma Stern Museum." *Artthrob*, July 2011, www.artthrob.co.za/Reviews/2011/07/Brandon-Edmonds-reviews-Two-by-two-by-Various-Artists-at-Irma-Stern-Museum.aspx. Accessed 18 Mar. 2014. Article last accessed prior to printing.

Efeoghene, Igor. "Rethinking the Egalitarian Potential of Postapartheid South Africa: Zanele Muholi's Intervention." *Radical History Review*, vol. 2016, no. 126, 2016, pp. 181–193.

Evans, Sally. "Minister Slams Porn Exhibition." *Times Live*, 1 Mar. 2010, www.timeslive.co.za/news/south-africa/2010-03-01-minister-slams-porn-exhibition/. Accessed 19 Apr. 2015.

Evaristo, Bernadine. *The Emperor's Babe*. London, Penguin, 2004.

Eversley, Shelly, and Jennifer L. Morgan. "Introduction: The Sexual Body." *Women Studies Quarterly*, vol. 35, nos. 1–2, Spring/Summer 2007, pp. 10–19.

"Famous Trends in British Food History." *Telegraph*, www.telegraph.co.uk/foodanddrink/foodanddrinkpicturegalleries/10000339/Famous-food-trends-in-British-history.html?frame=2545611. Accessed 18 Sept. 2019.

Fanon, Frantz. *Black Skins White Masks*. New York, Grove Press, 2008.

Farrington, Lisa E. *Faith Ringgold*. Petaluma, Pomegranate, 2004. Print.

———. "Faith Ringgold's *Slave Rape* Series." *Skin Deep Spirit Strong: The Black Female Body in American Culture*. Ann Arbor, U of Michigan P, 2002.

Fine, Ruth E. *The Art of Romare Bearden*. New York, Harry N. Abrams, 2003.

Foucault, Michel. "The Subject and Power." *Critical Inquiry*, vol. 8, no. 4, 1982, pp. 777–795.

Fuller, Lorraine. "Are We Seeing Things? The Pine-Sol Lady and the Ghost of Aunt Jemima." *Journal of Black Studies*, vol. 31, no. 1, 2001, pp. 120–131.

Garb, Tamar, contributor. "Zanele Muholi." *Somnyama Ngonyama, Hail the Dark Lioness*, edited by Renee Musai and Zanele Muholi, Reading, Aperture, 2018, p. 17.

Gay, Roxane. "Beyoncé's Control of Her Own Image Belies the bell hooks Slave Critique." *Guardian*, 12 May 2014, www.theguardian.com/commentisfree/2014/may/12/beyonce-bell-hooks-slave-terrrorist. Accessed 5 June 2019.

Geary, Daniel. "The Moynihan Report: An Annotated Edition." *The Atlantic*, 14 Sept. 2015, https://www.theatlantic.com/politics/archive/2015/09/the-moynihan-report-an-annotated-edition/404632/.

Genet, Jean. *The Maids and Deathwatch: Two Plays*. New York, Grove, 1994.

Gilman, Sander. "Black Bodies, White Bodies: Toward an Iconography of Female Sexuality in Late Nineteenth Century Art, Medicine, and Literature." *Critical Inquiry*, vol. 12, no. 1, 1985, pp. 204–242.

Glenn, Evelyn Nakano. "From Servitude to Service Work: Historical Continuities in the Racial Division of Paid Reproductive Labor." *Signs*, vol. 18, no. 1, 1992, pp. 1–43.

Gore, Dayo F. *Radicalism at the Crossroads: African American Women Activists in the Cold War*. New York, NYU Press, 2011.

Green, Alfred E., director. *Babyface*. Warner Bros., 1933.

Greene, Brenda. "Nandi Nanny Diaries." *Writers on Writing Radio Show*, 15 Nov. 2009.

Grigsby, Darcy Grimaldo. "Olympia." *Art Bulletin*, 1 Dec. 2015, pp. 430–451.

Gutiérrez Rodríguez, Encarnación. "The Hidden State of the New Economy: On Transnational Migration, Domestic Work, and Unprecedented Intimacy." *Frontiers: A Journal of Women Studies*, vol. 28, no. 3, 2007, p. 71.

Hall, Kim F. *Things of Darkness: Economies of Race and Gender in Early Modern England*. Ithaca, Cornell UP, 1995.

Hammonds, Evelyn. "Black (W)holes and the Geometry of Black Female Sexuality." *Differences: A Journal of Feminist Cultural Studies*, vol. 6, no. 3, 1994, pp. 127–145.

Harris, Kamala. "Harris, Jayapal Announce Domestic Workers Bill of Rights." Press release, 15 July 2019, www.harris.senate.gov/news/press-releases/harris-jayapal-announce-domestic-workers-bill-of-rights. Accessed 7 Oct. 2019.

Harris, Trudier. *From Mammies to Militants: Domestics in Black American Literature*. Philadelphia, Temple UP, 1982.

———. Introduction. *Like One of the Family: Conversations from a Domestic's Life*, by Alice Childress, rev. ed., Boston, Beacon Press, 1986.

Harris-Perry, Melissa V. *Sister Citizen: Shame, Stereotypes, and Black Women in America*. New Haven, Yale UP, 2011.

Hartman, Saidiya. *Scenes of Subjection: Terror, Slavery, and Self-Making in Nineteenth-Century America*. Oxford, Oxford UP, 1997, pp. 7–8.

Hayden-Guest, Anthony. "Took Care of the Kids and Very Good Notes." *New York Times*, 7 Feb. 2002, www.nytimes.com/2002/02/07/garden/took-care-of-the-kids-and-very-good-notes.html. Accessed May 2019.

Hennebelle, Guy. "Interview Ousmane Sembène, 1969." *Ousmane Sembène Interviews*, edited by Annett Busch and Max Annas, Jackson, UP of Mississippi, 2008, pp. 7–17.

Hepner, Tricia Redeker, and Randal L. Hepner. "Gender, Community, and Change among the Rastafari of New York City." *New York Glory: Religions in the City*, edited by Tony Carnes and Anna Karpathakis, New York, New York UP, 2001 pp. 333–356.

"Hidden Away: Abuses against Migrant Domestic Workers in the U.K." *Human Rights Watch*, 30 Mar. 2014, www.hrw.org/report/2014/03/30/hidden-away/abuses-against-migrant-domestic-workers-uk. Accessed 5 May 2015.

Hilgers, Lauren. "The Future of Work: Out of the Shadows." *New York Times*, 21 Feb. 2019, www.nytimes.com/interactive/2019/02/21/magazine/national-domestic-workers-alliance.html. Accessed June 2019.

Hondagneu-Sotelo, Pierrette. *Domestica: Immigrant Workers Cleaning and Caring in the Shadows of Influence*. Berkeley, U of California P, 2001.

hooks, bell. *Art on My Mind: Visual Politics*. New York, New Press, 1995.

———. *Black Looks: Race and Representation*. New York, Routledge, 1992.

———. "Selling Hot Pussy: Representations of Black Women's Sexuality in the Cultural Marketplace." *Black Looks: Race and Representation*. Boston, South End Press, 2010.

———. *Sisters of the Yam*. Boston, South End Press, 1993.

Hopkins, Pauline. *Contending Forces: A Romance Illustrative of Negro Life North and South*. New York, Oxford UP, 1988.

Iversen, Kristin. "White People Problems: On Kara Walker and the Way White People Interact with Black Art." *Brooklyn*, 2014, www.bkmag.com/2014/06/09/white-people-problems-on-kara-walker-and-the-way-white-people-interact-with-black-art/. Accessed 22 Mar. 2018.

Jansen, Ena. *Like Family: Domestic Workers in South African History and Literature*. Johannesburg, Wits UP, 2019.

Jewell, K. Sue. *From Mammy to Miss America and Beyond: Cultural Images and the Shaping of US Social Policy*. New York, Routledge, 1993.

Johnson, James Weldon. *The Autobiography of an Ex-Colored Man*. Rev. ed., New York, Penguin Books, 1990.

Johnson, William H. *Nude*. 1939, americanart.si.edu/artwork/nude-11856. Oil on burlap.

Jones, Claudia. "An End to the Neglect of the Problems of the Negro Woman!" *Words of Fire: An Anthology of African-American Thought*, edited by Beverly Guy Sheftall, New York, New Press, 1995, pp. 108–123.

Jones, Kirk, director. *Nanny McPhee*. Universal Pictures, 2006.

Kaltenback, Chris. "Monique Wins Big for Doing 'What Is Right.'" *Baltimore Sun*, 8 Mar. 2010, www.baltimoresun.com/entertainment/bs-xpm-2010-03-08-bal-ae-monique08mar08-story.html. Accessed 9 Sept. 2019.

Kariim, Una. "Beyond the Selfie: Renée Cox on the Power of Shooting Black Bodies." *Ebony*, 26 Mar. 2014, www.ebony.com/entertainment/renee-cox-talks-beyond-the-selfie-photos-323/. Accessed 7 Feb. 2016.

Kasinitz, Philip. *Caribbean New York: Black Immigrants and the Politics of Race*. Ithaca, Cornell UP, 1992.

Keyi, Nadi. *The True Nanny Diaries*. New York, Bread for Brick Publishing, 2009.

Kincaid, Jamaica. *Lucy*. New York, Farrar, Straus and Giroux, 2002.

King, Martin Luther, Jr. "Where Do We Go from Here?" Aug. 1967, kinginstitute.stanford.edu/king-papers/documents/where-do-we-go-here-address-delivered-eleventh-annual-sclc-convention. Accessed 22 Sept. 2019.

Koloane, David, and Ivor Powell. "In Conversation." *Seven Stories about Modern Art in Africa*, edited by Clementine Deliss, London, Whitechapel Art Gallery, 1995, pp. 261–265.

Krasner, David. *Resistance, Parody and Double Consciousness in African American Theatre, 1895–1910*. New York, Palgrave Macmillan, 1997.

Lacan, Jacques. "Of the Gaze as Object Petit a." *The Seminar of Jacques Lacan: Book 11, The Four Fundamental Concepts of Psycho-Analysis*, edited by Jacques-Alain Miller and Alan Sheridan and translated by Alan Sheridan, New York, W. W. Norton, pp. 65–119.

Lancaster, Sonja J. "Too Many Cooks: Contested Authority in the Kitchen." *Southern Literary Journal*, vol. 38, no. 2, 2006, pp. 113–114.

Landy, Marcia. "Politics and Style in *Black Girl*." *Jumpcut*, no. 27, 1982, pp. 23–25, www.ejumpcut.org/archive/onlinessays/JC27folder/BlackGirlLandy.html. Accessed July 2016.

Larsen, Nella. *Quicksand and Passing*. Edited by Deborah McDowell, New Brunswick, Rutgers UP, 1986.

Laurie, Alison. *The Language of Clothes*. New York, Random House, 1981.

Lauter, Paul. "Working Class Women's Literature: An Introduction to Study." *Radical Teacher* 15, vol. 100, 2014, pp. 63–76.

Lee, Felicia. "Nannies Still Draw a Keen Audience." *New York Times*, 13 July 2010, www.nytimes.com/2010/07/14/books/14nanny.html. Accessed 19 Aug. 2018.

Lee, Spike, director. *School Daze*. 40 Acres and Mule Films, 1988.

Levine, Lawrence. *Black Culture and Black Consciousness: Afro American Folk Thought from Slavery to Freedom*. Oxford, Oxford UP, 2007.

Lizzo. *Cuz I Love You*, Nice Life, Atlantic, 2019.

Lockard, Jon Onye. *No More*. 1967. Painting.

Lorde, Audre. *Sister Outsider*. Berkeley, Crossing Press, 1984.

Mabandu, Percy. "Ambition Made Flesh." *Mail and Guardian*, 31 July 2009, mg.co.za/article/2009-07-31-ambition-made-flesh. Accessed Oct. 2015.

MacDonnell, Judith A., et al. *Nursing Research and Practice*, vol. 2012. Article ID 57686, pp. 1–10.

Magona, Sindiwe. *Living, Loving and Lying Awake All Night*. New York, Interlink Publishing, 1991.

———. *To My Children's Children*. New York, Interlink Books, 2006.

"Maid of Hollywood." *Jet Magazine*, 11 Sept. 1952.

Manet, Édouard. *Children in the Tuileries*. 1861–1862. Oil on canvas. RISD Museum, Rhode Island. www.edouard-manet.net/children-in-the-tuileries/. Accessed 10 Oct. 2019.

———. *Le déjeuner sur L'herbe*. 1863. Oil on canvas. Musée d'Orsay, Paris. https://www.musee-orsay.fr/en/collections/works-in-focus/search/commentaire/commentaire_id/luncheon-on-the-grass-7201.html. Accessed 10 Oct. 2019.

———. *La Négresse*. 1862–1865. Oil on canvas. Pinacoteca Giovanni e Marella Agnelli, Turin. www.smithsonianmag.com/smart-news/what-black-maid-manets-olympia-tells-us-about-modernisms-models-180970708/. Accessed 10 Oct. 2019.

———. *Olympia*. 1863. Oil on canvas. Musée d'Orsay, Paris. www.musee-orsay.fr/index.php?id=851&L=1&tx_commentaire_pi1[showUid]=7087. Accessed 10 Oct. 2019.

Marshall, Paule. *Brown Girl Brownstones*. New York, Feminist Press, 1981.

Matebeni, Zethu. "Intimacy, Queerness, Race." *Cultural Studies*, vol. 27, no. 3, 2013, pp. 404–417.

May, Vanessa H. *Unprotected Labor: Household Workers, Politics, and Middle-Class Reform in New York, 1870–1940*. Chapel Hill, U of North Carolina P, 2011.

Mbue, Imbolo. *Behold the Dreamers*. New York, Penguin Random House, 2017.

McCormack, Donna. "Gender and Colonial Transitioning: Frantz Fanon's Algerian Freedom Fighters in Moroccan and Caribbean Novels?" *Journal of Transatlantic Studies*, vol. 7, 2009, pp. 279–293.

McDuffie, Erick S. "Esther V. Cooper's: 'The Negro Woman Domestic Worker in Relation to Trade Unionism': Black Left Feminism and the Popular Front." *Red Activists and Black Freedom: James and Esther Jackson and the Long Civil Rights Revolution*, edited by Michael H. Nash, et al., New York, Routledge, 2012, pp. 33–40.

McLaughlin, Emma, and Nicola Kraus. *The Nanny Diaries*. New York, Saint Martin's Press, 2002.

Meer, Shamin. *Women Speak: Reflections on Our Struggles 1982–1987*. Oxford, Oxfam Publishing, 1999.

Minding Ben. *Kirkus Review*. 4 Apr. 2011. www.kirkusreviews.com/book-reviews/victoria-brown/minding-ben. Accessed 10 Aug. 2019.

Mintz, Sidney. *Sweetness and Power: The Place of Sugar in Modern History*. New York, Penguin, 1985.

Miranda, Carolina. "How Alfonso Cuarón's 'Roma' Oscars Spark a Dialogue about the Faces We See on Screen." *LA Times*, 25 Feb. 2019. www.latimes

.com/entertainment/arts/miranda/la-et-mn-oscars-roma-20190225-story.html. Accessed 3 Aug. 2019.

Mirzoeff, Nicholas. Introduction. *The Visual Culture Reader*, edited by Nicholas Mirzoeff, New York, Routledge, 1998.

Mkandawire-Valhmu, Lucy, et al. "Surviving Life as a Woman: A Critical Ethnography of Violence in the Lives of Female Domestic Workers in Malawi." *Health Care for Women International*, 1 Sept. 2009, pp. 783–801.

"Modern Day Slavery." *BBC News*, 22 Nov. 2013, www.bbc.com/news/uk-25048307. Accessed Sept. 2020.

Mohr, Ian. "Fall Debut for Nanny." *Variety*, 28 Mar. 2007. www.variety.com/2007/scene/markets-festivals/fall-debut-for-nanny-1117962031/. Accessed 25 Sept. 2020.

Mokoena, Hlonipha. Rpt. "Work as Usual for Bester." *Sun News*, 13 Dec. 2002, in "Maid Chic." *PASS-AGES: References & Footnotes*, 2010, www.historicalreenactments.org/images/projects/Passages/15-1.pdf. Accessed 26 September 2020.

Monáe, Janelle. Acceptance speech. *Black Girls Rock*, 4 Nov. 2012.

Morgan, Ruth, and Saskia Wieringa. Introduction. *Tommy Boys, Lesbian Men and Ancestral Wives*, edited by Ruth Morgan and Saskia Wieringa, Auckland Park, Jacana Media, 2005.

Morrison, Toni. *Beloved*. New York, Alfred A. Knopf, 1987.

Muholi, Zanele. *Caitlin and I*. 2009. Print. Stevenson, Johannesburg, South Africa. archive.stevenson.info/exhibitions/muholi/caitlin.htm. Accessed 6 Oct. 2018.

———. *Bester I Mayotte*. 2015. Print. Somnyama Ngonyama, Zeitz MOCAA, Capetown, South Africa. zeitzmocaa.museum/art/bester-i-mayotte/. Accessed 9 Feb. 2019.

———. *Bester V Mayotte*. 2015. Print. Stevenson, Johannesburg, South Africa. archive.stevenson.info/exhibitions/muholi/somnyama/bester5_mayotte_2015.html. Accessed 9 Feb. 2019.

———. director. *Difficult Love*. Peter Goldsmid, 2010.

———. *Faces and Phases*. Munich, Prestel, 2010.

———. "I Have Truly Lost a Woman I Loved." *Reclaiming the L-Word: Sappho's Daughters Out of Africa*, edited by Alleyn Diesel, Oxford, African Books Collective, 2011, pp. 10–25.

———. "Internet Derica." 10 May 2011, derica.tumblr.com/post/5364557936/zanele-muholi-massa-and-minah. Accessed 7 Nov. 2016.

———. Interview with *Artnet News*. 28 Sept. 2018, https://news.artnet.com/exhibitions/zanele-muholi-art-21-1357777. Accessed 26 Sept. 2020.

———. *MaID X Durban South Africa*. 2015. Print. Stevenson, Johannesburg, South Africa. www.stevenson.info/exhibition/1440/work/88. Accessed 5 Aug. 2019.

———. "Mapping Our Histories: A Visual History of Black Lesbians in Post-apartheid South Africa." 2009, www.zanelmuholi.com. Accessed 5 Feb. 2018.

———. *Massa and Mina(h)*. 2008. Print. Brodie Stevenson, archive.stevenson.info/exhibitionsbs/muholi/index.htm. Accessed 2 Feb. 2014.

———. *Massa and Mina(h) 2*. 2008. Print. Brodie Stevenson, archive.stevenson.info/exhibitionsbs/muholi/index.htm. Accessed 2 Feb. 2014.

———. *Massa and Mina(h) 3*. 2008. Print. Brodie Stevenson, archive.stevenson.info/exhibitionsbs/muholi/index.htm. Accessed 2 Feb. 2014.

———. "Ngibonile (I have seen . . .)." *Uber(w)unden: Art in Troubled Times*, edited by Lien Heidenreich-Seleme and Sean O'Toole, Johannesburg, Jacana Media, 2012. pp. 40–55. Print.

———. "Photo of the Day." *INKANYiSO*, 22 Aug. 2013, inkanyiso.org. Accessed 14 July 2014.

———. *Somnyama Ngonyama. Stevenson*, 2012–2018. Print. www.stevenson.info/exhibition/1440. Accessed 27 Sept. 2020.

———. *Somnyama Ngonyama, Hail the Dark Lioness*, edited by Renee Musai and Zanele Muholi, Reading, Aperture, 2018.

———. "So They Have 'Eyes to See.'" 2009, Brodie Stevenson, archive.stevenson.info/exhibitionsbs/muholi/text.htm. Accessed 27 Sept. 2020.

Murphy, Carl. Letter to Alice Childress. 23 Feb. 1960. Alice Childress Papers, Archives and Manuscripts, Schomburg Center for Research in Black Culture, New York Public Library, Correspondence, 1950s–1970s, box 8, folder 1.

Murray, Derek Conrad. "Post-Black Art and the Resurrection of African American Satire." *Post Soul Satire: Black Identity After Civil Rights*, edited by Derek C. Maus and James Donahue Jackson, Jackson, UP of Mississippi, pp. 3–21.

Murrell, Denise. *Posing Modernity: The Black Model from Manet and Matisse to Today*. New Haven, Yale UP, 2018.

Nadasen, Premilla. *Household Workers Unite: The Untold Story of African American Women Who Built a Movement*. Boston, Beacon, 2015.

Ndlovu, Duma, and Mbongeni Ngema. "Sheila's Day." *Black South African Women: An Anthology of Plays*, edited by Kathy A. Perkins, New York, Routledge, 1998, pp. 142–158.

Ngcobo, Gabi. "It's Work as Usual: Framing Race, Class, Gender through a South African Lens." *AFRICAVENIR International*, 2014, www.africavenir.org/publications/e-dossiers/revisions/gabi-ngcobo.html.

Nichols, Mike, director. *The Graduate*. Lawrence Truman Productions, 1967.

Nottage, Lynn. *By the Way, Meet Vera Stark*. New York, Theatre Communications Group, 2011.

O'Grady, Lorraine. "Olympia's Black Maid: Reclaiming Black Female Subjectivity." *Feminism and Cultural Studies Reader*, New York, Routledge, 1992.

O'Leary, Elizabeth. *At Beck and Call: The Representation of Domestic Servants in Nineteenth-Century American Painting*. Washington, D.C., Smithsonian Institution Press, 1996.

Pattern, Phil. "Mammy, Her Life and Times." *American Heritage*, vol. 44, no. 5, 1993, p. 78.

Patterson, Louise Thompson. "Toward a Brighter Dawn." *CPUSA Journal Woman Today*, 1936 reprint. *Viewpoint Magazine*, Oct. 2015, www.viewpointmag.com/2015/10/31/toward-a-brighter-dawn-1936/. Accessed 9 Feb. 2016.

Patterson-Faye, Courtney. "I Like the Way You Move: Theorizing Fat, Black, and Sexy." *Sexualities*, vol. 19, no. 8, July 2016, pp. 926–944.

Peabody, Rebecca. *Consuming Stories: Kara Walker and the Imaging of American Race*. Berkeley, U of California P, 2016.

Pfaff, Francoise. "The Uniqueness of Ousmane Sembène's Cinema." *Contributions in Black Studies*, vol. 11, no. 3, 1993, pp. 13–19.

Pier, Carol, and Orville Schell. "Hidden in the Home: Abuse of Domestic Workers with Special Visas in the United States." Human Rights Watch. Accessed 1 June 2010, www.hrw.org/report/2001/06/01/hidden-home/abuse-domestic-workers-special-visas-united-states.

Powers, Nicholas. "Why I Yelled at the Kara Walker Exhibit." *Indypendent* blog, 30 Jun. 2014, www.huffpost.com/entry/why-i-yelled-at-the-kara_n_5552054. Accessed 2 July 2014.

Prat, Laurence. *Face a Face*. Photograph. Paris, Studio-Galerie Laurence Prat, 2017.

Redeker Hepner, Tricia, and Randal L. Hepner. "Gender, Community, and Change among the Rastafari of New York City." *New York Glory: Religions in the City*, edited by Tony Carnes and Anna Karpathakis, New York, New York UP, 2001, pp. 333–356.

Regester, Charlene. *African American Actresses: The Struggle for Visibility, 1900–1960*. Bloomington, Indiana UP, 2010.

Rivers, Larry. *I Like Olympia in Black Face*. 1970. Painting/sculpture.

Rocketto, Jess Morales. "Eva Longoria Offers Sweet Words of Encouragement to Roma Star Yalitza Aparicio." *In Style*, 25 Feb. 2019, ca.style.yahoo.com/eva-longoria-offers-sweet-words-224500979.html. Accessed 3 Sept. 2019.

Rollins, Judith. *Between Women: Domestics and Their Employers*. Philadelphia, Temple UP, 1985.

Romero, Mary. *Maid in the USA*. New York, Routledge, 2002.

Saar, Betye. *The Liberation of Aunt Jemima*. 1972. Mixed media.

Sassen, Saskia. "Women's Burden: Counter-geographies of Globalization and the Feminization of Survival." *Journal of International Affairs*, vol. 53, no. 2, Spring 2000, pp. 503–524.

Scales-Trent, Judy. "African Women in France: Citizenship, Family, and Work." *Brooklyn Journal of International Law*, vol. 24, no. 3, 1999, pp. 705–737.

Scott, Carole. "Magical Dress: Clothing and Transformation in Folk Tales." *Children's Literary Association Quarterly*, vol. 21, no. 4, 1996, pp. 151–157. Project Muse, web. Accessed 11 Nov. 2013.

Scott, James. *Domination and the Arts of Resistance*. New Haven, Yale UP, 1992, p. 4.

Sembène, Ousmane. *La Noire De* . . . Filmi Domirev, Les Actualités Françaises, 1966.

Senna, Danzy. *Caucasia*. New York, Riverhead Books, 1999.

Shonibare, Yinka. *How to Blow Up Two Heads at Once (Ladies)*. 2006. Fiberglass mannequins. www.artres.com/C.aspx?VP3=ViewBox_VPage&RAQF=1&

IT=ZoomImageTemplate01_VForm&IID=2UNTWAYZCTYS&ALID=2UN39YFM54M3&PN=9&CT=Search&SF=0. Accessed 23 Nov. 2017.

Shteir, Rachel. "Interpreting 'The Maids' through a Shifting Societal Lens." *New York Times*, 31 July 2014, www.nytimes.com/2014/08/03/theater/interpreting-the-maids-through-a-shifting-societal-lens.html. Accessed 22 Mar. 2019.

Sibande, Marie. *A Conversation with Madam CJ Walker*. 2009. Fiberglass mannequin. Institute for the Humanities Gallery, University of Michigan.

———. *Her Majesty Queen Sophie*. 2010. Archival digital print. www.marysibande.com/portfolio/im-a-lady/. Accessed 11 May 2016.

———. *I'm a Lady*. 2009. Archival digital print. www.marysibande.com/portfolio/im-a-lady/. Accessed 11 May 2016.

———. Interview with Mary Corrigall. "Interview with Mary Sibande." Incorrigible Corrigall, 2010, Web. Accessed 9 June 2015.

———. *Long Live the Dead Queen*. University of Michigan, Michigan Theater. 26 Sept. 2013. Penny Stamps Keynote Address.

———. "New Africa: The South African Artist Addressing Her Family's Past." *Guardian*, 25 Aug. 2012, www.theguardian.com/artanddesign/2012/aug/26/new-africa-south-african-artist. Accessed 2 Oct. 2014.

———. "*. . . Of Prosperity*." 2012. Fiberglass mannequin. Spencer Museum of Art, Kansas. Sculpture.

———. *The Reign*. Fiberglass mannequin. 2010. Iziko National Gallery, Cape Town. Multimedia.

———. *A Reversed Retrogress:* Mary Sibande. *YouTube*, uploaded by the British Museum, 25 Nov. 2007, www.youtube.com/watch?v=8C5YHIOHqus. Accessed 11 Feb. 2015.

———. *A Reversed Retrogress: Scene 1*. 2013 Fiberglass mannequins.

———. *Silent Symphony*. 2010. Fiberglass mannequin. Institute for the Humanities, University of Michigan.

———. *A Terrible Beauty Is Born*. 2013. Fiberglass mannequin. Institute for the Humanities Gallery, University of Michigan.

———. *They Don't Make Them like They Used To*. 2008. Fiberglass mannequin. Institute for the Humanities, University of Michigan. Archival digital print.

———. *Wish You Were Here*. 2010. Archival digital print. www.marysibande.com/long-live-the-dead-queen/. Accessed 7 Mar. 2019.

Sidman, Amanda. "*Minding Ben* Author Victoria Brown Drew from New York Nanny Experiences for New Novel." *Daily News*, 18 Apr. 2011, www.nydailynews.com/life-style/minding-ben-author-victoria-brown-drew-new-york-nanny-experiences-new-article-1.113291. Accessed 22 June 2019.

Simbao, Ruth. "Mary Sibande: *Long Live the Dead Queen*." *Gallery Momo*, 2010, www.gallerymomo.com/wp-content/uploads/2011/09/Mary-Sibande-English1.pdf. Accessed 9 Aug. 2014. Article last accessed prior to printing.

"Slavery in the UK." *Antislavery*, www.antislavery.org/slavery-today/slavery-uk/. Accessed 20 September 2020.

Smith, Gail. "Madam and Eve: A Caricature of Black Women's Subjectivity?" *Agenda: Empowering Women for Gender Equity*, vol. 12, no. 31, 1996, pp. 33–39.

Smith, Jaqueline Monique. "Black Princess Housewives and Single Ladies: Renée Cox's Housewife Enactments and the Politics of Twenty-First Century Wealthy Black Womanhood." May 2016. University of Texas at Austin, Dissertation.

Smith, Zadie. *The Emperor of Cambodia*. London, Hamish Hamilton, \2013.

Solovieva, Olga. *Fassbinder's France: Genet's Mise-en-Scene in Fassbinder's Films. A Companion to Rainer Werner Fassbinder*, edited by Bridgette Peuker, New York, Wiley-Blackwell, 2014, pp. 94–113.

Spillers, Hortense, et al. "Whatcha Gonna Do?—Revisiting 'Mama's Baby, Papa's Maybe: An American Grammar Book': A Conversation with Hortense Spillers, Saidiya Hartman, Farah Jasmin Griffin, Shelly Eversley, and Jennifer L. Morgan." *Women's Studies Quarterly*, vol. 35, nos. 1–2, 2007, pp. 299–309.

Staples, Brent. "Aunt Jemima Gets a Makeover." *New York Times*, Oct. 1994, www.nytimes.com/1994/10/19/opinion/editorial-notebook-aunt-jemima-gets-a-makeover.html. Accessed 9 June 2019.

Stern, Irma. "Maid in Uniform." *Pictify*, 1955, www.irmasternmuseum.co.za/portfolio-item/maid-in-uniform. Accessed 13 Jan. 2013.

Stevenson, Robert, director. *Mary Poppins*. Walt Disney Pictures, 1964.

Stockett, Kathryn. *The Help*. New York, G. P. Putnam's Sons, 2009.

Tate, Taylor, director. *The Help*. Walt Disney Pictures, 2011.

Thiong'o, Ngũgĩ wa. *Decolonizing the Mind: The Politics of Language in African Literature*. Portsmouth, Heinemann Studies in African Literature, 1986.

Thomas, Mickalene. *Ain't I a Woman (Sandra)*. 2009. Acrylic, enamel, and rhinestones on wood panel. www.mickalenethomas.com/works/Film%20and%20Video/WlO35CkAACkAGtoC. Accessed 20 Sept. 2019.

———. "Artist Mickalene Thomas: 'It Was Always a Political Statement.'" Interview by Julie L. Belcove. *Financial Times*, 31 Aug. 2018, www.ft.com/content/40f8bd16-ab1c-11e8-89a1-e5de165fa619. Accessed 19 Apr. 2019.

———. *Left Behind #2*. 2014, Relief. Intaglio, lithograph, digital, collage. www.mickalenethomas.com/works/exhibitions/V74PvSoAAIQfm9Zx/V74RhSoAAIQem92k. Accessed 20 Sept. 2019.

———. *A Little Taste Outside of Love*. 2007. Acrylic, enamel, and rhinestones on wood panel. Brooklyn Museum, New York.

———. *Mama Bush*. 2003. Acrylic, rhinestones, and resin. Vielmetter, Los Angeles. www.artnet.com/artists/mickalene-thomas/mama-bush-EnfjT5-2DG8eClKehNwOXQ2. Accessed 23 Mar. 2020.

———. *Marie Femme Noire Nue: Couchée #2*. 2014. Rhinestones, acrylic, oil, and enamel on wood panel. www.mickalenethomas.com/works/filter/paintings. Accessed 20 Sept. 2019.

———. "Mickalene Thomas." Interview with Sean Landers. *Bomb Magazine*, 1 June 2011, bombmagazine.org/articles/mickalene-thomas-1/. Accessed 3 Sept. 2019.

———. *Qusuquzah Lounging with Pink + Black Flower*. 2016. Rhinestones, acrylic, oil, on wood panel. www.mickalenethomas.com/works/exhibitions/WRtkYicAAPMTH3sE/WR3ZJicAAFM2Kk4c. Accessed 23 Mar. 2020.

———. *Sleep: Deux Femme Noires*. 2012, Mo-ARTGALLERY. Mixed media collage. Woodblock, screenprint and digital print. www.mickalenethomas.com/works/print/VrELPScAAPVC5p_4. Accessed 23 Mar. 2020.

Thomson, Allese. "Interviews Kara Walker." *Artforum*, 27 Mar. 2013, www.artforum.com/interviews/kara-walker-discusses-rise-up-ye-mighty-race-39955. Accessed 11 Mar. 2017.

"Trailer: *The Nanny Diaries* (2007)." *IMDb*, 1990–2020, www.imdb.com/title/tt0489237/?ref_=vp_back. Accessed 19 June 2018.

Trueman, Matt. Review of "Uzo Aduba in *The Maids*," directed by Jamie Lloyd. *Variety*, 1 Mar. 2016, variety.com/2016/legit/reviews/the-maids-review-uzo-aduba-1201719459/. Accessed 19 Mar. 2015.

Ulldemolins, Maria Gil. "A-dressing History." *Onafrica*, 10 Apr. 2010, Web. Accessed 17 Oct. 2015.

United States Department of Labor. *Domestic Workers' Bill of Rights*. labor.ny.gov/legal/domestic-workers-bill-of-rights.shtm. Accessed 2 Nov. 2018.

Van der Walt, David. "Mary Sibande: Reinventing Society." *A Look Away*, vol. 10, no. 1, 2008, pp. 23–25.

Van Onselen, C. "The Witches of Suburbia: Domestic Service on the Witwatersrand, 1890–1914." *New Babylon, New Nineveh: Studies in the Social and Economic History of the Witwatersrand, 1886–1914*, vol. 2, Johannesburg, Jonathan Ball Publishers, 1982, pp. 1–73.

Van Wyk, Lisa. "Public Art: A Microscope Trained on Our Society." *Mail and Guardian Africa's Best Read*, 22 Nov. 2010, mg.co.za/article/2010-11-22-public-art-a-microscope-trained-on-our-society. Accessed 9 Dec. 2014.

Walker, Cherryl. "Gender and the Development of the Migrant Labour System c. 1850–1930." *Women and Gender in South Africa to 1945*, edited by Cherryl Walker, Cape Town, Clyson Printers, 1990, pp. 168–196.

Walker, Kara. "Artist Kara Walker Draws Us into Bitter History with Something Sweet." Interview by Audie Cornish. *NPR*, May 2014, www.npr.org/2014/05/16/313017716/artist-kara-walker-draws-us-into-bitter-history-with-something-sweet. Accessed 18 July 2015.

———. *Gone: A Historical Romance of a Civil War as It Occurred b'tween the Dusky Thighs of One Young Negress and Her Heart*. 1994, Paper. MoARTGALLERY. www.moma.org/collection/works/110565.

———. Interview by Anna McNay. Camden Arts Center, 10 Oct. 2013, www.studiointernational.com/index.php/kara-walker.

———. "Kara Walker and Jad Abumrad Live from the NYPL." *YouTube*, 4 June 2014, Web. Accessed 8 Aug. 2015.

———. *A Subtlety, or the Marvelous Sugar Baby an Homage to the Unpaid and Overworked Artisans Who Have Refined Our Sweet Tastes from the Cane Fields to the Kitchens of the New World on the Occasion of the Demolition of the Domino Sugar Refining Plant*. 2015. Sugar and polyester resin. Domino Sugar Factory, N.Y. Sculpture.

———. "The Un-private Collection: Kara Walker and Ana DuVernay." *YouTube*, uploaded by Broad Museum, 11 Oct. 2014, www.youtube.com/watch?v=AA1brfeJfaw. Accessed Oct 15, 2019.

Wallace, Michele. *Black Macho and the Myth of the Superwoman*. Rev. ed., London, Verso, 1990.

Wallace-Sanders, Kimberly. *Mammy: A Century of Race, Gender, and Southern Memory*. Ann Arbor, U of Michigan P, 2011.

Walvin, James. *Sugar: The World Corrupted: From Slavery to Obesity*. New York, Pegasus, 2018.

Washington, Mary Helen. "Alice Childress, Lorraine Hansberry, and Claudia Jones: Black Women Write the Popular Front." *Left of the Color Line: Race, Radicalism, and Twentieth Century Literature of the United States*, edited by Bill V. Mullen and James Smethurst, Chapel Hill, U of North Carolina P, 2003, pp. 183–204.

Walters, Tracey. Interview by Lesley Perkes, Skype, 2014.

———. Interview by Marie Sibande, Skype, 2014.

Wellershaus, Elisabeth. "Sophie Is Not the Only Strong Woman Populating Our Art Scene at the Moment: A Conversation with the Artist Mary Sibande." *C&*, 24 June 2013, www.contemporaryand.com/magazines/sophieis-not-the-only-strong-woman-populating-our-art-scene-at-the-moment/. Accessed 12 July 2018.

Willis, Deborah. *The Black Female Body: A Photographic History*. Philadelphia, Temple UP, 2002, p. 187.

———. *Black Venus*. 2010. *They Called Her "Hottentot."* Philadelphia, Temple UP, 2010.

Wise, Robert, director. *The Sound of Music*. 20th Century Fox, 1965.

Yeung, Bernice. *In a Day's Work: The Fight to End Sexual Violence against America's Most Vulnerable Workers*. New York, New Press, 2018.

Zvomuya, Percy. "Suburban Dreams." *Mail and Guardian*, 26 Mar. 2010, mg.co.za/article/2010-03-26-suburban-dreams/. Accessed 13 Oct. 2015. Article last accessed prior to printing.

Index

About the Author

TRACEY L. WALTERS is an associate professor of literature in the Department of Africana Studies at Stony Brook University, where she also holds an affiliate appointment with the Department of English and Women's and Gender Studies. She has published three books on black women's literature—*African American Women and the Classicists Tradition: Black Women Writers from Wheatley to Morrison* (2007); *Zadie Smith: Critical Essays* (2008); and *Zadie Smith* (2012)—as well as numerous articles. Walters is cohost of the podcast *Black Girls with Accents.*